What Cities Say

What Cities Say

A Social Interpretation of
Urban Patterns and Forms

EMILY TALEN

OXFORD
UNIVERSITY PRESS

OXFORD
UNIVERSITY PRESS

Oxford University Press is a department of the University of Oxford. It furthers
the University's objective of excellence in research, scholarship, and education
by publishing worldwide. Oxford is a registered trade mark of Oxford University
Press in the UK and certain other countries.

Published in the United States of America by Oxford University Press
198 Madison Avenue, New York, NY 10016, United States of America.

CIP data is on file at the Library of Congress
ISBN 978–0–19–764777–6 (pbk.)
ISBN 978–0–19–764776–9 (hbk.)

DOI: 10.1093/oso/9780197647769.001.0001

Paperback printed by Marquis Book Printing, Canada
Hardback printed by Bridgeport National Bindery, Inc., United States of America

MIX
Paper from
responsible sources
FSC® C103567

Contents

Introduction

This is a book about how to "read" cities. It is a collection of interpretations—of cities, and parts of cities, as physical places. What do city forms and patterns say about social priorities, cultural values, and winners and losers in the game of city-making? What motivated a given pattern or form in the first place, and what does it mean to us now? Using samples of cities from all time periods and places, I work to understand motive and meaning.

Cities don't just build themselves. They are willed into existence. They reflect our values and priorities back to us, and we can learn to understand what they say. Understanding this reveals something of ourselves.

However, the aim of this book is not introspection. I wrote this book to help craft better arguments in the public discourse about why one type of pattern or form might be better than another in a given place. By exposing what urban patterns and forms mean and what values they hold, I believe we will be in a stronger position to articulate, and argue for, the kinds of cities we want.

The sources of these embedded meanings are varied: historical experience, behavioral and aesthetic effects, written critique, and the economic and social processes that generate pattern and form. Understanding why cities are built a certain way helps us interpret what they might mean. I summarize these meanings and offer an evaluation.

Cities are the result of a wide range of intentional acts, from the minute to the grandiose, from the desires of the homebuilder to those of the reigning despot. City shapes, forms, and street and building patterns are sometimes a product of blueprints, sometimes a product of gradual accretion, and sometimes the product of violent change. Forms and patterns might reflect the highest aspirations, or they might simply be responses to mundane, utilitarian needs. Perhaps a pattern or form boils down to nothing more than a financial calculus. Whatever the case, it is possible to develop a language of interpretation—and an understanding of meaning. Because behind every city pattern and form, whether for a complete city, a thoroughfare, or a small public space, there is a motive capable of being teased out and interpreted.

My topic is limited to physical evidence on the ground: two-dimensional pattern and three-dimensional form. Patterns are usually put down for an explicitly collective purpose (e.g., by governments), whereas forms are often privately held or market-based. Cities can have all kinds of mismatches between pattern and

What Cities Say. Emily Talen, Oxford University Press. © Oxford University Press 2024. DOI: 10.1093/oso/9780197647769.003.0001

form—streets too wide for low-rise buildings, buildings too tall for narrow streets, public spaces too large for a small town or too small for a big town. Sometimes this signals a disjuncture between public desires and what the market feels like delivering.

Urban patterns and forms can expose many possible meanings. Writers like Lewis Mumford, Jane Jacobs, Spiro Kostof, and Grady Clay exploited this understanding and were experts at urban interpretation, and I draw from them liberally. More recent writing has homed in on how to read urban problems like suburban sprawl—the land of highways, McMansions, and shopping malls has always been an easy read, readily exposing quick profit, individualism, and a lack of caring. Other writers, like David Harvey and Henri Lefebvre, emphasize the processes underlying urban patterns and forms, and knowing these processes is often the key to interpretation. I make use of all these approaches. The book is a summation of interpretations, an aggregation of my own and many others.

For some writers, any focus on the "pathology of space," where the interpretation of form draws from social and cultural factors rather than capitalism as the root cause, is suspect. Lefebvre derided planners attempting to be "doctors of space" as especially delusional.[1] But focusing too much on the economic and financial factors underlying urban form is limiting. It's true that financial systems and the workings of capital loom large in urban explanation, but financial calculus only goes so far in our attempt to understand meaning.

Lefebvre was also arguing that process is more important than form. This argument is found in books like *Cities by Design: The Social Life of Urban Form* or *The Cultural Meaning of Urban Space*, which focus on the processes of urbanization while de-emphasizing urban form as a physical presence to be interpreted in its own right.[2] But form and process are both important. Physical form is not the *only* way through which to understand the meaning and value of a place, but it is certainly one way.

There are numerous regularities that surface in interpreting pattern and form. For example, the desires of kings and other authoritarian figures tend to manifest in the form of monumentality and centrality. The money-making objectives of landowners tend to prioritize regularized, gridded land division. The desire to instill a sense of communal life tends to result in centralized public spaces. Not only does this imply a certain degree of hardwiring about how motivations pan out, but it also signifies that the range of possible forms and patterns is not unlimited.

Sometimes intentions were simply practical: avenues in ancient Chinese cities were based on the width needed to accommodate nine chariots; the width of streets in medieval cities accommodated a single wagon; a town square in England was triangular because it was originally the space where three roads came together to form a marketplace. But at other times there was an embedded cultural language, a "unitary code" that was not found in any practicality or official law. Lefebvre thought that Venice was a perfect example: "[W]ho conceived the architectural and monumental unity? The truth is that no one did."[3] Unity was a matter of cultural convention.

An understanding of motivation often requires knowledge of history and context—of the site, the land, the culture, the financial structures, the politics. The same urban form in one place can mean something entirely different in another. For example, freestanding houses built in early 20th-century Jewish settlements in Palestine were not simply emulations of a garden suburb. They were contrasts, the exact opposite of compact Middle Eastern cities with their mix of dense Arab neighborhoods and traditional Jewish row houses. A pattern of free-standing houses surrounded by green represented a "new start" for settlers: a "confident" Jew rather than a "diasporic" Jew. Front setbacks ensured that house gardens—under resident control—would be clearly visible, and the contrasting pattern symbolized autonomy, self-expression, and freedom from centralized authority, all of which was a marked departure from traditional form and governance.[4]

This is not to say that more obvious interpretations are the exception. The train tracks used to separate White and Black houses in Winter Park, Florida, couldn't be more obvious in terms of intent. An early 20th-century garden suburb in Indonesia, called Menteng, dictated the locations of seven different classes of residences—and therefore residents. The 17th-century town of Scherpenheuvel in Belgium had seven sides to honor the seven joys of the Virgin Mary. Dubai is an "immense, psychotic assemblage of fantasy kitsch" that expresses an affection for money and playtime, not unlike Las Vegas. Beijing's Olympic Village can be read not just as a collection of landmarks, but as the physical manifestation of a vast, exploitable workforce and a state capable of mass evictions whenever it needs to clear the land.[5]

One might also say that city patterns and forms reveal a society's attitude toward life. If there is great precision and uniformity—every house set back at the exact same distance, for example—it signals an adherence to rules and a love of predictability, uniformity, and conformance. City patterns can say something about religious beliefs, too. Venice with its multitude of churches can be compared to Amsterdam with comparatively few—Italians with their pride of place in contrast to a Dutch city where, although religious attitudes were stronger than in Venice, the "moral order of Calvinism took the place of churches."[6]

The Attachment of Meaning

We live with the city patterns and forms that those before us put in place, and our ancestors had their own reasons for building the way they did. Knowing prior motivations helps us articulate their meaning now. But do historical meanings still apply? How detachable are prior motivations? Do we need to forever associate baroque urbanism with despots? Is a circular city, designed to be a fortress, still so concerned with security? We might be able to make out the will of a tyrant, the whims of an aristocrat, the defensive posture of a medieval town, or the simplicity of Puritanical restraint—but what do these forms mean to us now? And if a city form was built through the suppression of people, does that mean that such a place should never be valued?

Divesting unwanted symbolic content seems especially hard with baroque form because of its association with imperialism and fascism. Can the monumentalism and grandeur, the axes, tree-lined avenues, and vistas terminating in landmarks be divorced from prior nefarious ends? Most often, baroque elements no longer hold the overt meaning they once did, so it is reasonable to argue that they can be valued in other ways. A grand building at the terminus of a grand avenue might still express grandeur as the original builders intended, but the object of adoration is likely to have changed. Perhaps the wide, straight street is no longer about monarchical pomp and riot control, but about prioritizing the street as a public space. One is reminded of Lewis Mumford's caution about making a distinction between the container and the contents. Rome during its Empire was a "veritable cesspool of human debasement and iniquity," but the container has remained "a marvel of formal dignity."[7]

These allowances might be conditional, however. It could be argued that an emphasis on unity and grandeur in a public setting makes sense only in the case of a city of great public importance. Thus, the baroque qualities of Washington, DC, are legitimately an expression of the ideals of a Republic—Greek, Roman, and early American. The use of monuments—those archives of collective memory—was entirely fitting. Even Beaux Arts architecture was appropriate because classical architecture reflects national heritage "in a way that Gothic, Romanesque, or commercial styles never could."[8] And while Americans were more attuned to small-town life and the American frontier than to ancient Rome—making the chosen style seem pompous and misplaced—small-town form would not have adequately expressed American ambitions. An eclectic mix of patterns and forms has the imprint of weak control, providing "no 'centerline' about which the city of democracy [could be] built."[9]

City interpretation—the attachment of meaning to pattern and form—is also complicated by the fact that one kind of desire, say, for a form to express communal values can have multiple built outcomes. And the same form can, in different times and places, have more than one purpose or motivation. For example, in the United States, garden suburbs are thought to be elitist; in the United Kingdom, at least until recently, they were the essence of middle-class mediocrity. Even more polysemous is the grid. It is sometimes a tool of capitalist exploitation, and sometimes a tool of egalitarian land division. Mumford observed that a grid "meant one thing to an Etruscan priest, another to Hippodamus, a third to the Roman legionary, and something else again to the City Plan Commissioners of New York in 1811."[10]

In addition, interpretations of city form can change. Where the dense, pedestrian-based city was once viewed as "a symbol of ecological and social crisis," our interpretation is now reversed: it is low-density sprawl that is the ecological and social disaster.[11] These changes make it challenging to proclaim the existence of inherent associations between particular forms and particular meanings. A grid can be equalizing or it can be a tool of social insularity. Curvilinear form enabled social mixing in antiquity but later facilitated suburban segregation. The best that one can do is to acknowledge that there is often more than one interpretation, and lay out the options.

This conjures up an age-old debate in architecture and urban design. One side believes that if the economic and social conditions that gave rise to a particular form no longer exist, then to replicate such forms in the present is illegitimate. It is better to aim for a contemporary zeitgeist—*of our time*. If new technologies of transportation and mobility emerge, city patterns and forms must change in response. The other side argues that there are limits to this because there are universal principles at play that are not dependent on underlying social and economic forces. The general size and structure of the human body is a constant, for example, as are certain preferences related to human scale. So if narrow and crooked medieval street patterns are produced in new developments in modern cities—a good example is Malmö's City of Tomorrow development (Figure I.1)—this is legitimate

Figure I.1 Malmö, Sweden. *The new development (left) uses medieval-like street patterns. The forces that gave rise to such patterns are no longer determinative, but the pattern is still valued.*

Figure I.2 Hikone Castle, Japan. *No longer an expression of dominance, the castle complex has acquired a new cultural meaning and symbolism that is set by Hikone residents themselves.* Source: z tanuki, CC BY 3.0 <https://creativecommons.org/licen ses/by/3.0>, via Wikimedia Commons

because it provides a scale related to the human body that people still value. And although the means of production and the forms of power that gave rise to medieval patterns are no longer determinative, the forms produced are valued now for other reasons.

Ultimately, of course, we can make whatever we want of the spaces, patterns, and forms put in place under completely different circumstances. Where, for example, castles once dominated the skyline and kept the population subservient, a castle might now simply provide a non-threatening connection to the past, a source of continuity and identity, a daily reminder of a resident's linkage to their historical roots. The castle complex that dominates Hikone, Japan, for example, has been released from its "authoritarian weight" and has acquired a new cultural meaning and symbolism that is set by Hikone residents themselves (Figure I.2). The relics of Naarden's 17th-century warfare defenses—bastioned walls and a double moat—are now parkland, so the meaning of these forms has obviously changed completely (Figure I.3). Current meaning might be nothing more than historical remembrance of what people used to do to protect themselves. Or it might be more profound, such as when cities once dominated by religion—cathedrals forming a landscape of the divine—are now dominated by profits in the form of tall office buildings and strip malls.

Planned or Unplanned?

It might seem easier to attach meaning to something deliberately planned, but the distinction between planned and unplanned is murky. As Kevin Lynch wrote, "no city is a natural growth, and therefore none is unplanned."[12] We might think of the medieval city as unplanned and haphazardly laid down, but in fact it was not spontaneous or unconsciously built. It had "esthetic unity," which was the result, as Mumford wrote, of "effort, struggle, supervision, and control."[13] By the same token, baroque planning was not always implemented as a complete system or through a master plan, but instead may have evolved through a series of "responsive efforts"

Figure I.3 Naarden, the Netherlands. *Warfare defenses are now parkland.*

over several generations. In the United States, the imprint of human intentions on city form seems to be nothing more than random acts of the invisible hand of the market. But even then there is an exchange of "conscious and unconscious" factors. The product of this interplay—the city—is no less a "willed artifact."[14]

But the outcomes might be indirect. For example, the location of housing and the deterioration of neighborhood quality might not be intentional and planned, but the prioritizing of industry, railroad, and retail—with profit-making as the operative goal—is usually deliberate. Cities often developed according to the desires of industry and railroads on the one hand, and retailers on the other, and housing was an afterthought, which meant that housing for workers was pushed to increasingly undesirable locations near various leftover domains.

Of course, that changed when financiers discovered there was money to be made in housing. Financial structures—especially the degree to which housing finance and capital markets are integrated—have had an enormous impact on the kind of housing produced.[15] In Europe's major cities, large, government-backed financial institutions favored large-scale apartment blocks; in the Anglo-American world, at least initially, the financial system was decentralized and involved small depositors taking out loans, which translated to single-family houses. When the government finally got involved in housing finance in the mid-20th century, suburban development exploded.

Figure I.4 Ancient Kamerios, Island of Rhodes, Greece. *The gradual development of rectangular squares is a cumulative outcome, but not unplanned.*

Kostof argued that even where development seems random, such as buildings dotted along a rural road, over time these "natural arrangements" tend to "turn self-conscious." In ancient Kamerios on the island of Rhodes, for example, the gradual accumulation of rectangular squares, still visible, is not the work of a single designer with a singular concept, but a cumulative outcome that should not be thought of as unplanned (Figure I.4). As M. R. G. Conzen writes of American towns of the colonial period, town plans were "incremental but not necessarily less thoughtful." And the reverse is also possible: places that we know were designed in blueprint fashion now look as if they hadn't been designed at all. The many planned garden suburbs of the early 20th century now benefit from decades of vegetative growth, giving them a patina of spontaneous authenticity.[16]

In sum, city patterns and forms might originate as elaborately and precisely drawn designs on paper, or they might simply be the product of spontaneous decisions. For the former, there are many different kinds, ranging from entire cities to component parts like subdivisions and plazas. Most cultures tend to plan by individual element—a plan for a street, a royal palace grounds, a waterfront—rather than planning for a complete unit with integrated parts, like a neighborhood. But it is less straightforward than one might think to determine the difference between blueprint plan and incremental intervention. The great early 20th-century planner Raymond Unwin admitted that it was "very difficult" to determine if "irregularity and want of symmetry" in city building was in fact consciously or unconsciously done. The asymmetry might have been done "on the ground by the eye" instead of "transferred from a paper plan," but it was every bit as planned.[17]

Even where cities are primarily the result of market forces and individual speculation, there are still deliberative actions and norms at work that can produce a coordinated pattern. Time period is a factor here, as an integrated assembly of individual plans appeared more coordinated in times when the range of possible building techniques and technological choices was more constrained.

Even patterns and forms that seem spontaneous most likely had some design motive, even if on a subconscious level. The 19th-century urban designer Camillo Sitte took the latter point to extremes, claiming that medieval irregularity was methodically designed. To his point, the medievalism of Siena looks "organic" and spontaneous, but it is the product of precise building codes issued by the city council starting in the 13th century (Figure I.5).[18]

In the end, the best we can conclude is that it is not always possible to determine whether a given city form is the result of conscious design or mere instinct. The positions of things, the configuration of places and spaces, may seem incidental, but someone at some point made a decision to put them there. Even if something happens out of inertia more than anything else, or if there seems to have been little forethought, it still has the mark of human intention.

Figure I.5 Siena, Italy. *The medievalism looks "organic" and spontaneous, but it is the product of precise building codes, starting in the 13th century.*

Why Is This Needed?

One might ask: why is this evaluation, this interpretative language of the city, important to have? The answer is that knowing what kinds of city patterns and forms we want requires knowing what city patterns and forms mean to us. As things stand, arguments for or against a particular city plan fluctuate between data analysis and strong opinion. Argument built on an understanding of what forms express—their embedded values and meanings—is an alternative, and I think underdeveloped, approach.

This kind of interpretation is possible because the built environment is loaded with social meaning. Patterns and forms have an impact on choice, access, opportunity, interaction, movement, identity, connection, mix, security, and stability, any of which can be the basis of meaning and interpretation. Patterns and forms are used to express power, establish alliances, or assert independence. Spaces can be thought of as embodied, gendered, inscribed, or contested, such that cities are capable of conveying, reinforcing, legitimizing, or overcoming social divisions. All kinds of social impacts—social interaction, sense of community, social capital, social engagement—have been attributed to cities patterned and formed in particular ways, meaning that one place might be "read" as being more socially oriented than another.[19] Is it better or worse for exclusion, social connectedness, opportunity, identity, or stability? What does it mean for quality of life, human happiness, social justice, or sense of community? Are the embodied values limited to maximizing profit, or are there values related to family life, respecting traditions, or providing social connectedness?

To understand the range of possibilities, we need to understand what meanings have been associated, past and present. The end goal is to create a vocabulary and a repertoire of possible meanings, from the mundane and practical to the spiritual and symbolic, all of which can be tapped to build a more convincing argument about the kinds of cities and places we want. We need this kind of interpretive skill—the ability to understand the implications of the patterns and forms we everyday live with—to be able to assess and interpret the meaning of city plans that are everyday proposed.

I believe the task of thinking through what city forms and patterns mean is underdeveloped. In part, this is likely because physical planning, in general, has lost favor. A century ago, the newly formed city planning profession was touting the power of the city plan, a message that resonated with the likes of Presidents Herbert Hoover and Franklin D. Roosevelt. Schoolchildren were taught the value of city plans in textbooks like *Wacker's Manual*.[20] But after World War II, city planning became less and less about physical plans and more and more about programs and processes—economic development, recreational programming, transportation modeling—none of which had a built form objective in mind. Planning cities in a literal sense—trying to change urban form in predictable, predetermined ways—was discredited. This was not without reason: city plans were being used to replace viable neighborhoods with highways, office towers, and shopping malls. Implemented city plans were justifiably dismissed as dystopian blueprints rather than physical manifestations of worthy ideals.

But there was a cost to this change: an inability to articulate the kinds of cities we want. I am not the first to observe that the planning field is insufficiently engaged with its traditional realm (physical planning). Some planners have argued that the physical realm—what Beauregard (2015) succinctly termed "things"—should be the core identity that the profession returns to. Campanella (2011) called for a more traditionally rooted planning field that is proactive and visionary, a profession with "disciplinary identity" focused on physical planning, placemaking, and a shared civic realm.[21]

I believe we will all be aided in this worthy objective if we know how to interpret, value, and understand the meaning of city patterns and forms, if we have a more explicit approach to interpretation that can be used to support reasoned debate about the pros and cons of alternative forms.

Approach

The subject matter of this book is limited to existing forms and patterns that are observable (I do not include idealized utopias that exist only on paper). The analysis makes use of all scales, from whole cities to small squares. Examples in each chapter, drawn from multiple time periods and places, are used to relate *what cities say*—or, how they can be *read*. The focus is on the intentional, human-generated habitat, and interpretations that can be derived.

I draw these connections explicitly. A statement proclaiming that "the built environment reinforces cultural stereotypes" may be true enough, but I want to say what, materially and literally, that interpretation can be based on. A few examples will help clarify:

- A skyline of church steeples and minarets can be read much differently from a skyline of corporate headquarters. One shows reverence to spiritual authority, the other shows the economic power of corporations.
- A city of separated functions—a shopping mall here, houses there—can be read as a machine with mechanical parts, whereas dense, multi-use urban neighborhoods can be read as settings for social interdependence and connectivity.
- A city with uniform, ordered buildings is a place with a culture that values stability and is perhaps fearful of disorder and what it might mean. A place lacking any visible order is either lacking such fear, or lacking the means of imposing uniformity.

Figure I.6 Heidelberg, Germany. *A castle towering above a town expresses power focused on subordination.* Credit: Hiroki Ogawa, CC BY 3.0 <https://creativecommons. org/licenses/by/3.0>, via Wikimedia Commons.

Figure I.7 Urbino, Italy. *A castle nestled in the urban fabric expresses confidence and an openness to collective life as the basis of power.*

- A castle towering above a town, as at Heidelberg, expresses power focused on subordination (Figure I.6), whereas a castle nestled within the urban fabric, as at Urbino, Italy, expresses an openness to collective life as the basis of power (Figure I.7).

Figure I.8 Heibei Province, China. *Settlement is clustered to leave room for agricultural fields.*

Although my focus is human intention, natural forces, beyond human control, play an indirect role—city patterns and forms are often a response to natural phenomena. Vitruvius' first-century (BCE) dictation of street and alley pattern based on wind direction is an obvious case. Or the way New Haven, Connecticut's town grid was angled to fit between two streams. Topography gave shape to harbors, hill towns, and river settlements. The ancient city of Pergamon (now a ruin) seems random unless viewed in relation to the site's steep site. Clustered settlement in China's Hebei province is in part a function of needing to maintain agricultural land (Figure I.8). British towns are said to be more horizontal and low-density than those on the European continent because Britain, being an island, had more "settled internal conditions" and there was no need to circle towns with defensive walls and constrain development to high-density apartments at the center (although cities on the continent became more prone to horizontal settlement when the cannon came along).[22] The impact of climate, too, cannot be overestimated. Houses built along the North Sea are clustered behind the dunes to avoid strong winds; neighborhood form in a Chinese village might be oriented to face the warmth of the sun.

I focus on patterns and forms as opposed to architecture, although sometimes architectural style cannot be ignored. It is worth noting that when architecture books first started to appear—as soon as printing presses became widespread in the 16th century—many contained as much material devoted to city patterns and forms as they did to the design of individual buildings.[23] So while my focus is city pattern and form, the relationship between a building and the space in front of it can be very much impacted by the architectural style of a building. Disney Hall in Los Angeles is a good example: a building style that seems to want to avoid "meaningful interface" with the sidewalk (Figure I.9).[24]

Figure I.9 Walt Disney Concert Hall, Los Angeles, California, USA. *An example of a building that avoids "meaningful interface" with the sidewalk.* Credit: Carol M. Highsmith, Public domain, via Wikimedia Commons.

An important consideration in selecting examples is choosing the right analytical scale. The goal is to choose a scale that best communicates or exposes a particular idea. This is tricky because any one place can be analyzed from multiple scales, involving an analysis of the whole plan, its street patterns, or its public spaces. Sometimes it is possible to interpret the totality of a city (e.g., a complete garden city), but in other cases the most illuminating feature is a particular place within it.

Interpretation is often a matter of social context, too. A cul-de-sac can be interpreted as a pattern that provides shelter and protection—or a pattern that is claustrophobic and socially determinist. This depends on context. Shelter and protection might be highly valued and relevant in societies where privacy is a concern, but less relevant in societies where the desire for privacy is low, which has been said of Scandinavian countries.[25]

Obviously, focusing only on the physical side of cities means that certain things are missed. I interpret the meaning of a public space based, for example, on its size, positioning, centrality, and connectedness—physically observable qualities— but whether it is also privately owned, policed to exclude certain populations, or surveilled with video cameras is a level of interpretation I can only allude to. Similarly, I do not know if certain areas, such as the open spaces of public housing projects, are being adequately maintained—if the answer is no, this would lead to an interpretation of societal neglect and a lack of caring.

Illustrations are essential to my approach, and I rely on a combination of two- and three-dimensional views. Two-dimensional images reveal the pattern of streets, the locations of buildings and public places, the treatment of edges, and sometimes the pattern of land use. Three-dimensional views show bulk, uniformity, and the relation of building to street. The same place can yield a different interpretation depending on which view is used. For example, in two dimensions, viewed from above, a suburban commercial street might look like a string of indistinct big box buildings. But on the ground, in three dimensions, the street often looks garish and chaotic for the interesting reason that it is trying to escape from an underlying homogeneity. Extreme variations in color, form, and texture are buildings crying out to be recognized amid an overbearing pattern of sameness.[26]

Except in a few cases, I avoid spending time on individual designers and planners because I want the focus to be on larger forces and social meanings. I agree with Mumford, who observed that in reviewing city plans "one should perhaps remember that the despot himself was an instrument in a larger movement of civilization: his arbitrary desires, or even those of his bureaucratic agents, were not the sole determinants of the new plan."[27] In other words, architects, planners, and developers are often the tools of larger systemic forces. Even places that *look* planned might not have had any planners involved. Gary, Indiana, for example, was the product of a board of directors (whose chairman was named Gary, incidentally) who wanted a steady supply of workers for US Steel Corporation. In laying out the town, "a city planner was not so much as considered."[28]

In this search for the motivation and meaning of city pattern and form, I draw from a rich urban literature: the writings of historians, architects, geographers, and planners. Each field approaches the subject differently. Historians are concerned with understanding the societal and cultural variables underlying urban form, and their interest is in ensuring that the built environment is "read" with historical accuracy. This task can be herculean. As Benevolo warned about seeking explanations for the medieval city, "there is an infinite variety of circumstantial factors which must be taken into consideration: the nature of the terrain, local tradition, even religion."[29] While this book is greatly informed by historical analysis, I pick up where the historian might leave off, focusing on what urban forms show about society and culture and what they might mean for us now.

Yet the historical record is an essential part of understanding the motivations behind patterns and forms. The plan of Shaker Village in Hancock, Massachusetts, looks like a simple utilitarian arrangement, but we know from the historical record that buildings and streets and their shape and positioning were arranged hierarchically and according to function (the Shakers were intentional in everything they did, from the design of a teacup to the design of a town).[30] In other cases, patterns and forms are highly symbolic and can be read at face value, such that an explicit historical reference about underlying intention isn't as necessary.

Architects have a different approach, often interpreting patterns, forms, and spaces like engineered building parts and avoiding any linkage to social meaning. Thus an urban space with tall buildings might be valued for its "vertical force," with streets transmitting "tension" between points that "penetrate" land areas. Zucker, in the book *Town and Square*, admired the "fluctuating rhythm" that created "visual freedom" in some Parisian squares, while Edmund Bacon described the Tuileries Garden in Paris as a "line of propulsion which thrusts farther and farther into the surrounding countryside." I try to steer clear of these kinds of subliminal (and sometimes phallic) architectural interpretations.[31]

Geographers like Conzen are an important source for social and cultural interpretation. Conzen called the arrangement of buildings, plots, and streets the "plan-unit" and identified forty-nine unique plan-units in the small market town of Alnwick in Northern England, each of which was derived from its "site circumstances." Researchers have taken this kind of analysis to a whole new level lately, analyzing city pattern and form using copious amounts of "big data."[32] There are tools to analyze the spatial structure of city blocks, to map millions of building outlines, to calculate street network distances, to measure the shape of every open space. There is a lot to learn from these analyses, but the goal is not to interpret what it might mean.

I have also learned from art historians, as I view the evaluation of city pattern and form as a kind of city planning version of what the art historian does. An art historian is able to look at a painting and reveal its significance in a way that most observers—untrained in art history—are not able to see. There is a formal analysis, involving the interpretation of lines, colors, shapes, and forms, and then an analysis of content and context. Combined, this formal and contextual analysis generates a deeper understanding of an artwork's meaning and value. Cities have more complex sources, but the goal of interpretation can be similar.

There is no standard way of categorizing city patterns and forms, although many have been proposed. Categorization in the early days of the city planning profession tended to be mostly concerned with drawing a line between cities that formed via "natural growth" and those that were the result of drawn plans. To early city planning advocates, the distinction was clear: "the town of natural growth embodies and displays the uncertainties and erratic tendencies of undisciplined growth." Town planning, on the other hand, was "prearranged and orderly."[33]

Most urban typologies are about divisions of types of cities rather than types of patterns and forms. For example, the French historian Fernand Braudel distinguished among the open city, in the sense of being open to the surrounding countryside (which was the practice in ancient Greek and Roman towns); the closed city, which was self-sufficient, insular, and distrustful of outsiders (which characterizes medieval towns); and the subjugated city, controlled by powerful rulers or the state (from the Renaissance onward). Spiro Kostof divided cities into pre-industrial (after Gideon Sjoberg's book of that title), industrial (pre-figured by capitalism), and socialist (anti-capitalist and under centralized control). Gordon Cherry saw two categories: cities designed to reflect "a dominant art form" in which "social, economic, technological and ideological influences compete for primacy" and cities that are focused on housing and sheltering people, mostly concerned with providing settings for social organization.[34]

It was Spiro Kostof, whose books most influenced my approach, who focused explicitly on plan interpretation and typology in his two great works *The City Shaped* (1991) and *The City Assembled* (1992). The first book was based on ways of seeing the city as patterns "from the air"—organic, grid, diagram, and grand manner. The typology used in the second book consists of extracted elements common to all types of cities: edges, divisions, public places, and streets. Kostof's goal in both books was to survey "how and why cities took the shape they did," bringing in a wide range of explanations, from site conditions to political power struggles.[35]

Two other typologies of urban form are important to note. Kevin Lynch, a prolific and influential 20th-century urban designer, differentiated among three types of city plans in order to summarize the motivations of city designers: cosmic (the holy city and expressions of power), practical (the city as a set of functional parts), and organic (the city as an organism, as in garden cities). Peter Hall's synthetic history of the profession, *Cities of Tomorrow*, presents another typology, mostly weaving a story of planning mishap: the "monstrous perversion of history" resulting from the misinterpretation and naiveté of planners as they amalgamated ideals across time and place.[36]

The Road Ahead

In the remainder of this book, I present thirty-five distinct city patterns and forms, summarizing their interpretations. The topics are not mutually exclusive—for example, the chapters on "The Baroque" and "Monumentalism" have an obvious overlap. But each chapter has a particular focus.

The topics generally progress from larger to smaller scale. The first chapters provide a reading of complete cities and towns. Here the interpretation of pattern and form is derived from the whole, rather than the parts. This includes entire cities (small, big, linear), followed by smaller planned examples (industrial villages) and suburbs in various guises (garden, planned).

Another set of categories might be described as modes, or ways of doing things, resulting in a distinct imprint on the land. These modes straddle multiple scales. They include the baroque, monumentalism, urban renewal, uniformity, variation, and sprawl. Here physical pattern and form are strongly influenced by a style, a manner, a system of thought. Modes overlap with many other topics—from linear cities to plazas—but modes need to be discussed in their own right. The interpretation of pattern and form stems from an underlying ideology that is often explicit—about what cities should be, how they should be built, and who should build them.

There are seven chapters devoted to street and block patterns—for example, grids, curved streets, diagonals, and superblocks. Patterns created by streets and blocks provide numerous opportunities for interpretation. Street patterns can reflect a desire for social exclusion or a desire for exposure. They can determine how people move through space, and therefore the frequency with which people are provided opportunities to interact. Street patterns can appear inert, with streets that lead nowhere, or they can seem alive, with people and places interconnected.

The last set of chapters is devoted to distinctive, often smaller parts of the city. Here the object of interpretation is the design of a specific kind of place, like a center, a boundary, or a plaza. These places often form discrete sections of cities, like government complexes or "towers in a park" housing developments. Often set apart, they provide the basis for particular design interpretations.

Finally, I conclude with a set of evaluative questions that summarize how to "read" cities. I hope people will draw from this material to craft their own interpretations of the cities in which they live and the daily spaces they encounter. I hope readers will want to engage with the art of "reading" cities, to learn what cities and places seem to be saying.

1

Greek Polis

The Greek city-state, the polis, had the imprint of a political philosophy—democracy and equality—at least as far as free males were concerned. There were three zones: private houses, places for worship (the acropolis), and public space (such as the agora, which was a place of assembly and a marketplace). There was one architectural style. The size of houses varied internally but it was not pronounced, at least not during classical antiquity. This is because in the fifth century, "a display of affluence was not consistent with the tenets of democracy."[1] Houses adjoined and did not have private gardens. Modern Greek cities like Athens have a few remaining remnants of the original polis, notably the Acropolis, but in smaller cities it is possible to see the imprint of the ancient form. One example is Argos (Figure 1.1).

There are other meanings attached to the Greek city-state besides politics. For one, the polis is said to exemplify nature in the sense that the parts of the

Figure 1.1 Argos, Greece. *Remnants of the Greek city-state, the polis, are still visible.* Credit: Karin Helene Pagter Duparc, Own work, CC BY- SA 4.0

What Cities Say. Emily Talen, Oxford University Press. © Oxford University Press 2024. DOI: 10.1093/oso/9780197647769.003.0002

town were connected to the whole of the town. Thus, the city emulated the "perfection of nature" by "imposing the same close relationship between individual elements and the whole." The two- and three-dimensional shapes of the city were also interrelated, and the buildings sometimes seem to be carved right into the blocks. There was also a sense of limits, which constituted another connection to nature. When a polis reached a certain size, a new polis was formed rather than expanding the original town. "Smallness and limitation" were part of the moral code.[2]

Greek cities were especially well known for taking their public spaces very seriously. There was a deep integration between public and private realms, since although public life and public space were paramount, the structure of the town was based on the dwelling. Houses were simple because citizens spent most of their time in these public spaces; monuments were scattered throughout as a reminder that the city "was, quite literally, the common property of all its citizen."[3] Cities thus mirrored an underlying social structure, and public spaces were the enablers of social life. It was also a form that relied on an organized workforce. Of course, one has to always bear in mind that citizenship was selective and did not extend to women or slaves.

2

Medieval Towns

Most cities and towns take shape gradually rather than being formed all at once. This is how the medieval town mostly evolved: one road, one block, one building added to another. There was no preconceived end product, but in this gradual and incremental development, there was abundant intentionality. That the final plan was not present at the beginning does not mean that "rational considerations" were not present. And given the medieval town's love of irregularity, it is especially important not to confuse orthogonality with purposefulness and "organic" with "intellectual confusion" or "technological incompetence." Today, the medieval towns that dot the European landscape would never be thought of as confused or incompetent— only beloved and admired.[1]

There are always unique circumstances, but if one were to generalize, the medieval European town typically evolved like this: castle first, small settlement of feudal servants in an adjoining cluster, gradual prosperity and growth of the settlement into a village, construction of a surrounding wall, and then the commencement of the transformation from village to town, where all available sites, apart from those reserved for public spaces, cathedrals, and the castle area, were gradually filled in. Old village paths became the town's streets.[2] An excellent example of the quintessential medieval town is Brugge, Belgium, now a mecca for tourism thanks to the centuries of economic stagnation that kept Brugge from growing. We can still see the imprint of the feudal mode of production, whereby the houses of villagers were clustered around the lord's castle or a church (Figure 2.1).

The medieval city is dense and tightly packed, and originally this was the result of needing to be within city walls. Because building new walls was a major, expensive undertaking, cities just got denser to accommodate a growing population. New walls were postponed until there was "positively no room left." The resulting density and compactness exuded security. Thus, it was not only a surrounding wall that brought safety, but the narrow streets and multistory buildings: "the less the length of the wall in relation to the number of citizens the better the chances of beating back the attack of the enemy."[3]

Originally, houses were the primary generators of form, not the streets. In between the main streets, access to what seems like a jumble of structures was maintained via all kinds of smaller thoroughfares, closes (small semicircle roads), narrow passages, blind alleys, and intimate squares that served "most efficiently the community's purposes." With houses tightly clustered together, there were a lot of hard surfaces and not much in the way of open space and grass, but there really was

What Cities Say. Emily Talen, Oxford University Press. © Oxford University Press 2024. DOI: 10.1093/oso/9780197647769.003.0003

Figure 2.1 Brugge, Belgium. *The quintessential medieval town: pattern and form are largely unchanged because of centuries of economic stagnation.*

no need to be otherwise—open fields were close at hand. As the city opened up and streets widened in the Baroque period and later, landscape entered in, initially in the form of aligned street trees or parks or landscaped medians. It was then that streets became the primary elements that defined the form of the city, and houses were "fitted in between them" without much thought given to the basic needs of the houses or their occupants.[4]

Towns from the Middle Ages are mostly thought of as "organic," which means not a lack of planning but a lack of monumentalism, formalism, grids, or street axes. The outcome of this incremental, but collectively minded, evolution was a town that was thought of as a work of art. However, it was a conceptualization of art that was very different from the aesthetic imagery of baroque urbanism, which also regularly invoked the "city as a work of art" idea. Jane Jacobs was disdainful of the notion in either case, whereby utopianists substituted "the order of art" for the "order of life."[5]

Irregularity and informality give the impression that small-scale change is possible—large and ordered form implies control from the top down, and therefore less opportunity for incremental change. It also seems less static. Rooflines and streets seem to go in every which way, as though the whole town were in constant motion. But growth was gradual. Some historians view irregularity as an indicator of slowness in the city-building process. In the case of the Jewish quarter in Fez, Morocco, for example, an irregular street plan and a diversity of building types within the walls supported "a slow process of organic growth" (Figure 2.2). The advantage of slowness was that it enabled adaptation. In the medieval town, as needs and opportunities evolved, there was "continuity in change" and urban adaptations

Figure 2.2 Mellah, Fez, Morocco. *The irregularity of the street plan and the variety of building types imply a slow process of organic growth.*

became "increasingly coherent and purposeful." The resulting town form was "hardly less unified than a pre-formed geometric pattern."[6]

There is a key social distinction about the medieval town. Unlike the monumental places found in more modern cities, the medieval town had tight spaces and a labyrinthine street system that was not conducive to big social gatherings, anonymity, or popular uprisings. It was conducive to a more intimate form of social exchange.

3

Small Cities

The Greek polis and the medieval town are two types of small cities, but more can be said about small cities in other contexts. A small city—and up until the 19th century, most were—can be read in several ways. One interpretation is that they simply lack gravitas. And in fact an earlier era of city planners thought that city size correlated with knowledge. Thomas Adams, writing in the 1930s, lauded big cities because they gave "almost unlimited power in the harnessing of nature to their service."[1] By this logic, small cities were the result of limited knowledge, a highly questionable interpretation. Small size does have something to do with technological constraint, but obviously that is not the whole story.

There are many examples of small city size as a deliberate goal, enforced not in a way that citizens felt constrained or boxed in. In antiquity, as discussed above, smallness was a natural outgrowth of the limits of what the polis could do administratively, as well as how many people it was possible to interact with and how close people needed to be to the surrounding fields. In the 17th century, French Huguenots, fleeing annihilation in France, founded towns in Germany of limited size with no expansion or growth in mind. This was because they equated stasis with lasting peace. In American colonial settlement, small size was a conscious act of town planning rooted in communal ways of thinking, and these small villages are still a dominant feature of New England, for example in Vermont. To architect Léon Krier, this all made sense: there should be limits on size not because of abstract ideals, but because "like a tree or a man," a human community that exceeds its normal growth becomes a monster (Figure 3.1).[2]

Small size also makes the integration of the urban and the rural realms seem less problematic. The earliest American small towns, including New England colonial settlements as well as the pueblos influenced by the Spanish *Laws of the Indies*, were successful in treating urban and rural development as one integrated unit—the town, village green, or central plaza integrated with the surrounding fields. And yet town and country were distinct and separate, not blurred as in suburban sprawl. The small town, in other words, was the antithesis of sprawl because it was a town with defined limits, a place with an embodied sense of the limits of physical growth.

There is a social aspect to small city size as well, at times involving a prescribed kind of social life. A New England village reflects a communally oriented, puritanical social structure (although the New England "common" also served the function of military display). In theory, small size is better at sustaining face-to-face communication so that residents stay socially connected. Whether this is life-sustaining or

What Cities Say. Emily Talen, Oxford University Press. © Oxford University Press 2024. DOI: 10.1093/oso/9780197647769.003.0004

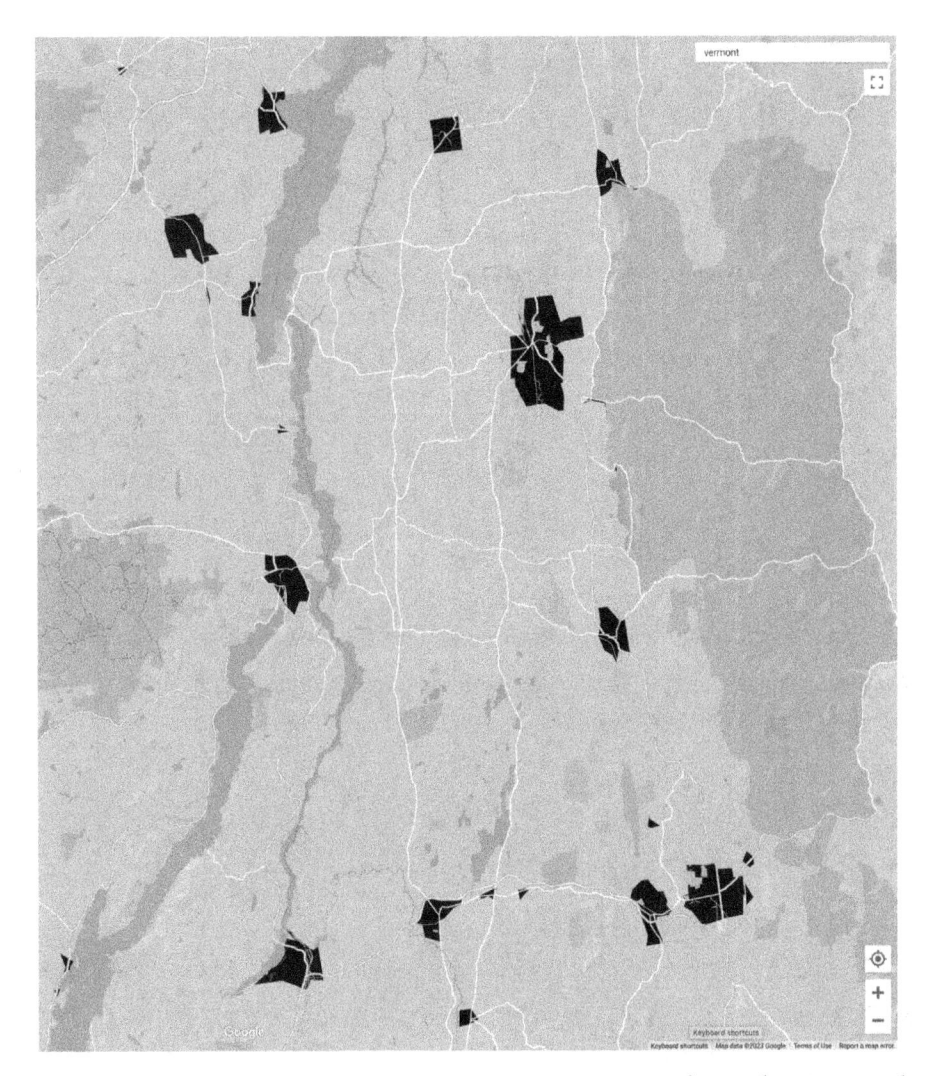

Figure 3.1 Vermont, USA. *Limiting town size is a conscious act of town planning rooted in communal ways of thinking.*

socially stifling is a matter of debate. Meinig thought of the New England village, or at least the image of it on Christmas cards, as symbolizing a tangible bond between the past and the present, "an intimate, family centered, Godfearing, morally conscious, industrious, thrifty, democratic community."[3] It certainly reflected modesty, a quality in stark contrast to the bold aggrandizement of other city forms and sizes.

The small city in circular form had a more overtly social meaning. The round patterns of 19th-century utopianists—Howard's garden city model, for example—suggest a desire to draw resident attention inward and toward each other. The added desire for access to nature kept things compact as well as circular. Kostof surmises that there was "something about the round form" that "suggested a unified pioneering community," "the will to endure," and a desire to reflect the fact that "all the

Figure 3.2 Nahalal, Israel. *The circular kibbutz suggests a unified, pioneering community—but also defense.*

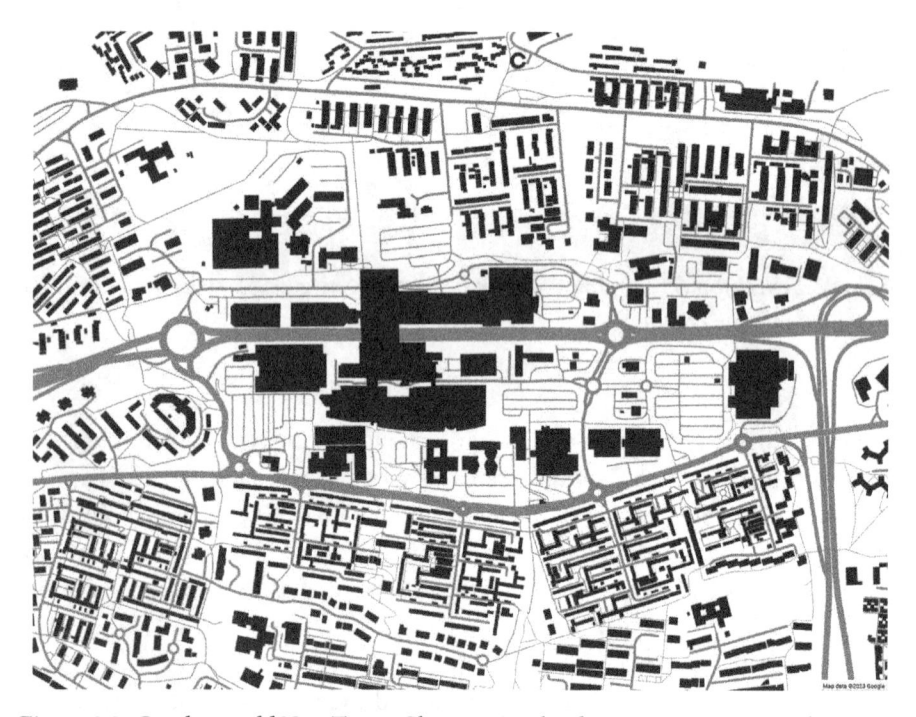

Figure 3.3 Cumbernauld New Town, Glasgow, Scotland. *A mega-structure at the center signals single ownership, as well as separation from surrounding neighborhoods.*

grand forms of nature are round." This is likely the motivation behind the rounded design of the 20th-century kibbutz, such as Nahalal, although it also reflects a defensive posture (Figure 3.2).[4]

The small, compact town has been difficult to sustain, however. In the case of small villages in the American frontier, farm lots consolidated to create larger and larger landholdings, and easy access to town by sufficient numbers of people was no longer feasible. Over time, the compact settlement was no longer needed for defensive purposes either, as conflicts with Native Americans declined.[5] Of course, towns could adamantly refuse to grow for other reasons quite different from socialization or urban-rural balance goals—more a matter of maintaining homogeneity and control over a settlement of peers.

Small cities seem vulnerable in certain contexts. Although they might have the ability to be flexible and adaptable, and therefore resilient, this falls apart if their cores are singularly owned rather than composed of multiple owners and uses. For example, if composed of a single commercial mega-structure and owner, as at Cumbernauld, Scotland, it signals that there is a great deal of money and centralized authority involved, with few individual business owners (Figure 3.3). This makes it more difficult to adjust to changing circumstances. A mega-structure at the core of a small town lacks flexibility, and therefore resilience. If the mega-development fails, so does the town.

4

Big Cities

If big cities are old and dense, centuries in the making, they reflect a certain level of resiliency. An old, big city reveals itself as a place that has been able to count on at least some people sticking around to help it survive. This is an apt description of American rust belt cities, which have faced cycles of abandonment followed by slow and patchy rejuvenation—but they're still there. To some observers, the most important point about big, old cities is how they compare to places planned all at once from scratch: new towns, industrial villages, garden cities, and especially planned suburbs—thought to be no match for big, old cities. Thomas Sharp summed up the sentiment when he wrote about garden cities in 1932: "They are unworthy of us. We want something to reflect our achievement, our great over-topping of Nature; something that is a worthy symbol of civilization . . . [garden cities] will never give it. Only sheer, triumphant, unadulterated urbanity will."[1]

There is something else revealed by modern cities that have reached a large size: an implicit attitude that there are no limits, and that more is better. This was certainly the 19th-century view of cities: the bigger the better, because quantity was indicative of success. And so, we might interpret a very large city, most likely with vast amounts of surrounding sprawl, as the physical form of an ideology espousing limitless "freedom." The freedom derives from the fact that there is no boundary, no definite shape, in fact no easily describable form. There might be an attempt to bring nature close in via private green space (the suburban lawn), but the countryside is pushed further and further out.

Another interpretation of big cities is that their sheer size and spread has tended to engender multiple forms of separation. This is somewhat paradoxical, since big cities, with their large consolidated populations, not only indicate that people want to come together in one place, but that they are willing to share in the costs of doing so. But it was under industrialized urbanization and the rise of big cities that new forms of separation and residential differentiation emerged. Previously, in places like the European quarter, shopkeeper and landlord lived alongside working-class neighbors, creating what has been described as a "collectivist moral economy."[2] But industrialism in the form of factory-based employment increased the distance between work and residence, even in the pre-automobile city, and factory workers who had once lived close to their jobs were now burdened with long commutes. The transition "from industrial to finance to corporate capitalism" that took place in big cities did not have the effect of producing "higher levels of consumption to successively lower strata" but instead had the effect of sorting people into differentiated

What Cities Say. Emily Talen, Oxford University Press. © Oxford University Press 2024. DOI: 10.1093/oso/9780197647769.003.0005

neighborhoods. Affordable mass transit played a role in this sorting, too. Lewis Mumford blamed social segregation on "wheeled vehicles" and "the domination of the avenue" in city-making, but it was after 1880 that mass transit provided the means for people to segregate into income-defined neighborhoods in a way that had not existed before.[3]

If big city neighborhoods were sorted but nevertheless linked to each other by rail, like beads on a string, that would be different. There was a brief moment when American streetcar settlements fanning out from big urban cores had this kind of linkage. But the nodes of modern cities are linked by highways rather than rail lines, creating fragmented urbanism, not interconnected beads on a string. Dubai has been described in this way: a series of disconnected centers with only desolation in between, forever looking like a construction site (Figure 4.1).[4]

But if large cities are clustered and dense, they have been likened to living organisms. Jane Jacobs, for one, made no apology for the big, messy, 20th-century city in all its complexity, and instead championed it as an essential setting for creative life. She saw the city not as social pathology but as the peak of human productivity and a setting that inspired adaptation. Where some have observed chaos, she observed the power of social connection. Not everyone agreed, of course, with the living organism analogy. Kevin Lynch rejected the notion that cities are in fact organisms: they do not "grow and change of themselves" or "reproduce or repair

Figure 4.1 Dubai, United Arab Emirates. *Dubai is a series of disconnected centers with only desolation in between, forever looking like a construction site.* Credit: Gary Denham from Edinburgh, Scotland, CC BY-SA 2.0 <https://creativecommons.org/licenses/by-sa/2.0>, via Wikimedia Commons

themselves," he wrote. They do not "run through life cycles," nor do they have even have organs.[5]

Big cities do, however, have districts, such as the central business district (CBD), or a warehousing district or an industrial district. As evidence of adaptation, sometimes the function of these districts changes radically. A stadium plopped down in the middle of a big city, most likely surrounded by highways to promote suburban access, is an indication that the city is courting tourist dollars and valuing out-of-towners over local residents. Loft districts have replaced industrial districts whose warehouses have been converted or repurposed as luxury lofts with restaurants and entertainment. To some observers, these district conversions create an "amusement park mood" and only an "illusion of urban vitality." What has been created is a passive district of residences and entertainment venues where there once flowed the city's economic lifeblood.

There are many examples of this attempt at district adaptation, a phenomenon especially associated with big, old cities. The conversions often represent some kind of loss. At the river's edge in St. Louis, Missouri, vacant 19th-century buildings are a reminder of a formerly thriving, working harbor, replaced with vacant land that further separates citizens from their waterfront (Figure 4.2). Finger piers, boardwalks, and high-density development along the water's edge in downtown Boston show the transition from using water as a source of livelihood to using water as an aesthetic object to be looked at. It is the "commoditization" of water views, elite replacing working-class conceptions of water, and a transition in which the water's "exchange value" is deemed more important than its "use value."[6]

Figure 4.2 St. Louis, Missouri, USA. *At the river's edge, vacant land separates citizens from their waterfront.*

Figure 4.3 Greenwich Village, New York, USA. *Human-scale and walkable, the Village has at least the veneer of a localized texture, although it now lacks the social and economic interconnectedness that generated it.* Credit: Felix Stahlberg, CC BY 2.0 <https:// creative commons.org/ licenses/ by/ 2.0>, via Wikimedia Commons.

Big cities are thus prone to dramatic change. Remnants of the past—pieces of old urbanism—are still visible and stand as a reminder of what a previous century of leaders, and the economic system they operated under, did not value highly enough to protect: small-scale, pre-automobile urban form. This was the form that played a role in supporting localized networks of social and economic interaction. The benefits of small-scale, localized urbanism have been documented by numerous writers, in addition to Jane Jacobs: Berman in *All That Is Solid Melts into Air* (1988), Von Hoffman in *Local Attachments* (1996), and Rae in *City* (2003). Perhaps the retention of small-scale urbanism and the loss of localized networks under urban renewal was thought irrelevant, or unstoppable, in light of the new "mass consumption economy," one that channeled consumer markets to suburban areas.[7]

Now, the older residential districts in big cities, places like Greenwich Village in New York City, have at least the veneer of a localized texture, a human-scale, finely grained, walkable urban context, with street-facing windows and doors, an interconnected street pattern, and a fine-grained mixture of land uses (Figure 4.3). Unfortunately, such places most likely lack the social and economic interconnectedness that once generated them.

5

Linear Cities

Linear cities are often the result of natural phenomena, for example when cities are sandwiched between ocean and mountains. Bern, Switzerland, is linear because it developed between two rivers formed by a deep bend in the meandering River Aare (Figure 5.1).

Commerce is also a common factor. Medieval towns were often essentially "street villages," for example Appleton-le-Moors in North Yorkshire, UK (Figure 5.2). The modern American equivalent is the arterial commercial strip. Both the street village and the commercial strip elevated commerce and movement simultaneously. But there is an important difference. The medieval street village contained the whole of town life; the strip was and is an abstraction of town life, offering only a car-based, and therefore individualized, commercial experience. As Grady Clay observed, the strip says a lot about Americans: that they value convenience, and that they are "determined to simplify" life as much as possible. This translates to the "open road" rather than the "closed city."[1]

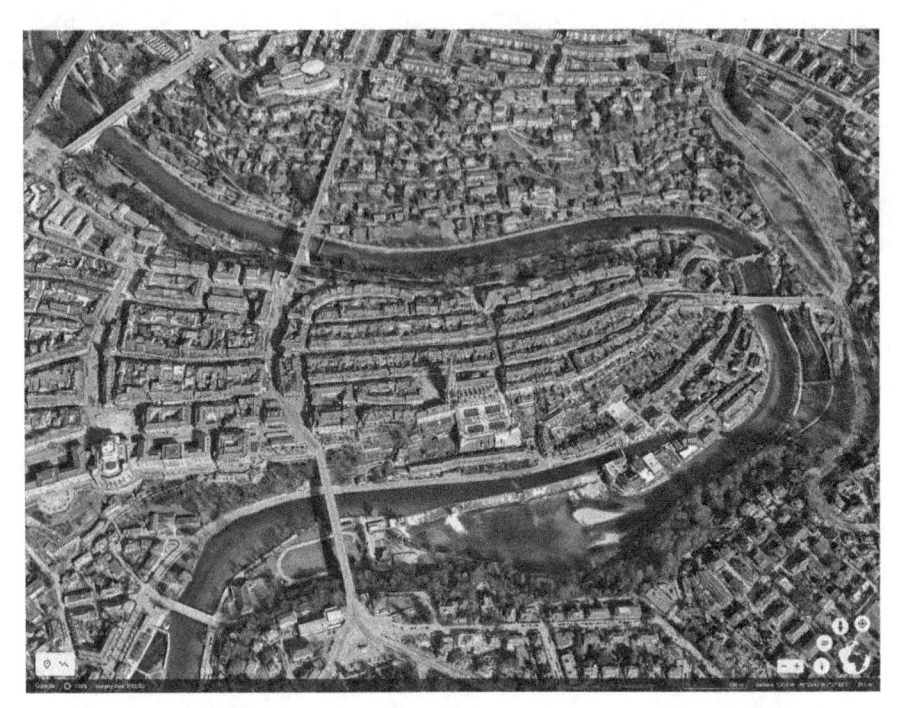

Figure 5.1 Bern, Switzerland. *The city's linearity is a function of being fit within a deep bend in the River Aare.*

What Cities Say. Emily Talen, Oxford University Press. © Oxford University Press 2024. DOI: 10.1093/oso/9780197647769.003.0006

Figure 5.2 Appleton-le-Moors in North Yorkshire, UK. *The medieval street village elevates commerce and movement simultaneously.*

Figure 5.3 La Ciudad Lineal, Madrid, Spain. *The linear city was expandable and had no population limit, but it was swallowed up by Madrid, obscuring its novel rail-based linearity.*

The most famous explicitly planned linear city is La Ciudad Lineal in Madrid, devised by Arturo Soria y Mata in the late 19th century (Figure 5.3). The idea was to devise an infinitely expandable urban form, since a city without limits has to expand, either by spawning new colonies or by growing vertically or horizontally. La Ciudad Lineal's growth concept was intended to bring services into the countryside along rail lines, a very different approach from populating the countryside with nodes and clusters of houses. In theory, the linear city was expandable and had no population limit. It was also made for commuters, which means it could strengthen the urban core and keep people close to both amenities (via transit) and green space. And it was not directed inward, as British garden cities were.[2]

Kevin Lynch labeled La Ciudad Lineal, somewhat sarcastically, an "excellent mechanical form," with its quality of "infinite expression." But he also knew that mechanical form, while seemingly economical and rational, could mask the fact that cities, and societies, were becoming completely dominated by the transportation sector.[3] The translation of Soria's concept into strip malls and arterial-based development has been a source of critique—although not a fair one, since strip development is an incomplete applications of linear city form. The problem for La Ciudad Lineal in Madrid is that it got swallowed up by Madrid, obscuring its novel rail-based linearity except for the name of its central avenue.

Linear development can have certain advantages and efficiencies. It can be compact while still keeping open space, perhaps even "nature," close at hand. And it can make transit systems more accessible. Manhattan is fairly linear, and as a result subway lines run north and south and everyone is close to a station—but in Chicago, with its spoke-and-wheel system where all lines point to the center, wide areas are left stranded. The concentric form is less efficient in terms of commute cost. And, unlike the concentric garden city model with its higher land values concentrated at the core, the linear city involves a more logical declension of values from the axial road.

The movement-based linear city is an idea that still appeals, although not in the form of strip malls along arterials. The Line, a linear city under construction in Saudi Arabia, has all the hallmarks of La Ciudad's top-down utopian vision. More modest is the idea of repurposing arterial roads. For cities that have developed in function of cars, the linear city provides a model for retrofit: a way of making something of value out of the arterial. The arterial is mostly a commercial wasteland with no social value—and also often quite deadly, as pedestrians attempt to cross commercial strips that never had a walking human in mind. The creation of transportation-based ribbons of urbanism through sprawl, perhaps edging close to something more akin to the medieval street village, has been presented as a way to transform endless miles of commercial corridors into more complete, transit served communities, a 21st-century vision of the linear city.[4]

6

New Towns and Colonial Outposts

New towns and colonial outposts are a category of "whole places" that occur earlier than garden cities, planned suburbs, and company towns. Like all planned communities, new towns reflect aspirations about lifestyle and how people are supposed to conduct their daily lives. In this sense, the form of the new town embodies a social order—who is supposed to live where, how much land they are supposed to have, how integrated the functions of the town are supposed to be, and what level of collective life is imagined.

The mere act of town-founding—staking out a town location and building it from scratch—can have considerable symbolic value. To Lefebvre, Spanish-American town founding under the *Laws of the Indies* (discussed below) was an "instrument of production" and a way for an economic and social "superstructure" to gain a foothold in a foreign land. As such, town founding to further Spanish economic goals symbolized a violent takeover of existing space.[1]

Monarchical town planting was not particularly natural nor responsive to social or economic need. The town might even be planted in a place with no natural reason for accommodating a town. Such towns were unlikely to be good at inspiring self-organization or adaptation, since deviation from the plan would be viewed as an affront to the town creators. New towns can thus be dehumanizing and regimenting in a way that goes against human nature. Sometimes, the diagrammatic new town is thought to be created by "dreamers" who are operating in a world of control and fantasy, wanting "the complexity and richness of urban structure without the problems, tensions and volatility."[2]

One could say that new towns—building a complete town from scratch—is an extreme case of instilling order. The order is not only about laying out streets and public spaces, but about ensuring that all the pieces are there to make the town complete. On the positive side, controlling where those pieces are located can ensure reasonable access and proximity between things. It might also evoke commitment, confidence, and a sense of optimism. Perhaps order saves money by eliminating waste that might come from haphazard development. And planning in totality—all the parts of the whole conceived together—has the ability to communicate a strong message.

But town founding was often also a matter of empire-building, a desire to control territory by establishing towns as colonial outposts. Roman military encampments, medieval bastides, colonial outposts of the British Empire, Early American cities, and US railroad towns all share this trait—town founding for the purpose of

What Cities Say. Emily Talen, Oxford University Press. © Oxford University Press 2024. DOI: 10.1093/oso/9780197647769.003.0007

Figure 6.1 Williamsburg, Virginia, USA. *Vestiges of baroque spatial form symbolized that Williamsburg was the center of an empire.*

Figure 6.2 Pavia, Italy. *The Romans liked their towns gridded and regularized; the blocks of Pavia and Verona measure exactly the same size.*

territorial expansion. Even Williamsburg, Virginia, has been described as a town devoted to inscribing colonial power and control, suppressing and exploiting indigenous peoples, and using its baroque spatial form to symbolize that Williamsburg was "the center of an empire" (Figure 6.1).[3]

The Romans were prolific town founders—and they liked their towns gridded, with large square blocks. The Roman military played a part in standardizing town form, translating militaristic discipline to neat, standardized blocks and a central axis. So, for example, the blocks of Verona and Pavia, Italy, measure exactly the same size: approximately 265 feet square (Figure 6.2). Another example is the town of Timgad, Algeria, a gridded ruin, with square blocks and centrally positioned

Figure 6.3 Timgad, Algeria. *Square blocks and centrally positioned public spaces: "the Roman grid at its most perfect."*

public spaces (Figure 6.3). The Romans founded the town in 100 CE. The forum, baths, and amphitheater are just below the central crossroads, and around them the blocks become slightly larger, but the main effect is of coherence and centrality. Kostof heralded Timgad as "the Roman grid at its most perfect."[4]

The medieval bastides, which were new towns developed in the Middle Ages throughout Europe, are an important category of town founding. The bastides were highly regularized and driven by basic functional requirements in order to attract population. As they were the first settlements in Europe no longer attached to a feudal castle, the possibility of living a life apart from serfdom was a huge draw. There was a market square, church, and surrounding walls, and the regularized structure, overseen by founders who lived far off in places like London or Paris, enabled "efficient remote control."[5] Like Roman towns, these strategically located enclaves and outposts, set to claim land and resources, were almost always gridded.

Like most new towns and colonial outposts, there was a strong profit motive involved. Most of the bastides were developed as market towns by powerful noblemen (kings, dukes, counts, lords) who wanted to "return a profit to their sponsors" and concentrate population "in secure places for ease of administration." Though built

Figure 6.4 Monpazier, Provence, France. *Bastide towns were supposed to return a profit; the church is just outside of the marketplace.*

for profit-making, Braunfels labeled the bastides "sterile" speculations that "paralyzed the entrepreneurial spirit" (they were kept small because success just meant more taxation). Kostof argued that religion was also a motivation, citing Thomas Aquinas' 13th-century writing that "building cities is the duty of kings." The towns, however, did not reflect religious centrality. A centralized marketplace, either square or rectangular, had an associated market building, but the positioning of the church was often in a corner of the market or even a couple of blocks away. For example, in Monpazier in Provence, one of the many extant bastide towns, the church is just outside of the marketplace (Figure 6.4).[6]

Another main category of town founding, or more specifically, colonial outposting, occurred under the rules of the *Laws of the Indies*, the well-known 16th-century ordinance imposed by the Spanish monarchy for laying out colonies in the "new world" (although not all Spanish colonies were based on the *Laws*). Like the sponsors of the medieval bastides, the king used the *Laws of the Indies* to achieve his objective of regulating from a distance. Spanish colonialists had the option of three types of settlements for three different purposes: missions (religious), presidios (military), and pueblos (civilian), although these functions were not always kept distinct. The *Laws* were meant to apply only to pueblos.

It is possible to see traces of the *Laws* today in places like Los Angeles, Tucson, and Santa Fe, but very few towns followed the specifications exactly. The City of La Plata in Argentina, laid out in the late 19th century, merged the historical specifications of the *Laws* with 19th-century ideas about the hygienic city and the need for air, light, and green. The result is a highly regularized pattern (every sixth

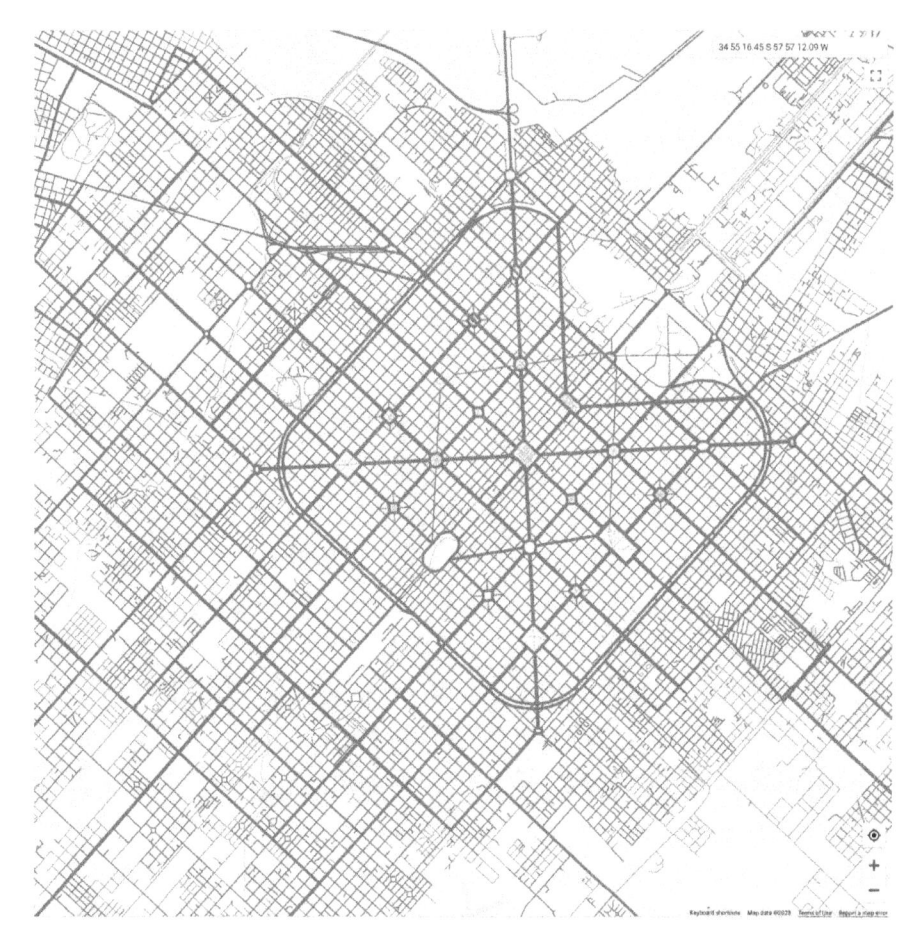

Figure 6.5 La Plata, Argentina. *A highly regularized merger of the Laws of the Indies with 19th-century ideas about the hygienic city. Smaller blocks toward the center are meant to improve access to it.*

block has an intersecting diagonal avenue) employing what was the latest in scientific thinking: smaller blocks toward the core to improve access to the center, green areas at the intersections of avenues, and lavish, strictly aligned tree planting (Figure 6.5).[7]

Unlike the bastides, which were enclosed towns positioned as discrete and self-contained nodes, the Spanish model of town founding had an open configuration and a "logic of infinite expansion." This was accomplished by designating a commons at the town's periphery that could accommodate future growth. In addition, the main square at the center of town, initially proportioned relative to population size, was meant to be extendable as the population grew. But, somewhat paradoxically, the *Laws* emphasized the importance of completeness by forbidding the entry of Indians into new towns until they were "complete": "so that when the Indians see them they will be filled with wonder and will realize that the Spaniards are settling there permanently and not temporarily."[8]

Figure 6.6 Kanbawzathadi Golden Palace, Bago, Myanmar. *Square cities built in Myanmar were based on planet mythology: the magic of nine squares.*

Another motivation for town founding was religious or cosmological symbolism, in which case town form might be based on cardinal points or the movement of the stars. Amos Rappaport called these "high-level meanings."[9] For example, in the first century CE, square cities built in Myanmar (formerly Burma) were based on planet mythology: the magic of nine squares (Figure 6.6). The town of Madurai in India was meant to be a model of the cosmos, an explicit reflection of symbolic holiness and a way of stabilizing communities on earth so that humans could be given a secure place within it. Gates and walls functioned as encircling enclosures that inspired a sense of sanctity and helped the inhabitant move progressively inward, literally and spiritually (Figure 6.7).[10]

In the Christian world, cross-shaped towns were a popular new town design, for example the little Moravian settlement of Schoenbrunn, Ohio, laid out in the shape of a cross in 1772 (Figure 6.8). More elaborate is the town of Scherpenheuvel in Belgium, laid out in the 17th century with seven sides and seven roads leading to a church (Figure 6.9). This was done because the number seven is a highly symbolic and religiously meaningful number, corresponding to the number of the Virgin Mary's seven joys and seven sorrows. Because of its holy plan, the town was, and still is, a pilgrimage destination believed to bestow healing powers.

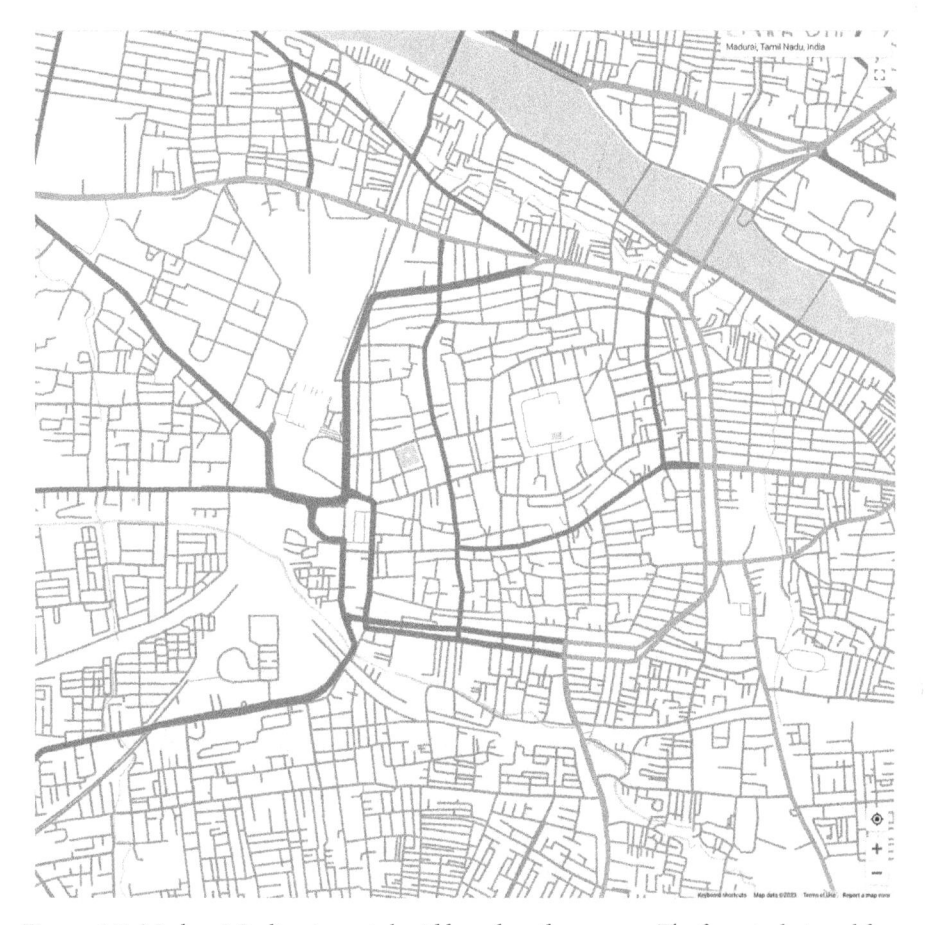

Figure 6.7 Madurai, India. *A special grid based on the cosmos. The form is designed for rituals like processions.*

Figure 6.8 Schoenbrunn, Ohio, USA. *An 18th-century Moravian settlement in the shape of a cross.*

Figure 6.9 Scherpenheuvel, Belgium. *Seven sides and seven roads leading to a church, symbolic of the Virgin Mary's seven joys and seven sorrows.*

Other new towns based on numbers emerged out of the "Age of Reason" that started in the late 17th century. Gutkind gives examples of the "symbolism of numbers" that became a basis of these new towns: the towns of Willemstad, Deventer, and Enkhuizen in the Netherlands, all of which had seventeen bastions corresponding to the country's seventeen counties, as well as the "sacred character" of that number. Palma Nova's nine bastions were in honor of the nine families of Venetian nobility.[11]

In the United States, religious separatists founded utopian towns of "refuge" that were planned so that communitarianism would balance with individualism.[12] Examples include New Harmony, Indiana, and Economy, Pennsylvania, built by the 19th-century religious sect the Harmony Society (Figure 6.10). Although they were simple grids, they embedded a social theory that stressed the importance of one's surroundings and its effect on morality and thoughtfulness. There was care and thought put into building placement in which buildings went right up to the sidewalk and engaged with the street—and thus public life. Such towns can be contrasted with towns built not according to social theory or spiritual need, but according to economic fact. In time, the latter tended to have a more prosperous outcome, at least economically.

Figure 6.10 New Harmony, Indiana, USA. *Simple grids with an embedded social theory about the value of community.*

Colonial outposts in Asia and Africa constructed in the early to mid-20th century embodied a profound incongruity. In some cases, for example British colonial town-building in Africa, new towns were built with a rigid kind of order not at all in keeping with the multipurpose and integrated spaces the local population wanted and needed. Suddenly people were forced to construct functions and uses for village life with a town form not at all conducive to flexibility and adaptation.

In other places, the modern "New Towns" movement of the mid-20th century started with utopian and social egalitarian motives. Gradually, the devotion to "green" seemed to eclipse these goals, and the new towns ultimately translated to just another form of sprawl, with its car dependence and social and economic separation. For example, the highways and large-scale gridded arterials traversing the British new town of Milton Keynes, while "lined with fine planting," created inwardly focused neighborhoods and pedestrian routes sequestered and "invisible" (Figure 6.11). Development is contained within landscaped grids and because of the separation, local shopkeepers struggle for viability. There are similar examples in the United States. The newer peripheral parts of Peachtree City, Georgia, a 1960s-era new town, show residential neighborhoods that are disconnected from, though geographically close to, the village shopping center (Figure 6.12). One might say that this reveals a lack of interest in the communal life that the new town was supposed to embody. The lifeline for the storeowners is that the shopping center is next to a highway exit.[13]

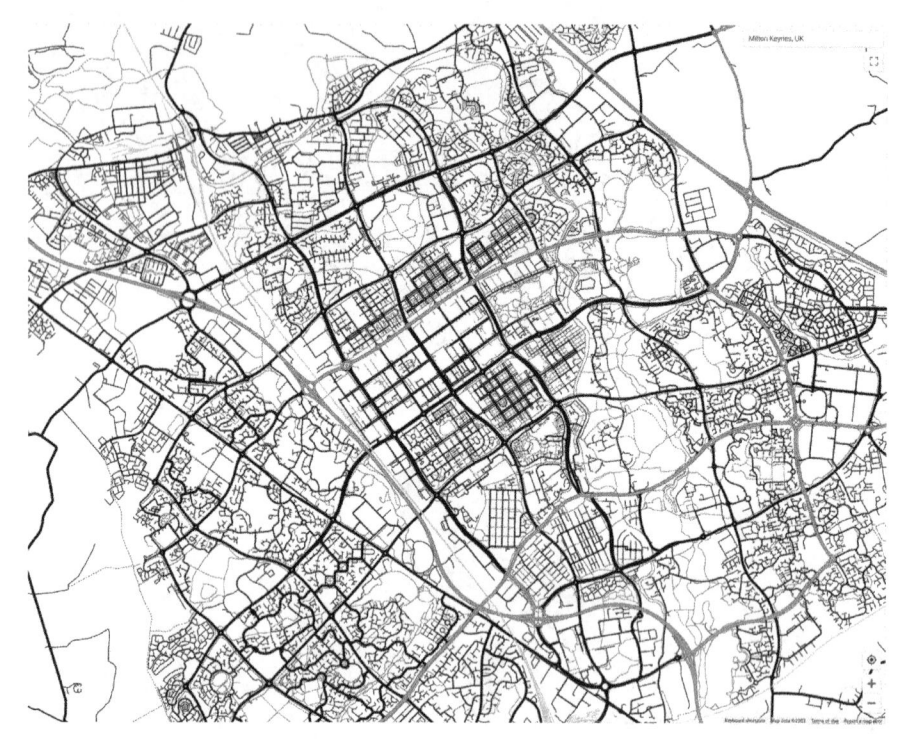

Figure 6.11   Milton Keynes, UK. *The large-scale gridded arterials create inwardly focused neighborhoods and sequestered pedestrian routes.*

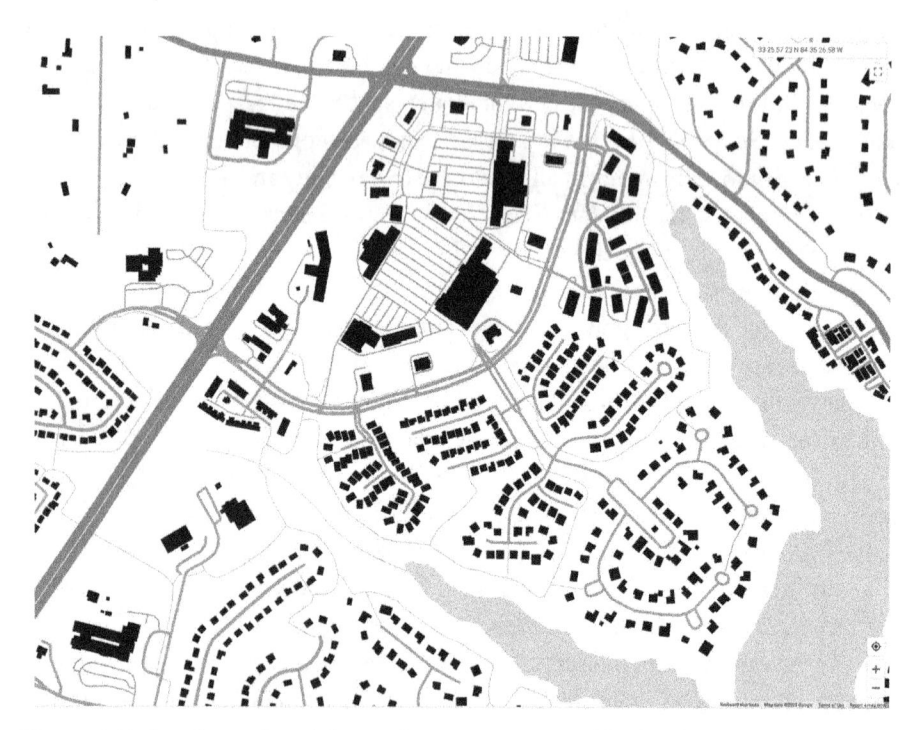

Figure 6.12   Peachtree City, Atlanta, Georgia, USA. *Neighborhoods can be completely disconnected from, although geographically close to, a shopping center.*

Figure 6.13 Rawabi, West Bank, Palestine. *A symbol of Palestinian aspirations for middle-class security: town founding need not symbolize escape or aggression.*

Since the 19th century, the whole idea of creating a new town from scratch has been regularly, and strongly, criticized. Hans Blumenfeld summed it up, writing that the "fixation" on the new town "is rooted in a conscious or unconscious desire to escape from the complexities of our rapidly changing times into a simpler and stable world that probably never existed and certainly cannot exist today."[14] However, town founding need not symbolize escape or aggression, and in fact can symbolize hope and aspiration. The Palestinian new town of Rawabi is a good example, a mark of Palestinian aspirations for middle class security. Located in the occupied West Bank, the town stands for nothing less than the dream of a better future for the Palestinian people (Figure 6.13).

7

Industrial Villages and Company Towns

The defining element of an industrial village or a company town is that it is a human settlement that does not exclude the industry it depends on. Industry is not covered up or shunned; it is an integral part of human habitation. The difference between the two terms is subtle. "Industrial village" is a slightly more modern term than "company town." Both are based on the idea that the employer should provide homes and daily life services for workers, in the same locale as industry.

This makes the company town quite different from a planned community like Riverside, Illinois, developed in 1869 (discussed under "Garden Suburbs," below). Undergirding the latter was a desire to purposefully escape industry, relying on a distant city for employment, attractions, and cultural diversity. Since diversity was desirable only from a distance, the towns created what Christopher Alexander called "the plastic unreality of sheltered residential neighborhoods." Better, Alexander argued, to integrate industry, make it a "real part of life" that could be "woven into the fabric" of the town in a way that properly reflected "its huge importance in the scheme of things."[1]

Because of manufacturing requirements, industrial villages were often planned and built along waterways. Internally, the layout could be symbolic and almost allegorical. Saltaire in the UK, founded in 1851 in Yorkshire and built in a neo-Renaissance style, placed the church across from the mill as a kind of symbolic pairing of functions—a proclamation of the godliness of industrial ingenuity. Creese admired Saltaire's urbanity, noting that those who thought the model village was in general too low-density would "find comfort in Saltaire."[2]

The industrial village that emerged in the late 19th and early 20th centuries was often planned in the "organic" tradition (the other organic tradition, according to Kostof, was the "picturesque suburb," which was exclusively for the affluent). Two early examples from the 19th century are Port Sunlight, developed near Liverpool in 1892 by the soap manufacturer W. H. Lever (Figure 7.1); and Bournville, near Birmingham, started in 1895 and developed by the chocolate manufacturers the Cadbury brothers. Both were greatly admired at the time by city planners in the United States and Europe, and, symbolic of their stature, were the sites of the first two garden city conferences held in 1901 and 1902. Mumford thought the design of Port Sunlight was overblown, ridiculing it for its "almost comic" baroque approach to the civic center, which he thought revealed "the influence of princely absolutism even under an industrial disguise."[3]

What Cities Say. Emily Talen, Oxford University Press. © Oxford University Press 2024. DOI: 10.1093/oso/9780197647769.003.0008

Figure 7.1 Port Sunlight, Birkenhead, UK. *Baroque absolutism under an industrial disguise; rich and poor lived side by side, their houses indistinguishable from the exterior.*

Port Sunlight popularized the picturesque, with its irregular street plan and neo-vernacular architecture. According to Kostof, this is where the "superblock" was first introduced, where houses faced an interior green space rather than the street (a technique later popularized at Radburn, New Jersey). Another notable feature was that the town included housing intended for a range of incomes, and design regularity was used to minimize the distinction between single-family and multiple-family dwelling types. Thus the attention to a unified architectural style went beyond being merely picturesque: it was also a social integration strategy, as large houses and worker's cottages, all adhering to the same architectural vocabulary, could be integrated seamlessly. This practice became a regular feature of garden city and garden suburb design. A good example is found in the garden city of Hellerau, outside Dresden (Figure 7.2). Bournville was also successful in maintaining social diversity, but the approach was programmatic: there was a limit on how many of the company's employees could make their residence there. George Cadbury believed it should be limited to one-half the town, to avoid the closed-in feeling of other industrial villages (Figure 7.3).[4]

Industrial towns in the early 20th century were often modeled after garden cities. This included the Krupps family town established outside Essen, Margarethenhohe, and Hellerau. Such towns were not the usual modus operandi of the 19th-century industrial capitalist. They were the product of patricians who wanted to construct a holistic environment thought to be wholesome, morally uplifting, and a better place for workers to live. But this was not all altruism: the towns were believed to be conducive to increased worker productivity. Nelson P. Lewis, an engineer-planner, reported that the towns were run at a financial loss that was offset by an increase in worker efficiency—a direct result, he surmised, of the improvement in living

Figure 7.2 Hellerau, German. *A 1911 postcard, showing curved streets for the purpose of artful groupings that form "street pictures," a characteristic of picturesque design.* Credit: Brück & Sohn Kunstverlag Meißen, CC0, via Wikimedia Commons.

Figure 7.3 Bournville, Birmingham, UK. *An early model industrial village and a garden city in miniature. Houses and gardens are communally arranged, but slightly staggered.*

conditions. Thus, the industrialists' goal of providing better living conditions has to be seen for what it was—a business decision.

Industrial villages and company towns do have a major flaw: they suffer from having a singularity of purpose, rising and falling based entirely on the strength of one industry. Tyrone, New Mexico, a short-lived copper-mining town that was deserted when the price of copper dropped, is one example. A company town is

Figure 7.4 Pullman, Chicago, Illinois, USA. *The most famous company town in the United States was a model of control; the provision of civic spaces was tempered by the fact that all spaces were company owned.*

also thought of as too controlling and socialistic (and in the United States, un-American). This control is why the company town has been interpreted as anti-city—because it constrains economic structure. The merger of factory and town is an artificial alliance, since cities are made up of complex interactions drawn from a diverse set of enterprises that go beyond a factory, housing, and services for factory workers. What is missing is reciprocity: people, housing, and services living in direct function of work productivity, not in function of their own needs for investment or the production of capital.[5] The industrial village thus subsumed the social life of the town, combining urban life and economic productivity in such a way that the city was, in a sense, annulled. There was no system of growth outside of the factory.

The most famous company town in the United States was Pullman, Illinois, built ten miles south of downtown Chicago in 1881 (Figure 7.4). Pullman was a model of control, from the architectural design of the buildings, to determining where workers were supposed to live and shop. The provision of civic spaces was tempered by the fact that all spaces were company owned, a condition that made it seem less like a real town and more like an exercise in pure social control. Gans described Pullman as a "beautiful and efficient reformatory . . . for people who had done nothing wrong."[6]

The town of Vandergrift, Pennsylvania, was a model company town attached to a large steel mill outside of Pittsburgh (Figure 7.5). The town provided housing for workers, which, as with all company towns, was intended to soothe labor unrest. But the town lacked a center, or even a logical commercial focus, perhaps as a way of tamping down communalism or to ensure that the steel mill was not upstaged as the heart of the town.

Figure 7.5 Vandergrift, Pennsylvania, USA. *The town for factory workers lacked a center, perhaps as a way of constraining communalism.*

How should we judge industrial villages and company towns? One metric is to consider whether the population was provided for and protected. Most often, despite the rhetoric, little thought was given to the needs of the population—the very workers who would be essential for keeping the factories rolling. Instead, the factories and railroads took the choicest locations and blocked access to waterways and other natural features. Worse, the wind direction carrying smoke, the location of waste disposal, and the shielding of residences from the noise and soot of industry were all concerns that were usually given no thought whatsoever.[7]

8

Garden Cities

True "garden cities" are rare because the concept requires communal ownership of land and an integrated employment source—hard to pull off under capitalism. Much has been written about the concept's originator, Ebenezer Howard, whose 1898 garden cities proposal was an anarchic, utopian vision of communal living. There have been countless variations on his basic theme of complete communities surrounding by "nature," developed outside of the city. Many are called "garden cities" but are located at the outskirts of cities with no integrated employment source like a factory, which means they are not technically garden cities in the Howardian sense. But these distinctions became muddled over time. The 1913 book *Garden City Movement Up-to-Date* distinguished garden cities as a) self-contained towns; b) garden suburbs that provided a way for the growth of existing cities to be along "healthy lines"; and c) garden villages, such as Bournville and Port Sunlight, that were "garden cities in miniature" dependent on "some neighbouring city for water, light and drainage."[1]

The interpretation of a garden city changes significantly depending on context. Outside of a 19th-century industrial city, it was an escape from urban degradation and a chance to be close to nature and tend to a garden. In an early 20th-century Brazilian context, the sinuous curves of a garden city meant foreign, and especially English, influence, which were highly revered at the time. In that case, the meaning had little to do with escaping to a garden because for Brazilians, who were "descendants of a slavery society," there was "no dignity" in garden work.[2]

Long before the garden city idea emerged out of the 19th century, there was a long tradition of garden design having an influence on city form. One example is the Champs Elysées in Paris, which was originally the bucolic private entrance to the king's palace. Garden designs from the Renaissance and Baroque periods were also influential, and highly diagrammatic. The gardens at Versailles, or the grounds of the Château de Sceaux, six miles from Paris (Figure 8.1), were formal gardens that provided a necessary intermediate link between nature (the sacred) and the city (the profane). In an especially literal transfer, the garden of the Villa Lante, adjacent to the town of Bagnaia in Italy, seems to be a near copy of the town square (Figure 8.2).[3]

With the rise of industrial urbanization, reformers contemplated the idea of putting housing in a garden. An early 19th-century writer spelled out the implications: it meant that the "cottager" could be attached "to his home and to his country," which would not only have the effect of "inducing sober, industrious, and domestic habits"

What Cities Say. Emily Talen, Oxford University Press. © Oxford University Press 2024. DOI: 10.1093/oso/9780197647769.003.0009

Figure 8.1 Château de Sceaux, Paris, France. *Formal gardens provided an intermediate link between nature (the sacred) and the city (the profane).*

Figure 8.2 Bagnaia, Italy. *The garden of the Villa Lante is a copy of the town square.*

but would produce a "feeling of independence," which in turn would be "the best security against pauperism."[4] The garden city of Bawarda in Abadan, Iran, built a century later, had similar moralizing objectives (Figure 8.3). The smaller size meant that not only was it easier to control, but the "social pathologies" of the overcrowded cities, which were unable to expand (or prevented from so doing), could at least be dispersed.[5]

The main objective of a garden city was to have all the diversions of urban life contained within the settlement, minus the associated incivilities like pollution and crime—a best-of-both-worlds, town-country arrangement. This was thought possible because of the small size involved. Kept small, garden cities fought against

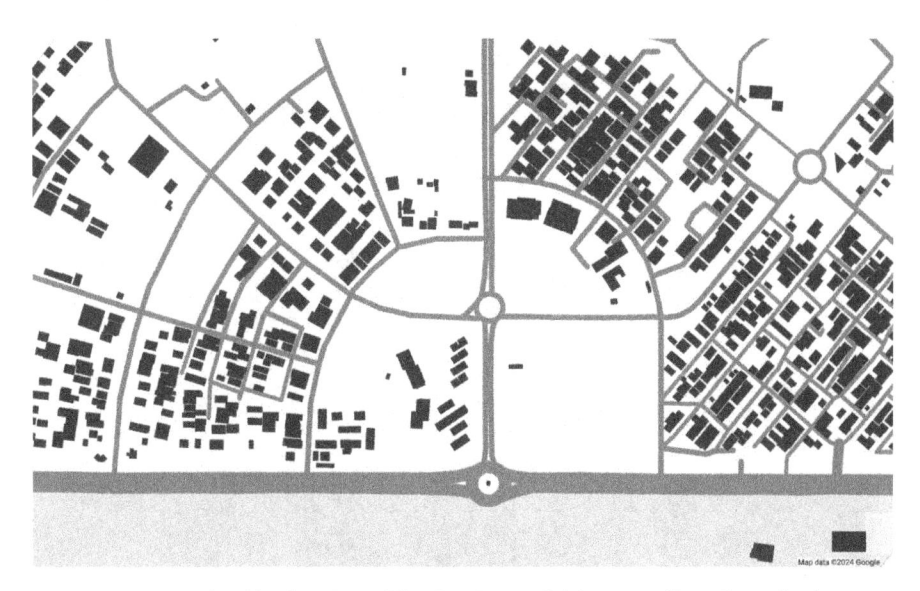

Figure 8.3 Bawarda, Abadan, Iran. *The City Beautiful for a small garden suburb; scattered housing ignores the formality of the ceremonial axes.*

the aggregative tendencies of cities, which were in a continual campaign to concentrate wealth and power.[6] Fortunately, with the right architecture to emulate a romanticized English village, the ideology behind Howard's more radical socialistic vision could be neutralized. But is it legitimate to combine urban material advantage with nature-inspired tranquility in an attempt to be "Hamiltonian by day and Jeffersonian by night"?[7]

Sir Patrick Abercrombie saw Howard's vision as a logical replication of a planetary system, whereby growth would be coherently distributed to "sun city and satellites."[8] The organization of cities into small, discrete units "embedded in a decentralized society" was critical for Howard's vision of a civilization based on cooperation. But it was a tall order, and according to planning historian Peter Hall, only three true garden cities were ever actually built. One of them, Howard's Letchworth Garden City, is more garden than city (Figure 8.4).

Of course, not all garden cities are small and village-like. New Delhi is one example. Another is Canberra, the capital of Australia, which is essentially a garden city organized around City Beautiful–like monumental centers. It is an odd mix. The garden city is devoted to communalism, while the City Beautiful is associated with social hierarchy. Ceremonial axes presenting "a great imperial display of ethnic and political hierarchies" are lined with the "rhetoric of historical assimilation" in the form of rows of worker housing.[9] Despite the incongruity, there are many examples of the Garden City–City Beautiful merger, such as the affluent Mount Royal in Montreal (where the blocks align north-south to maximize sun exposure) (Figure 8.5). Bawarda, Iran, is a near–ghost town of City Beautiful ceremonial axes, with only scattered housing that seems to ignore the formality.

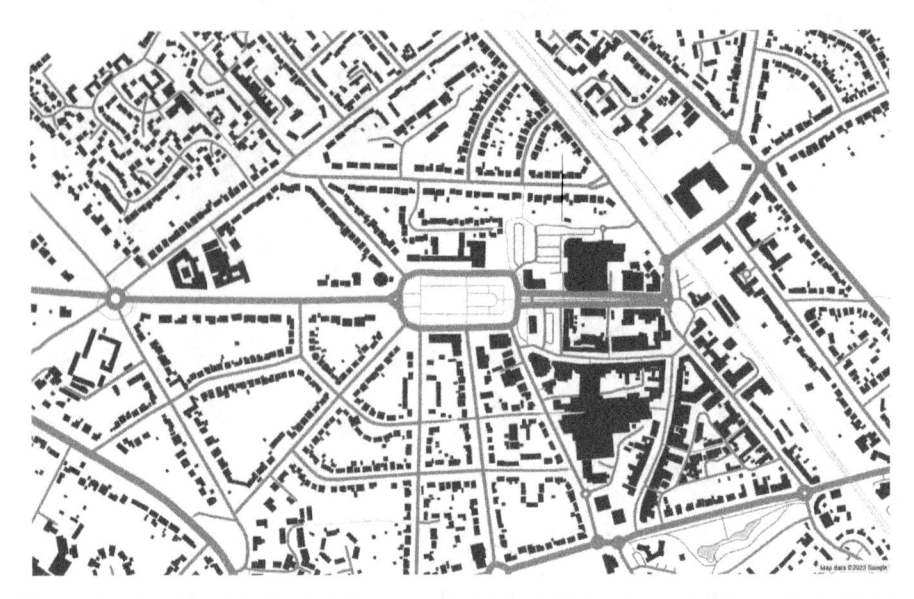

Figure 8.4 Letchworth Garden City, near London, UK. *Letchworth was the first official Garden City. Peter Hall criticized it for having a "weak" center, with streets that seemed to go nowhere.*

Criticism of the garden city model has been strong. It would be one thing to withdraw from the dehumanizing "modern" world and seek out "nature" for escape, comfort, and a sense of release, but garden cities, in seeking to isolate themselves from the city, are said to engage in a "cult of isolation." The insistence on ruralized housing style doesn't help and has been labeled "aesthetic cowardice." Winding lanes and detached houses are an aestheticized version of "the country" and essentially fake, especially as there is often no "countryside" left.[10]

But there have always been strong supporters, too. Walter Creese's treatise *The Search for Environment* (1966) was a sympathetic look at the garden city, which he described as an attempt to find a middle ground between "the cottage of the hand weaver and the town of the manufacturer."[11] It certainly tried to overcome the problem of spatial mismatch—workers and work were brought together in one place. Where this integration was successful, the garden city could be conceived of not as limiting to the individual, but as a conduit for freedom—freedom from the tyranny of the city, from social pressures, from financial worries, from want of the basic needs of daily life. Speculative development, in contrast, does not provide more freedom; it only homogenizes living options.

Garden city design emphasized access to green space and careful management of traffic, both strategies seen as promoting wholesomeness and moral uplift. For example, one strategy was to use open and connected green space as the organizing physical framework of the town, rather than using a street system as the framework. The open space was to be shared and networked, the idea being that this arrangement would be better at community-building than a street system. It was a

Figure 8.5 Mount Royal, Montreal, Canada. *A Garden City–City Beautiful merger. Blocks align north-south to maximize sun exposure.*

Figure 8.6 Margarethenhöhe, Essen, Germany. *A garden city for industrial workers. Moral uplift was intended by keeping the marketplace and school off the main through-traffic roads and embedding them in residential blocks.*

Figure 8.7 Mariemont, Cincinnati, Ohio, USA. *In this version of the garden city, there are single-family houses on larger lots, separated from duplexes and rowhouses in separate sections—but the distances between them are short.*

greenbelt "turned inside out."[12] At Margarethenhöhe in Germany, a related aspect of the intended moral uplift was to make sure the town's main attractions—the marketplace and the schools—were kept off the main through-traffic roads and were instead embedded in residential blocks (Figure 8.6).

But social segregation seemed to be baked in. In Letchworth, Welwyn Garden City, and Mariemont, Ohio, one can see housing separated by economic class. What can be said in their defense, however, is that in these older versions of the garden city model, the segregation is often a smaller and tighter version of the socially segregated housing pods production builders later employed to build residential sprawl. Housing variety is distinct, but there is proximity. At Mariemont, Ohio, it is easy to pick out the single-family houses on larger lots, separated from the duplexes in a separate section, and the rowhouses in another—but the distances among them are short (Figure 8.7).

9

Urban Suburbs

The earliest suburbs were either relatively close in to the existing city or linked by public transit. Railroad suburbs were physically distinct, initially separated from the city by plenty of open land, but in many cases, these early suburbs now have a very urban feel. Often, suburbs that were first developed adjacent to large cities have by now been swallowed up by the surrounding city. Their origin as separate suburbs is barely recognizable—they started out as suburbs but they are now just urban neighborhoods. Boston's Back Bay (Figure 9.1) and Brooklyn's Brooklyn Heights (Figure 9.2) are examples: technically suburbs but essentially extensions of the city. Suburbs are thus not always easy to identify; in Los Angeles, there is barely a way to tell where the city ends and the suburb begins.

Initially, suburbs were connected to the existing city via railroad or streetcar; it was only later, and much more destructively because of the infrastructure required, that they were connected via the automobile. Linked by transit, these urban suburbs were not focused on rejecting or undermining the city in the way later planned suburbs were. In Chestnut Hill, outside of Philadelphia, the railroad suburb strengthened the urban core because the core was where the institutions suburbanites still depended on, like offices and hospitals, were located. For a brief time, writes Fishman, there was a "functional unity" between city and suburb, a

Figure 9.1 Back Bay, Boston, Massachusetts, USA. *The earliest suburbs were technically suburbs but essentially extensions of the city.*

What Cities Say. Emily Talen, Oxford University Press. © Oxford University Press 2024. DOI: 10.1093/oso/9780197647769.003.0010

Figure 9.2　Brooklyn Heights, Brooklyn, New York, USA. *The earliest suburbs were later absorbed by the city.*

"precarious equilibrium." Nevertheless, the classic railroad suburb was still a place of exclusion, often underscored by the use of English Gothic architecture.[1]

The streetcar suburb, so well chronicled by Sam Bass Warner, is usually so much closer to the central city that it is sometimes hard to think of it now as a suburb. Streetcar suburbs occupied what Chicago School sociologists termed "the zone of emergence"—meaning emergence out of the much less desirable tenement house neighborhoods.[2] Warner's study showed that the streetcar suburbs surrounding Boston in the late 19th century were essentially street layouts, not communities and neighborhoods organized to promote public life. Commercial development tended to be strip-oriented and centerless, and institutions like schools were often located in function of land price rather than accessibility. Thus, residents were forced to construct their own bespoke versions of community life from a set of spatially disaggregated social functions. And yet, the peripheral communities that developed outside of Boston between 1830 and 1870 were fully mixed in population and services. They were more city than suburb, even possessing their own industrial potential, motivated by a desire to "re-create the conditions of Boston."[3]

Frederick Law Olmsted was fine with the idea that the railroad suburb was to be an escape from the city, but he thought that Riverside, Illinois, his iconic commuter railroad suburb outside of Chicago, was an integral part of the city by virtue of the rail connecting city and suburb. Based on this connection, he insisted that the metropolis included both city and suburb.

10

Planned Suburbs

A suburb can be, simply, any group of houses slapped up by a housing developer, perhaps with an amenity like a golf course. Or a suburb can be laid out with a conscious identity and asserted attention to the totality of its design. The former is sprawl, the latter is the planned suburb. The distinction is not black and white, but rather a gradient. A planned suburb typically consists of single-family homes carefully arranged in a picturesque design that integrates collective space, shared amenities, and green space. Sprawl, at the other end of the suburban spectrum, does not pay attention to design quality.

Geographic and cultural context play a significant role in how the planned suburb is interpreted. In the United States, planned suburbs have historically been affluent or middle-class, often signaling a rejection of the urban core in favor of family-oriented suburban life. But in other places, such as France, the suburbs are less likely to be affluent enclaves. Historically, wealthier groups claimed the more central locations and pushed industry, and the working classes, to the periphery. This is not to say that Europe doesn't have wealthy enclaves built away from cities. Tunnard observed that the planned enclave in the United States had nowhere near the level of exclusivity that European countries experienced. "Newport was not Versailles," he noted.[1]

To David Harvey, any planned community is suspect because it is seeking a "fixed" spatial form that excludes "the temporality of the social process" and avoids "the dialectics of social change." Planned communities are spatially fixed and ordered, and as such are part of "the fetish of commodity culture" aimed at inducing "nirvana rather than critical awareness." Planned suburbs thus deaden political sensibilities and, according to Harvey, "do as much to signal the end of history as the collapse of the Berlin Wall ever did."[2]

The classic counter response to this criticism is that the fixed form of the planned community, such as the planned suburb, offers stability as well as the ability to withstand pressure to disintegrate into sprawl. It is built to last and operates under a restraint that respects community above unfettered individualism. The physical form of the planned suburb is supposed to create social unity, achieved by designing holistically, with much thought given to common areas. All the elements of culture and society are to be physically linked and their relationship organized into an "organic whole" that would otherwise be "a mere conglomeration of buildings."[3] It is a unity often achieved, despite not having nearly the kind of control that the industrialists, with their company towns, had. Proportion and symmetry are the

What Cities Say. Emily Talen, Oxford University Press. © Oxford University Press 2024. DOI: 10.1093/oso/9780197647769.003.0011

primary tools for achieving integration and unity, although the easiest kind of unity is a suburb built for a single class.

The planned suburb is paradoxical, as Fishman observed, in that it is the product of "two opposing forces . . . attraction and repulsion." It is both "an explosive urban expansion and a desperate protest against it." The goal of the bourgeois elite was "to enjoy all the advantages of the massive urban economy while escaping its perils."[4] Thus the bourgeois elite created the urban industrial world but used the planned suburb to escape it. And there is another embedded paradox: the expanding suburban periphery of the middle class helped create an urban core that, as the concentrated center of capital accumulation and wealth generation, became increasingly unaffordable.

The communitarian aspect of the planned suburb is something to admire, but it too has paradoxical claims. Fishman points out the inherent inconsistency: on the one hand, the planned suburb is something separate, which is supposed to facilitate internal community-building; but on the other, a suburb is usually composed of single-family detached housing, a form that is the manifestation of separation from one's neighbors. Single-family houses denote individualism. The quest for separation, as if houses were built into a forest, is evident in Brentmoor Park, Missouri, a suburb of St. Louis. Limited access from surrounding streets strengthens the idea (Figure 10.1).[5]

Jane Jacobs read the planned suburb as an attempt to block future growth and freeze life in place. Its focus was inward rather than outward. Much before Jacobs, suburban growth around London in the last decades of the 19th century was interpreted disdainfully as a search for a sedentary, un-aspirational life. One commentator wrote of the "homogenous civilization" being created in places like

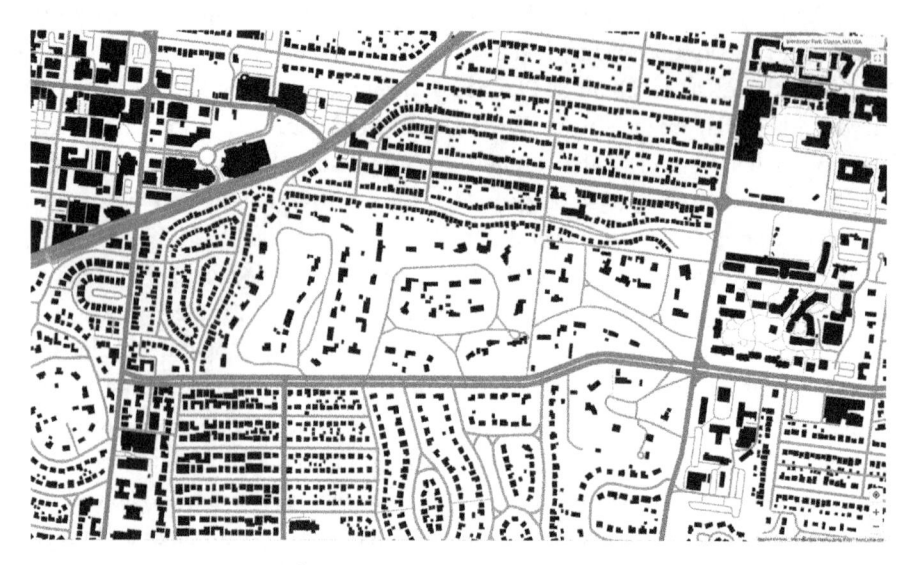

Figure 10.1 Brentmoor Park, Missouri, USA. *Contrasting pattern and separation of estates in an early planned suburb, with houses arranged to escape community.*

Figure 10.2 Bedford Park outside of London. *A pastoral suburb of single-family houses that offered security, a sedentary occupation, and respectability.*

Bedford Park: it embodied "a life of Security; a life of Sedentary Occupation; a life of Respectability . . . little red houses in little silent streets" (Figure 10.2). A critic from the 1930s, Thomas Sharp, wrote that the suburbs were sterile and neutral, "haemaphrodite beastliness" arising from a "pitiful attitude of escape."[6]

Fishman built the case that suburbia, whether in England or the United States, can never be understood on its own, but always "in relation to its rejected opposite: the metropolis." The planned suburb was built on "a nightmare image of eighteenth century London." Later, in the United States, the Protestant suburb was an escape from cities increasingly populated with Catholics and Jews. But in addition to rejecting city life, it also represented something more vulnerable: insecurity about the "fragility" of the economic system it relied on. The planned suburb was a monument built not to express faith and assurance, but to construct the "appearance" of confidence. The "dual legacy" of the planned suburb is, on the one hand, the beauty that suburban design could be, but on the other, a physical expression of "bourgeois anxieties" and hatred for the "others" inhabiting the city.[7]

At the same time, as Fishman argued, the planned suburb's constraint on use— they were residential only, with perhaps a few facilities mixed in—mirrored new conceptions of domestic life. Prior to suburban expansion, urban families were not sequestered and separated. The merchant's house was "open to the city" and families were integrated into "wider networks of urban amusements." But planned suburbs undermined the mixed-use urban townhouse, which transitioned to office-only, "now dedicated to intensified, unremitting work." London became "a specialized office district" rather than the diverse mix it had been. There were significant social ramifications. For one, clerks were no longer regarded as family members. There emerged a new, profound division between home and work, between "the feminine/natural/emotional world of the family and the masculine/rational/urban world of work."[8] The planned suburb offered a way to manifest these new conceptions of family and the role of women; essentially, city and family were put in contradiction.

Fishman also sees the imprint of 18th century Christian Evangelicals, a group unique to England and America at the time. The planned suburb was an apt expression of their "emotionally charged" ideal of family life, in which the home was "more sacred to the bourgeoisie than any place of worship." The nuclear family reigned supreme. Work and residence were kept separate and the close-knit family—women in particular—were to be insulated and freed not only from city life but from economic life. Suburbia was for a single function—domesticity. Meinig points out that decades later, the California version of the suburb revealed a break with Puritanism in which a leisure lifestyle and a focus on personal gratification were considered fine pursuits.[9]

Interpretations of the planned suburb have always been mixed. Whereas some will view the planned suburb as an embodiment of civic spirit, functionality, beauty, and plain common sense, others will see it as escapist, exclusionary, and controlling. Where one observer will see something logical and reflective of the best in place-making, another will see it as nothing more than an insidious quest to find the most bankable version of an exclusionary enclave. Any endeavor that involves the laying out of human settlement according to abstract principles of geometry and picturesque design can be interpreted as an attempt to oversimplify the true nature of the human habitat.

11

Garden Suburbs

Garden suburbs are a distinct subset of the planned suburb. Robert A. M. Stern and associates produced a definitive study of the "garden" version of the planned suburb called *Paradise Planned*. The authors argue that garden suburbs, which flourished globally in the late 19th and early 20th centuries, "hold the key to the future of our cities" because of their ability to meet material and spiritual needs, enable "complex social relationships," and combine "the intensity of the inner-city and the passivity of nature." Kostof was less sanguine, labeling garden suburbs as "housing schemes" involving "a suburban grid with some curves."[1]

Like the garden city, the garden suburb was trying to merge the best of two worlds: town and garden. They were to be places where people could have access to rural tranquility without having to give up access to the amenities needed for a high quality of life. One such garden suburb, Country Club District in Kansas City, invented its own downtown for this purpose (Country Club Plaza) (Figure 11.1). More often, there was a constrained set of functions, which is what separated the garden suburb from the garden city or company town. There was to be no adjoining factory or source of employment, and the mixing of uses was limited to a few amenities for residents. This is one reason Jane Jacobs labeled them paternalistic: "very nice towns if you were docile and had no plans of your own and did not mind spending your life among others with no plans of their own."[2]

The garden suburb is laid out with great attention to detail and a focus on holistic design, made possible by building on unfettered land. Building on a clean slate provided the ability to perfect the human settlement, offering a kind of replacement of what had been tried before. Even the earliest suburbs were idyllic versions of the feudal villages they were replacing. Contemporary suburbs, with names like "Eagle Run" and "Pine Forest," are still at it: creating idealized versions of what they replace.

Thinking holistically means that no one element of settlement is allowed to dominate—not the streets, not the buildings, not the recreational spaces. Planning, architecture, and gardening are united in a "real concern with art in shaping the human environment." The garden suburb provides a way of relating elements to each other in a unifying way, creating an overall composition. At Riverside, Illinois, whatever variation there might be—there is some variation in lot sizes, for example—the plan is completely unified, a singular conception in stylistic terms (Figure 11.2). Some observers believe that this enables innovation and thus outweighs the associated elitism.[3]

What Cities Say. Emily Talen, Oxford University Press. © Oxford University Press 2024. DOI: 10.1093/oso/9780197647769.003.0012

Figure 11.1 Country Club Plaza, Kansas City, Missouri, USA. *A downtown was created close to the suburb to merge the best of two worlds: rural tranquility without having to give up access to amenities.*

Specialization could undermine the principal asset of the garden suburb, which was its ability to offer a system of integrated conditions that were in balance, and able to express permanence and stability. Unfortunately, the coherence of the garden suburb eventually morphed into "suburbia," which had no such coherence. As Robert Fishman points out, the economic system propelling suburbia—instant

Figure 11.2 Riverside, Illinois, USA. *The quintessential bourgeois utopia; curvilinearity was thought to be more natural, but the iconic block shapes can be disorienting.*

change, quick profit—was never going to sustain communities defined by permanence and stability.[4]

Riverside, like other early garden suburbs, was meant for the affluent—or as Olmsted put it, "the more intelligent and more fortunate classes," although housing for domestic servants was provided near the railroad tracks. It was the quintessential "bourgeois utopia," to use Robert Fishman's phrase, "a collective assertion of class wealth and privilege as impressive as any medieval castle." Here the wealthy elite fostered their own "collective creation" that remade the world according their values. Social dominance was expressed through location and architecture. Tuxedo Park in New York, what Stern et al. call a "resort garden suburb," was "an English country estate on a colossal scale," the "country club and its clubhouse stood in for the lord of the manor and his 'power-house'" (Figure 11.3). Under the weight of the industrial city and mass immigration, and absent government policy aimed at retaining the middle class at the core, class segregation was maintained not by luxury apartment houses lining boulevards (as in Paris), but by relocating to the suburbs, where "distance alone sufficed to isolate the bourgeoisie."[5]

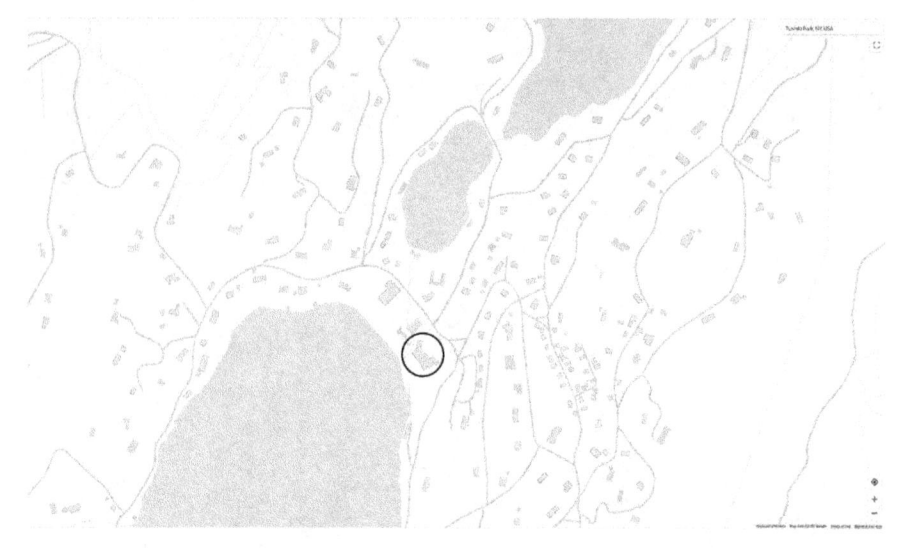

Figure 11.3 Tuxedo Park, New York, USA. *The resort garden suburb: social dominance was expressed through location and architecture; the clubhouse (circled) stood as the lordly manor house.*

In addition to maintaining social elitism, the garden suburb reflected a desire for green, leafy realms. It was another aspect of exclusion: cutting out the grayness of cities, with their concrete and noise. A ruralized aesthetic, it was hoped, would better connect people to "nature" and to "the land." This inspired certain design regularities: lots of green lawns, relatively low-density housing, and low building height—which allows inhabitants to be even closer to the ground, that is, nature.

The desire to be close to all things "nature" implies that it is possible, by living in a garden suburb, to withdraw from the social, economic, and environmental problems of the city to which it is connected. It implies freedom from toil. This is ironic since this is the exact opposite of what living in the country would actually be like, at least historically, if one were trying to make a living there and needed to work the land. Other societies had alternative ways of connecting to nature that did not involve living in a detached garden suburb. The Mormon town, for example, sought connection to nature by siting houses so that they looked at the surrounding land or at least an adjoining garden, instead of the neighbors' front door.[6]

While garden suburbs seek to withdraw from urban problems, they do attempt to cultivate a sense of collective life by way of green space. Each individual home contributes to the illusion of living in a park, and thus the landscape, which might take decades to coerce into manicured perfection, becomes the basis of a communal existence. It is the selling of "a triple dream, house plus nature plus community." Each family maintains their own piece of the park, and thus fulfills a civic duty. In Llewellyn Park, New Jersey, for example, lots merge into a singular landscape design (Figure 11.4). In Riverside, small green islands are sprinkled throughout the plan, the residuals of the intersections of oddly shaped blocks. And while there are

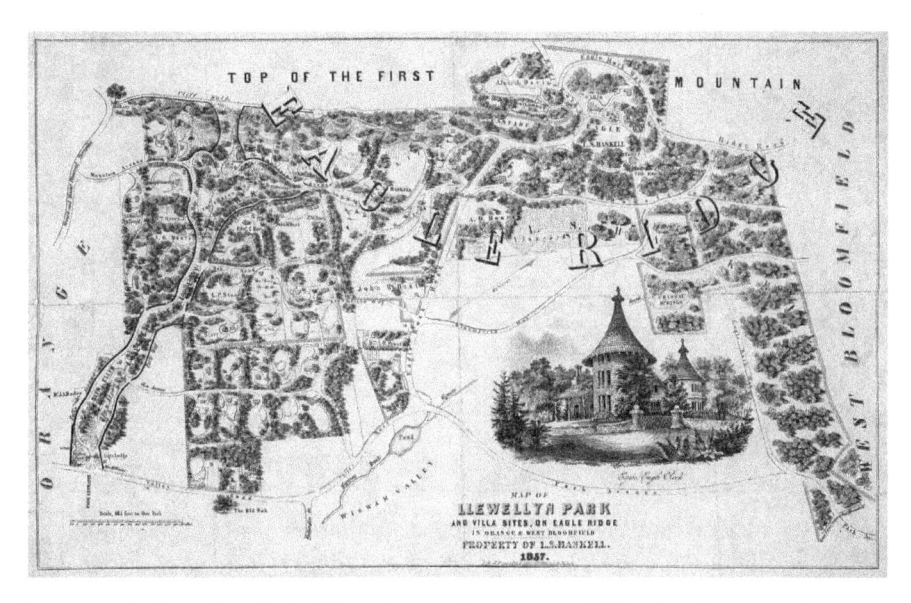

Figure 11.4 Llewellyn Park, West Orange, New Jersey, USA. *Landscape as the basis of a communal existence: each family maintains their own piece of the park and thus fulfills a civic duty.* Credit: Alexander Jackson Davis, CC0, via Wikimedia Commons.

plenty of public areas (constituting one-third of Riverside's total area), it is the generous front lawns—too public to be part of private family life—that provide the impression of a singular community united in a natural setting.[7]

In pursuit of the imitation of nature, garden suburbs rejected urban forms more conducive to a unified design, like attached row housing and squares, and relied instead on family homes embedded in greenspace. Villas might be clustered around an unimproved central common, but if houses around it were clustered (and thus urban-ish), the illusion was somewhat harder to maintain. More likely than a central commons was the front lawn—not really private family space, but collectively, at least, an institution.

Living in a park could be picturesque, a word that aptly describes the earliest garden suburbs. Picturesque settings were derived from painting—specifically Northern European Renaissance landscape painting, where the vanishing point is hidden and distance is revealed by the diminishing size of elements. This is the opposite of the Italian Renaissance conception of formalized nature, where greenery is coerced into straight lines. It is instead a nature of manipulated variety, the facade of "unspoiled nature," with imitative curves and planned irregularity. The goal is "natural 'intricacy,' not formal clarity."[8] Ironically, however, this imitation of nature does not come "naturally"; it is an aesthetic that requires strict rules and extra effort and attention. The burden was somewhat lower if streets and blocks were curvilinear, which automatically attached a vestige of "nature" to the design.

The picturesque suited the garden suburb. In Blaise Hamlet in Bristol, UK, said to be the first garden suburb (1810), nine "cottages" were carefully positioned around

Figure 11.5 Blaise Hamlet, Bristol, UK. *In this early 19th-century garden suburb, cottages were positioned around a green in a way that defined a foreground, a middle ground, and a background, just like a painting composition.*

Figure 11.6 Bournemouth, UK. *Pretty as a picture, at least originally: a picturesque setting was created by detached houses carefully aligned along curving roads. The scheme has since been "invaded" by high-rises for the masses.*

a green in a way that defined a foreground, a middle ground, and a background, just like a painting composition (Figure 11.5). Bournemouth, in England, started in 1830 as a seaside resort, was similar, where a picturesque setting was created by detached houses carefully aligned along curving roads (Figure 11.6). Later, garden suburbs in the early 20th century were said to be based on the paintings of the Impressionist painter Cézanne. One is reminded of Stilgoe's quip about Forest Hills Gardens: it was not just "pretty as a picture, it *was* the picture." At least at Forest Hills Gardens each house was not given its own front lawn, a wasteful practice,

Figure 11.7 Forest Hills, Queens, New York, USA. *The picturesque arrangement of houses offered a sharp contrast with the surrounding grid.*

but houses were grouped around a shared green space. Small neighborhood parks sprinkled throughout "aerated the plan" (Figure 11.7)[9]

Park settings, nature, rural life, the picturesque: applied to the garden suburb, these descriptive qualities signal an infusion of nature, but not necessarily a more sustainable, "green" approach to human settlement.

12

Modernist Urbanism

Starting in the 1920s, but especially after World War II, much urbanism around the globe was constructed under the tenets of modernist urbanism. Country capitals, communist cities, new towns, suburbs, and neighborhood units were all rendered in this iconic, anti-historical, often placeless form: segregated uses, extreme uniformity, car dependence, stripped-down architecture, and a rejection of the street with its aligned frontages and spatial definition. Plans tended to separate land uses, prioritize the automobile over the pedestrian, reject the street as public space, create superblocks that promoted containment and insularity, treat buildings as isolated objects in space rather than as part of a larger interconnected urban fabric, reject traditional elements like squares and plazas, demolish large areas of the city to make unfettered places for new built forms, and create enclosed malls and sunken plazas that deadened public space. It was the design of cities turned inside out: what was once space became solid, what was once solid became open, and what was once integrated became discrete.[1]

Making city-building more "natural" was a priority. This could be done, proponents thought, by setting buildings in green space, or by making them look more natural by curving them a bit, as at the Park Hill apartment complex in Sheffield, UK (thought to be more "organic" but notoriously lacking in pedestrian life) (Figure 12.1). Another way to align with nature, the thinking went, was to replace streets with parks. However, the reality was that fewer streets meant more separation, which translated to more cars. And cars needed to be put somewhere, acquiring a newfound claim to special storage sites: garages and parking lots now occupying prominent places within cities.

Modernist urbanism broke the traditional bond between two-dimensional pattern and three-dimensional form. Writing in 1935, Thomas Adams observed that the medieval city's informal street system fit Gothic architecture just as the architectural classicism of ancient Greece and Roman cities harmonized with their two-dimensional formality. But as modernist building style gained ground, these associations no longer held. Barnett critiqued Regent Street in London for losing the association: the "unity" of Regent Street's "new architecture" had severed the careful relationship between building and street that was once the hallmark of the street's design. By the late 20th century, the New Urbanists claimed in their charter of principles that the urban pattern "transcended" architectural style.[2]

The impulse to erase historical building tradition—a key tenet of modernist city-building—started early in the Balkan region, in the 1920s. By the time of

What Cities Say. Emily Talen, Oxford University Press. © Oxford University Press 2024. DOI: 10.1093/oso/9780197647769.003.0013

Figure 12.1 Park Hill, Sheffield, UK. *If modernist towers curved a bit, they were thought to be an "organic" approach to city building, but they were notoriously lacking pedestrian life.*

the collapse of the Ottoman Empire, Balkan cities reflected political and cultural turmoil: fragmented street patterns, few civic centers, and rural areas that were allowed to cultivate within city limits. New regimes in the early 20th century, with centralized authority, were eager to modernize and "catch up" with the Western world, which translated to forms that were geometrical, undiversified, and had no connection to historical building traditions. The loss of connection was exactly the point, "making history a mystifying riddle rather than a process of national self-knowledge." The idea was to "minimize all common traditions and local particularities," as "everything local seemed a reminder of foreign rule."[3]

New towns built after World War II in the modernist vein have the unmistakable imprint of functionalism, which, in practical terms, means separation. A good example is Cumbernauld New Town, Scotland. The downtown core does attempt to mix certain functions like shopping and entertainment, but only to a constrained point: it is completely separated from the surrounding neighborhoods. Without connection to the places where people live, the visible functionalist paradigm creates a segregated world that is radically different from the previous millennia of city development, which was gradual and diverse. The components of cities, from streets to land uses, are kept mono-functional, discrete, separated, and designed for a single purpose, which fits the modernistic worldview. And if the city is put together mechanically, there really is no need to consider context. It presents an attitude that planners who understand "the science of urbanism" are the only ones who should be tasked with city-making.[4]

The street pattern of modernist housing developments was used to separate people by minimizing street connection. Perhaps there would be only one or two street intersections, which created an unfortunate aggregation of traffic at these

Figure 12.2 Rochelle Park, New Jersey, USA. *To promote exclusivity, links to the exterior street system were kept to an absolute minimum.*

junctures. For example, Rochelle Park, New Jersey, has an internal street system to serve resident needs, but links to the exterior street system are kept to an absolute minimum (Figure 12.2). Street patterns were also used to distinguish lower- from higher-income neighborhoods. Diagonal roads could be used to provide a clear contrast with neighboring (lower-income) areas, if the latter had a rectangular layout.

Speed and quantity are appropriate interpretations of modernist urbanism. Incremental development is conducive to retaining historic fabric; the clean slate required by modernism is conducive to building quickly, and in large quantities. The approach was common in post–World War II Europe. Suburban development in modernist form was composed of high-rises or maybe a mix of low- and high-rise,

Figure 12.3 Vällingby, Stockholm, Sweden. *After World War II in Europe, housing was needed in great quantities, and modernism prevailed; there was no time for attached row housing in picturesque settings.*

as at Vällingby, Sweden (Figure 12.3). The impression left is that housing was needed in great quantities, and fast (there was indeed an acute housing shortage). Ravaged countries did not have the luxury of building single-family detached homes, or even attached row housing, in picturesque settings, as was the norm in pre–World War II suburban development.

Some modernist housing arrangements, like Dammerstock in Karlsruhe, Germany (Figure 12.4), or the housing complexes of the southern part of Amsterdam, were driven by a formulaic attachment to the principles of maximizing exposure to sun and green space. Houses fronted green space rather than streets, and the orientation was north-south to maximize sunlight to every room. In similar, single-purpose fashion, the attached housing of Aluminum City Terrace near Pittsburgh reveals that the only real consideration was solar orientation (Figure 12.5). However, as Gallion and Eisner point out, the requirement of uniform sun orientation (although not uniform exposure to green space, nor equalized privacy) is not new, and is reminiscent, for example, of Greek towns in the fifth century BCE.[5] For modernist developments, the sun exposure requirement, worked out mathematically to dictate the space between buildings, was prioritized at the expense of any social priorities, like the creation of enclosed space or the recognition of streets as a setting for social encounter. Arranging buildings for social life or pedestrian circulation was not a priority. Social exchange via the street was eliminated since there was to be no traffic—and thus no street—between buildings, and housing was placed perpendicular to the street. Streets were treated like service lanes.

And yet, if there was hope that the open green space would absorb the street's function and provide a setting for social connection, it didn't happen. Green space is a passive social space, not a space in which social interaction naturally springs

Figure 12.4 Dammerstockstraße, Karlsruh, Germany. *Formulaic application of the principles of maximum exposure to sun and green space.*

Figure 12.5 Aluminum City Terrace near Pittsburgh, Pennsylvania, USA. *Buildings arranged solely for solar orientation, with no other intent shown, such as arranging buildings for social life or pedestrian circulation.*

from people engaged in daily tasks. In this sense, the approach is naïve, as if people are being told "here is open green space, now go interact." In contrast, traditional city form with its spatial definition, continuous building frontage, integrated elements, mixed uses and unambiguous spaces enabled social encounter in an unprogrammed and organic way: spontaneous social interaction was woven into the flows of everyday social exchange.

To eliminate shadows, buildings could be set at right angles to the street, not facing them. Untethered in this way, buildings seem to float in open space, as at

Dammerstock. Modernist theory applied to urbanism thus prioritized mathematically derived orientation above all else, which tended to create uniform, geometrical shapes. City-building by geometrical shape facilitated repetition, and repetition, in turn, facilitated the standardization of types. Uniformity translated to sterile places of institutional quality.[6]

Experiencing the city mechanically would seem the perfect reflection of capitalist abstraction—an abstraction necessary because capitalism is notoriously bad at expressing the substance and materiality of life. Matters of context, of the spaces between buildings, of the perspective of residents as they move through the built environment, of the city's experiential qualities—these matters were subordinated to efficiency, speed, and rationalized separation. It was as if the "Org Man," the 1950s sociological conception of the anonymous, mobile urbanite, had found expression in built form.[7]

But socialism was also aligned. The Soviet version of modernist urbanism was rendered at the scale of the mikrorayon ("micro-district"), composed of clusters of five to eight superblock neighborhoods of apartment blocks (sometimes five stories but often much taller). An example is the mikrorayon in Tbilisi, Georgia (formerly part of the Soviet Union) (Figure 12.6). The highly regularized mikrorayon formed the basis of massive residential growth in the postwar period. It was the grouping of buildings that was the basis of the communist city—apartment buildings arranged around open spaces. This grouping was thought to give the clusters a kind of totality. The apartment building, as the authors of *The Ideal Communist City* put it, was "unthinkable apart from the existence of the whole."[8]

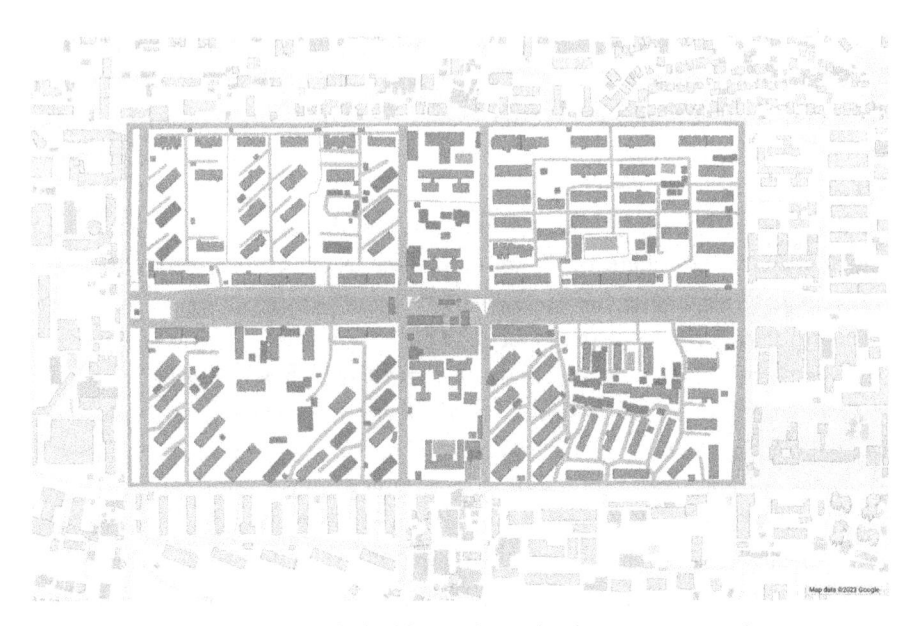

Figure 12.6 Tbilisi, Georgia. *The highly regularized mikrorayon grouped apartment buildings around open spaces, giving the clusters a kind of totality.*

In the socialist city, there is no private space, no strict separation of public and private, which means that buildings are "free" to go anywhere. On the positive side, there is freedom to experiment with building placement. Set in open space, this might translate to easily traversable sites, going from point A to B with no obstacles. In traditional urbanism, aligned buildings and disciplined street frontages restrict movement. But in reality, the placement was mechanistic. The form of the mikrorayon superblocks is sometimes called "crane urbanism," as the site layout was related to the maximum reach of a crane machine. Building height—five stories—was dictated by the maximum number of stories one could reasonably walk up without an elevator.

The mikrorayon sought to embody socialist principles, a settlement based on class unity, public ownership of land (there were no individually sold plots of land), a planned economy, and "equality and friendship" among residents. It was considered the perfect socialist antidote to the "bourgeois necropolis of slums, traffic jams, pollution, noises and hot concrete." Instead of an elite center surrounded by a poor periphery, land intensity was to be more uniform across the landscape. An urban periphery of apartment blocks seemed the right way to even things out.[9] Sometimes there was a mix of dwelling types—one-story apartments, two-story flats, and hostels (which could be up to 16 stories)—a mix based on assumptions about varying family size as opposed to income variation, as the latter was not a relevant basis for planning in the socialist city.

But while the physical design of the mikrorayon was intended to stimulate "collectivist habits" with their "organic" integration of housing and services, they failed as systems of self-governance. Statistically, all the elements of "community" were there, including centers designed to have schools, playgrounds, small shops, and communal kitchens, with few cars, and residential buildings linked via footpaths. But administration was top-down and opaque, public services were often lacking, and there was excessive standardization. By the 1980s, the high-minded social principles of the original mikrorayons seemed a distant vision, leaving only vast expanses of underserviced blocks of drab and cheaply constructed apartment buildings.[10] Free-standing buildings disconnected from the street, with no attempt to spatially define the public realm, reinforced the sense of top-down control.

The Soviets also built complete socialist cities before and after World War II—"Sotsgorod," which means "socialist city"—to exemplify rational, machine-based perfection.[11] These communist new cities—for example, Dimitrovgrad in Bulgaria, Eisenhüttenstadt in East Germany, Dunaújváros in Hungary, Poruba in Czechoslovakia, and Nowa Huta in Poland (Figure 12.7)—were thought to be both utopian and revolutionary because they were built from scratch: there was no need to constrain to old building patterns—or old social structures. They were centered on industrial plants, specifically steel and iron mills. Here the socialist commitment to the collective good could be demonstrated via the provision of schools, libraries, and community centers. There was usually a large central plaza fronted by administrative buildings, an unsubtle reminder of the central place of the communist party.

Figure 12.7 Nowa Huta, Kraków, Poland. *A top-down, all-at-once production of a complete city in the Stalin era. There was no need to be constrained to old building patterns—or old social structures.*

The plaza was linked by a central boulevard to the factory, giving physical expression to Marxian unity between politics and economics. Nature was integrated by putting a greenbelt between housing and factory, and workers could access the factory through green corridors rather than streets. There were no private backyards, apparently in an effort to prevent new residents, who came from the countryside, from bringing along their farm animals (which they did anyway).[12]

These modernist towns, with their separations and uniformity, read like cold calculations intended to manipulate the masses. The rebuilding of Bucharest along socialist lines in the 1970s had the goal of eliminating single-family houses not only because they represented "bourgeois fabric," but because people in single-family structures, especially where dispersed on winding roads, were less controllable (Figure 12.8). Diversity of building types and forms was also to be eliminated because it reminded people of former social and cultural values, which the new regime (under Nicolae Ceausescu) was trying to eliminate.

The relationship between old and modernist urbanism was awkward. Collective, stripped-down, and standardized apartment buildings eradicated any remembrance of things past and instilled the "ideals of discipline" right into the urban fabric. At the same time, monumentalism and grandeur in modernist form were imposed in public spaces to impress foreign visitors and hail "the grandeur of Romania." The resulting merger of old and new created an unfortunate pattern of modernist islands surrounded by, but disconnected from, the historical city.[13]

Modernist impositions that created stark dichotomies between old and new was a problem in many other parts of the world. The agenda of postcolonial urban plans, for example in the Bulaq area of Cairo, was to eliminate traces of colonialism, and so ordered rows of buildings were inserted to represent a radical departure

Figure 12.8 Bucharest, Romania. *Modern high-rises surround historic single-family houses (which were thought bourgeois and less controllable), creating an awkward, disconnected pattern.*

from Cairo's colonial history (Figure 12.9). These kinds of gestures tend to represent control more than change. The irony, of course, was that the modernist planning models that were used were imported from Western powers—the very occupiers the Egyptians were trying to reproach.[14]

Brasília, the capital of Brazil, is an especially iconic example of modernist city form. From overhead, the pattern resembles an airplane, abstract and diagrammatic, based on an affinity for nature's curves (Figure 12.10). The segregated functions are easily revealed from overhead too: circulation arteries that create the overall shape, public space forming the core, dwelling superblocks that form the wings, work areas running along the spines, and surrounding recreation space. Charles Jencks called it a perfect illustration of "Platonic purism"—giving physical expression to an abstract ideal about what cities should consist of: a set of discrete functions. This was the modernist aim, to create something completely novel, with no historical context, no connection with the past, no precedent. The uniformity, in residential space and in the elimination of any division between public and private space that was the hallmark of traditional urbanism, was supposed to embody—and create—an egalitarian society. But the top-down aspect of its design and construction meant that there was no ability to yield to citizen input. Brasília was so totalizing in its conception that it gave the impression that there was nothing any citizen could possibly contribute.[15]

Figure 12.9 Cairo, Egypt. *The Bulaq area of Cairo tried to eliminate traces of colonialism by inserting rows of modernist buildings (at left).*

Figure 12.10 Brasília, Brazil. *From overhead, the abstract and diagrammatic plan resembles an airplane, but it is also based on an affinity for nature's curves.*

In the United States in the 1960s and 1970s, the "New Towns" movement, which produced places like Columbia, Maryland; Irvine, California; Reston, Virginia; and The Woodlands, Texas (Figure 12.11), produced modernist versions of the garden city. There was great thought put into the design of these towns, especially how

Figure 12.11 Panther Creek, The Woodlands, Texas, USA. *Modernist versions of the garden city used design to foster social integration and connection to green space.*

Figure 12.12 Soul City, North Carolina, USA. *A government-backed new town laid out in separatist fashion, with discrete sections and an embrace of suburban form.*

their design might foster "community," social integration, and connection to "green space"—the best of town and country. The aim was an "improved middle ground" between congested cities and suburban homogeneity.[16]

Soul City, North Carolina, was a government-backed new town that emerged out of the civil rights era, essentially an economic development project for poor African Americans, although intended for all races. The failure of Soul City—it never attracted sufficient industry or population—was blamed on politics and fund-raising, but one can surmise that its modernist form likely also played a role. The town was laid out in classic separatist fashion, with the site divided into "discrete" sections that separated offices into an industrial park, with retail outlets in a separate area and housing subdivisions in another (Figure 12.12). Soul City was not a bedroom community and was meant to be a complete city with jobs and amenities, but its curvilinear plan set in "the gently rolling countryside" signaled its paradoxical intention to be suburban.[17]

13

New Urbanism

Hundreds of self-identified New Urbanist developments, from infill blocks to complete planned communities, have been constructed since the mid-1980s, mostly in the United States. The most visible New Urbanist communities are greenfield developments outside of existing cities. This opens them to the critique that they are simply a slightly better designed version of suburban sprawl and an embodiment of suburban escapism.[1]

There are certain design principles common to all New Urbanist developments. An exemplar is Kentlands, Maryland, where the pattern and form is aimed at walkable human scale (Figure 13.1). There are small buildings, integrated and varied housing types, narrow, traffic-calmed streets, and dispersed public spaces in a variety of sizes and forms. There are gridded streets lined with multistory row houses intended to create spatial definition and therefore elevate the street's role as a public space. Cars are not allowed to dominate the design. The automobile is accommodated, but its disruptive tendencies are kept in check. Car storage is dispersed rather than consolidated in surface parking lots. Privatism is tempered by an insistence on communal elements, like porches and balconies, seen as essential devices for stimulating social connection, or at least helping residents observe and potentially engage in communal activity. Densities are not high, consistent with planned suburbs rather than older cities, but in comparison to standard suburban housing, they are higher.

The focus on pedestrianism and traditional architecture has generated an authenticity critique. The design precedent is pre-automobile, using plans that grew out of economic, social, and technological systems very different from those of today—plans in which the private automobile did not dominate and social and economic networks were localized. To some observers, the attempt to replicate past forms, generated under vary different circumstances, presents a fake reality, since, they argue, development form is mostly the product of economic and transportation systems.[2]

This is not a new critique. The same observation was applied to residential neighborhoods around London constructed in the 19th century. Choay wrote that the design of these neighborhoods was "born in the seventeenth century," and to build similarly in the 19th century meant they were "no more than a relic, an anachronism." Instead of branching out and devising new, more responsive patterns and forms, some interpret the application of recurrent elements in New Urbanism as demonstration of ignorance at the multiplicity of forms available.[3] And yet,

What Cities Say. Emily Talen, Oxford University Press. © Oxford University Press 2024. DOI: 10.1093/oso/9780197647769.003.0014

Figure 13.1 Kentlands, Maryland, USA. *Pattern and form aimed at walkable human scale; the automobile is accommodated, but its disruptive tendencies are kept in check.*

Figure 13.2 Melrose Arch, Johannesburg, South Africa. *An upscale reproduction of a traditional town stands as a reminder of South Africa's socially fragmented past.*

co-opting the past by using traditionally evolved urban patterns and forms—say, the small streets and squares of an early 20th-century garden suburb—seems a valid reaction to the dehumanizing mechanization that new transportation and economic systems brought to bear on cities.

The replication of walkable, human-scaled, mixed-use urbanism, even if in suburban contexts, can alternatively be interpreted as a welcome change from car-dependent, modernist form. But where the development amounts to an "upscale themed entertainment" district it can stand as a reminder of a socially fragmented past. The New Urbanist Melrose Arch development outside of Johannesburg, affordable only to the affluent and under single ownership, has been ridiculed as an inauthentic attempt to re-produce a traditional town, a stage set for "a theatrical re-enactment of a lost civic ideal" (Figure 13.2). Everything about it is orchestrated, with nothing left to chance. Even inclusiveness is "staged" as a form of "seduction." The development is strictly surveilled.[4]

It is not uncommon for New Urbanist developments to be equated with theme parks—simulations, not actual villages. Within these constructed imaginary worlds, critics argue, rules become essential; personal freedom would shatter the village illusion and mess with property values. As one critic summarized the problem with Seaside, Florida, the iconic New Urbanist town that launched the movement, its "seductive appeal only fosters the illusion of solving problems by avoiding them."[5] But New Urbanism does not claim to solve all problems. It only claims to provide a more walkable and more diverse alternative to sprawl.

14

Neighborhoods

Within cities, people naturally cluster into residential precincts—neighborhoods. These differentiated areas can have religious, political, or sociological motive and meaning. Mormon towns are a classic religious example. Joseph Smith's "City of Zion," Salt Lake City, has equal-sized parcels in a strictly orthogonal grid of equal blocks, and the blocks are grouped into delineated neighborhoods (wards) that are oriented around a Temple (Figure 14.1). The square blocks are biblical in origin, called for in Numbers 35:1–5, Leviticus 25, and proposed by Ezekiel for building Jerusalem. The dimensions involved are often critiqued as overly generous and not particularly pedestrian-oriented.[1]

Sometimes neighborhoods are delineated to accommodate a system of political organization. Savannah's planned system of wards is an example of how the grid facilitated cell-like expansion—a system of wards—consisting of plots of housing and public buildings clustered around public squares (Figure 14.2). John Reps referred to them as "little neighborhood units" that created a social life driven by "co-operation and neighborly assistance," or at least that was the goal. The wards constituted a system of taxation and political representation. It was a centered, rather than bounded, approach to neighborhood delineation: gravitational nodes around which neighborhoods developed. In other cities, these centers could be landmarks or strong intersections, really anything with the ability to "extend their influence into the less articulate areas around them."[2]

The neighborhood as a basis of urban pattern tended to be more sociological than political. In the early 20th century, Charles Horton Cooley, inspired by the German sociologist Ferdinand Toennies (who thought that the condition of urban society was deplorable), instilled the idea that face-to-face local communities were everything. Cooley made the case that neighborhoods, along with family, were on the front line of socialization, and this made neighborhoods important in a fundamental way. Writing in 1912, Cooley argued that family and neighborhood were "ascendant in the open and plastic time of childhood" and this meant that in adulthood they were "incomparably more influential than all the rest."[3]

This was not just theoretical. Under the influence of Cooley, Clarence Perry, a sociologist, debuted his "neighborhood unit" in the early 20th century, and its imprint can be seen in post–World War II development throughout the United States. The neighborhood unit was to be village-like and self-contained, adopted as a method of social organization, reform, and discipline. It was protected by surrounding arterials. One can make out Perry's neighborhood structure in the areas

What Cities Say. Emily Talen, Oxford University Press. © Oxford University Press 2024. DOI: 10.1093/oso/9780197647769.003.0015

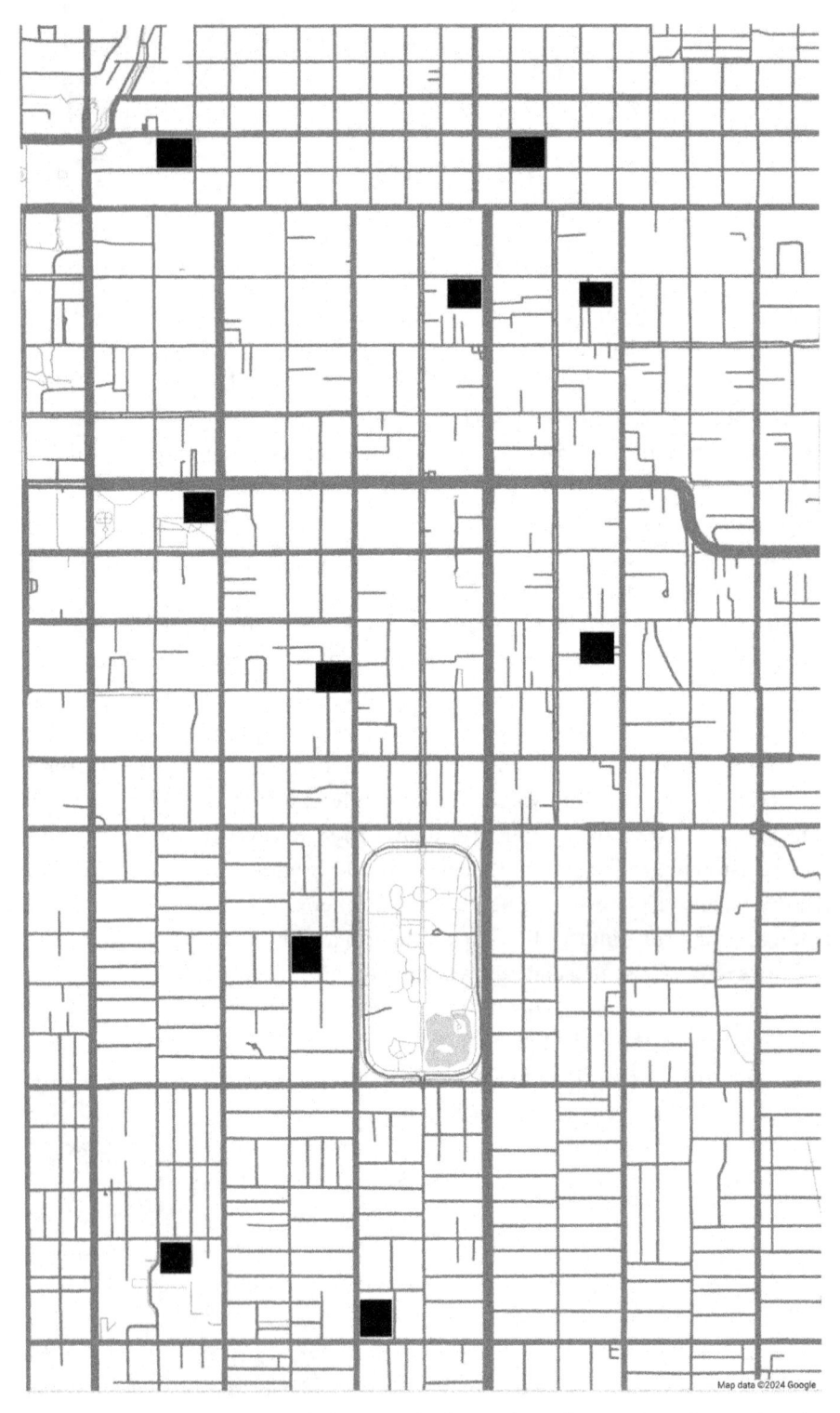

Figure 14.1 Salt Lake City, Utah, USA. *In the "City of Zion," a strictly orthogonal grid of equal blocks are grouped into wards, and the delineated neighborhoods are oriented around a center, the Temple (black rectangles).*

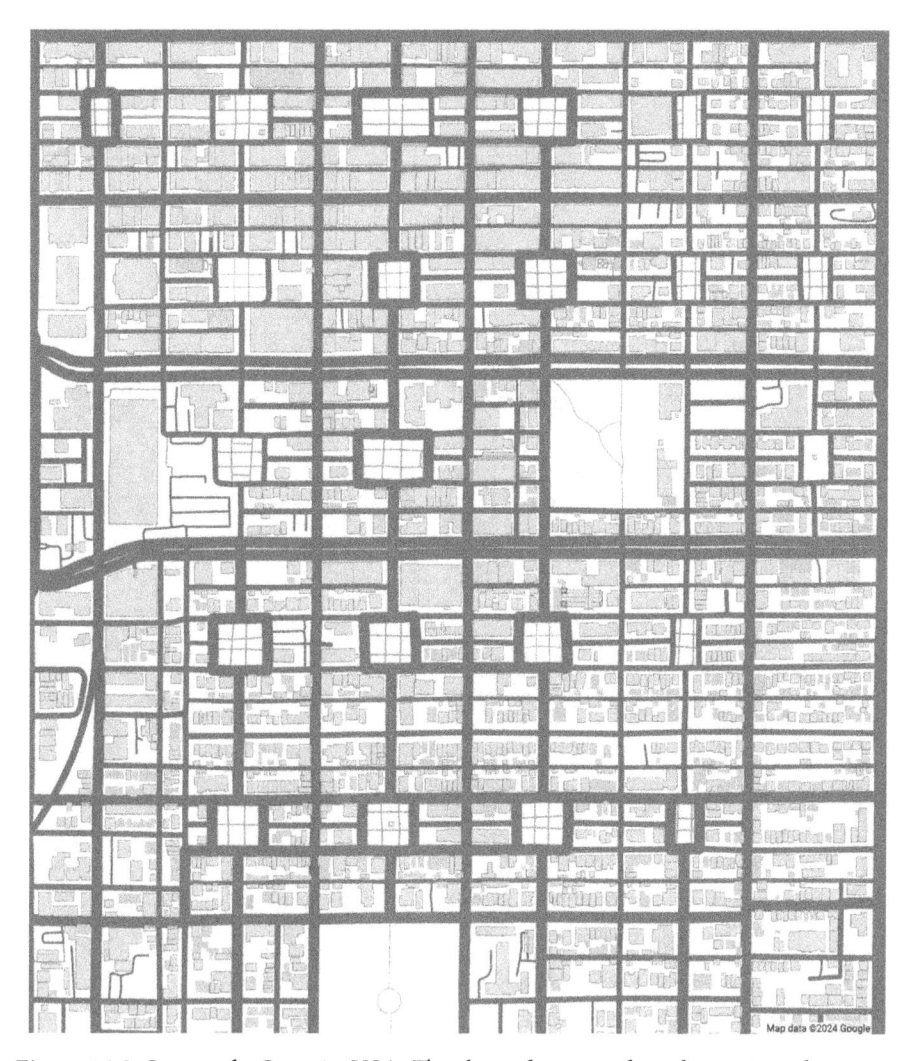

Figure 14.2 Savannah, Georgia, USA. *The planned system of wards constituted a system of taxation and political representation.*

surrounding cities like Phoenix, Arizona, the physical manifestation of a quest to organize an otherwise disorganized pattern and shield families (i.e., women and children) from urban harm (Figure 14.3).[4]

In an urban context, the village-like urban neighborhood was imbued with a pastoral, communal spirit in places that would otherwise simply be row upon row of housing blocks. Cities were anonymous and uncaring; neighborhoods as villages, it was argued, counteracted alienation and enabled closeness and a sense of belonging. If urban neighborhoods could function as villages, they could combine the close bonds of Toennies' *Gemeinschaft* villages within a larger *Gesellschaft* community. It was a reform idea with early antecedents: anthropologists believe the practice of villagers re-creating village life in the city by establishing neighborhoods was a feature of ancient cities.[5]

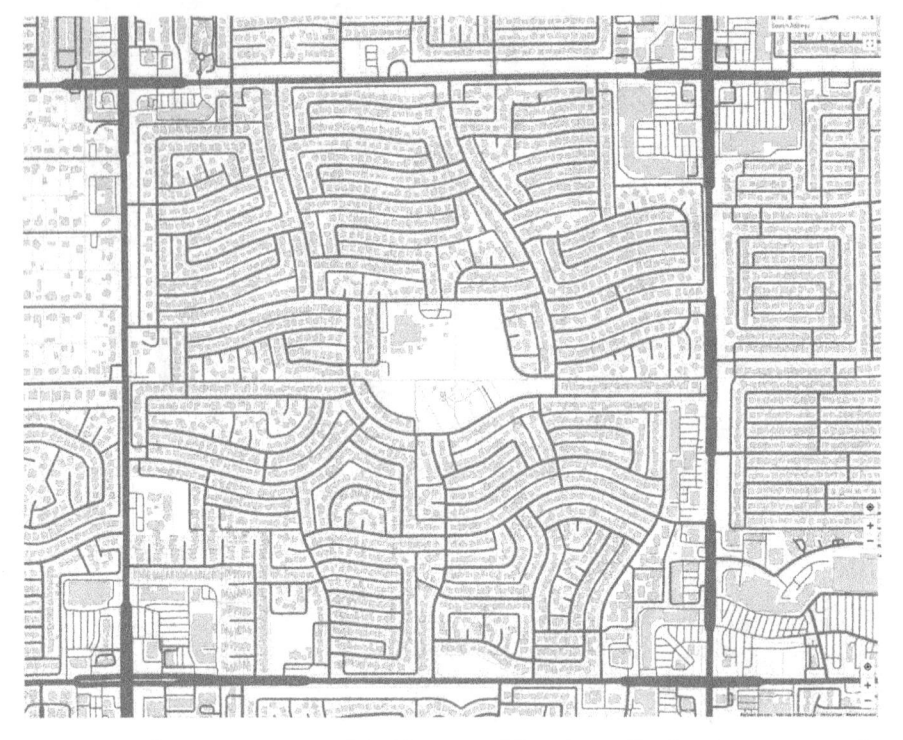

Figure 14.3 Phoenix, Arizona, USA. *Elements of Perry's neighborhood structure can be seen in this suburban development.*

Neighborhoods sometimes emerged around important buildings and their attached civic space. Medieval neighborhoods were likely to have developed around a prominent place like a manor, the church, a street, the market, or, in the case of Jerusalem's 15th-century Jewish Quarter, a synagogue. The *Laws of the Indies* dictated that important civic buildings like churches needed to have their own block—basically their own neighborhood—so that they did not to find themselves adjacent to incompatible uses. In Renaissance Italy, the area around the residence of a ruling family was its own neighborhood, the nucleus of a "defensible urban compound." The adjoining neighborhood was socially diverse in that it included servants and tenants clustered around the nexus of a wealthy family. Adding to the cohesion and identity, strong families exerted design control on the areas surrounding their residences, ensuring the "alignment of facades, the regularization of massive blocks, and the opening of spacious piazzas."[6]

Sometimes entire cities were formed as aggregations of neighborhood-like cells. The neighborhood basis of Canberra is easily discernible, and as Canberra was built out over the decades, the neighborhoods exhibited a uniform, production built aesthetic. One critic described Canberra as a "Sausage Machine that squirts out ready-made neighborhood modules" (Figure 14.4). The family-oriented, socially segregated "domestic communities" centered on community buildings that were never supposed to be more than three blocks away from

Figure 14.4 Canberra, Australia. *A neighborhood sausage machine: the socially segregated neighborhoods are said to exhibit a uniform, production built aesthetic.*

any household. However, Canberra was also known to be modeled on German Expressionism, an art philosophy that valued geometrical abstraction, which was somewhat in conflict with the social pragmatism of Perry's neighborhood unit ideal.[7]

Discerning the neighborhoods of a city is often a matter of finding the physical features that act as boundaries. It has been argued that without some kind of neighborhood delineation there is less sense of territory and identity, which are necessary to establish neighborhood meaning. Boundaries are essential to ethnic neighborhood identity, and though signifying "both inclusion and exclusion," boundary "enforcement" may be necessary to define economic and political power.[8] Boundaries are the basis of certain freedoms, then.

Natural features are one source of delineation. In the British new towns and later in the US "New Towns" of Columbia, Maryland; Reston, Virginia; The Woodlands, Texas; and Irvine, California, natural buffers were used to establish neighborhood boundaries. Kentlands, Maryland, makes use of a lake, wetlands, and green belts to define and differentiate its neighborhoods.

More commonly, however, wide or busy streets are used to delineate where neighborhoods begin and end. Major thoroughfares might serve the dual purpose of bounding neighborhoods and directing traffic around rather than through them. Larger streets formed at the intersection of unaligned grids almost always function as neighborhood boundaries, as people tend to resist crossing them. As Grady Clay observed, breaks create psychological barriers and "relationships that confuse," so that neighborhoods on the "other side" seem foreign: "land beyond the break has an uneasy look to it." The "confusion zone" of these breaks is often where highways and urban renewal developments were placed.[9]

Thus neighborhood delineation using streets has complications. Streets bound neighborhoods, but they are also supposed to function as neighborhood centers, acting like social seams that pull the surrounding residential areas together. But if they are overly trafficked, social seaming is unlikely, and certainly doesn't conjure up the street-based neighborhoods of poor and working-class areas of the early 20th century. And thoroughfares that surround have the tendency to create the "border vacuums" that Jane Jacobs thought so destructive.[10]

Separating arterials carrying heavy traffic from smaller side streets carrying local traffic might be one remedy, but that can result in the loss of the street as a defining social space if smaller residential streets became unused. In effect, segregating out the "movement function" of the street has the impact of segregating out their social function. Streets became traffic conduits rather than integrative social spaces.[11] This seems especially true where these streets are simply too wide (a good example is Stony Island Avenue in Chicago; Figure 14.5), often fronted by car-dependent strip malls and wide lanes designed to accommodate fast-moving traffic, not pedestrians. Social seaming seems unlikely in such places.

Any method of delineating neighborhoods as "units" is open to critique. The practice has been labeled "inorganic" in the sense that, first, neighborhoods thus defined have limited ability to grow and evolve, and second, they are unlikely to be well integrated within the whole urban fabric surrounding them. More naturally evolved neighborhoods, for example, the barrios of Hispanic American cities, were at one time permitted to adapt incrementally, whereby residents appropriated

Figure 14.5 Stony Island Avenue, Chicago, Illinois, USA. *Social interaction is unlikely along wide streets fronted by car-dependent strip malls.*

space (such as alleys) for specialized trades, evolving into street patterns of varying widths. But bounded neighborhoods seem unable to embrace this sort of temporal change.[12] Additive units are not an organic system of growth, either; they are mechanical—when nature adds a new part, "the whole" changes too. The planned neighborhood is thus too standardized and simplistic, too static and inflexible. It pays no attention to how the part (the neighborhood) relates to the whole (the city), thereby attempting to elevate the part above the whole.

Christopher Alexander, in his "A City Is Not a Tree" essay, was a particularly potent critic of neighborhood designs in places like Columbia, Maryland, and the Greenbelt Towns, which he said were isolating and not at all in keeping with cities as places that interconnect. Often the critique boils down to the hyper-insularity that tends to follow predesigned neighborhoods. Lakeview Terrace, completed in 1937 and one of the first public housing projects in the United States, is a prime example of a "complete" neighborhood cut off from surrounding neighborhoods (Figure 14.6).

And yet, the static simplicity of the neighborhood designed as a unit is one reason it has endured. Well-structured and identifiable neighborhoods bring a "human scale" to cities and facilitate social exchange, whereas socialization at the scale of a whole city is unworkable. Mumford believed that neighborhood-scale social functions had the benefit of preventing "institutional overcrowding and needless

Figure 14.6 Lakeview Terrace, Cleveland, Ohio, USA. *One of the first public housing projects in the United States and a prime example of a "complete" neighborhood cut off from surrounding neighborhoods.*

Figure 14.7 Venice, Italy. *Piazza San Marco (top) was repeated in miniature in each Venetian parish (bottom), allowing citizens to feel the Piazza's magnificence in their own neighborhood.*

circulation," keeping "the whole town in scale" by distributing "small structures, small numbers, intimate relations." This contrasts with larger cities, with their "crazily competitive fortress towers" that, Mumford thought, were a symptom of "social pathology." Smallness and decentralization at the scale of neighborhood spurred creativity.[13]

Delineated neighborhoods have been thought of as microcosms of the larger city, the whole town a united "congeries of little cities," each with some degree of self-sufficiency. This describes the medieval town, whose neighborhoods contained functions and elements based on the needs of the local populace, with all the functions needed for daily life within them. In an emblematic way, San Marco's Plaza (Piazza San Marco) was repeated in miniature form in each Venetian parish, each with its own square in much smaller size (Figure 14.7). Perhaps this correspondence allowed each citizen to feel "a reflection of the total civic magnificence" of Piazza San Marco in their own neighborhood.[14]

The delineated and designed neighborhood, like the planned suburb, also provides an opportunity to design in an integrative way. At Sunnyside Gardens in New York, neighborhood design was adapted to a dense urban grid, with housing units organized around a shared commons (Figure 14.8). Here the neighborhood unit was conceived as the antidote to the austere rationalism of urban expansion led by developers who had little interest in differentiating space for social purposes. The monotonous grid was psychologically and socially harmful,

Figure 14.8 Sunnyside Gardens, Queens, New York, USA. *Neighborhood design was adapted to a dense urban grid, with housing units organized around a shared commons.*

whereas the neighborhood unit was in service to the creation of complete and protected social clusters.[15]

But does the differentiated space of delineated neighborhoods play a role in elevating consumption over production? Is it a means of capitalist exploitation, the controlling of space to exert power? One might see the physical manifestation of Lefebvre's thesis in *The Production of Space* in the delineated neighborhood. Where there are bounded, identifiable neighborhoods in the urban pattern, are we witnessing the undermining of a wider political identity and the thwarting of class-based solidarity and activism?[16]

15

Districts

Not every separated area of the city can be defined as, or is attempting to be, a neighborhood. Sometimes separate areas are better defined as "districts," especially if they aren't residential or if they are simply aggregated buildings confined to an area. Districts are created for specific purposes, such as to define college campuses, religious compounds, or public housing projects. The created districts are freed from constraint, emerging as places of inwardly focused, individualized experience and functionality. There are now districts devoted to every kind of purpose: entertainment districts, warehousing districts, innovation districts.

Historically, districts emerged out of the street-platting habits of surveyors who resisted aligning with other plats. American cities often have multiple intersecting street patterns at different angles showing the imprint of platting and development in different stages. The initial grid would be at right angles to a waterway, subsequent grids would latch on, and eventually grid patches would align with the national imprint of Jefferson's grid, with its strict cardinal orientation. The rest of the city's grid would straighten up. Over time, jogs, awkward intersections and weirdly shaped properties in cities would create separate districts. Historical land holdings also played a role. In New Orleans, for example, it is possible to see the imprint of former plantation boundaries (Figure 15.1).

Singular focal points, if they are well placed, can grow into recognizable districts that impact the whole shape of a town. In European cities, three kinds of places had this impact: the manor and the land around it (called the demesne), the church and its fronting plaza, and the marketplace. Ensembles emerged, such as the combination of church, market square, and a royal residence. In some countries, the areas surrounding the church created the city's most important district. The marketplace would then be located nearby to take advantage of assembled church crowds. What types of buildings were most prominent varied by country, reflecting what function dominated civic life. In France, the church dominated; in Germanic towns, it was more likely the castle.[1]

Sometimes these separated districts are peaceful, secluded enclaves, such as the Beguinage in Brugge, Belgium, a small district in the heart of the city established as a convent (Figure 15.2). The quiet repose within the district is the result of being insulated from traffic. It was a superblock-like separation later favored by modernists.

If districts are created by an outside power like an imperialist government, they can be disruptive, even violent, and wildly out of step with existing settlement

What Cities Say. Emily Talen, Oxford University Press. © Oxford University Press 2024. DOI: 10.1093/oso/9780197647769.003.0016

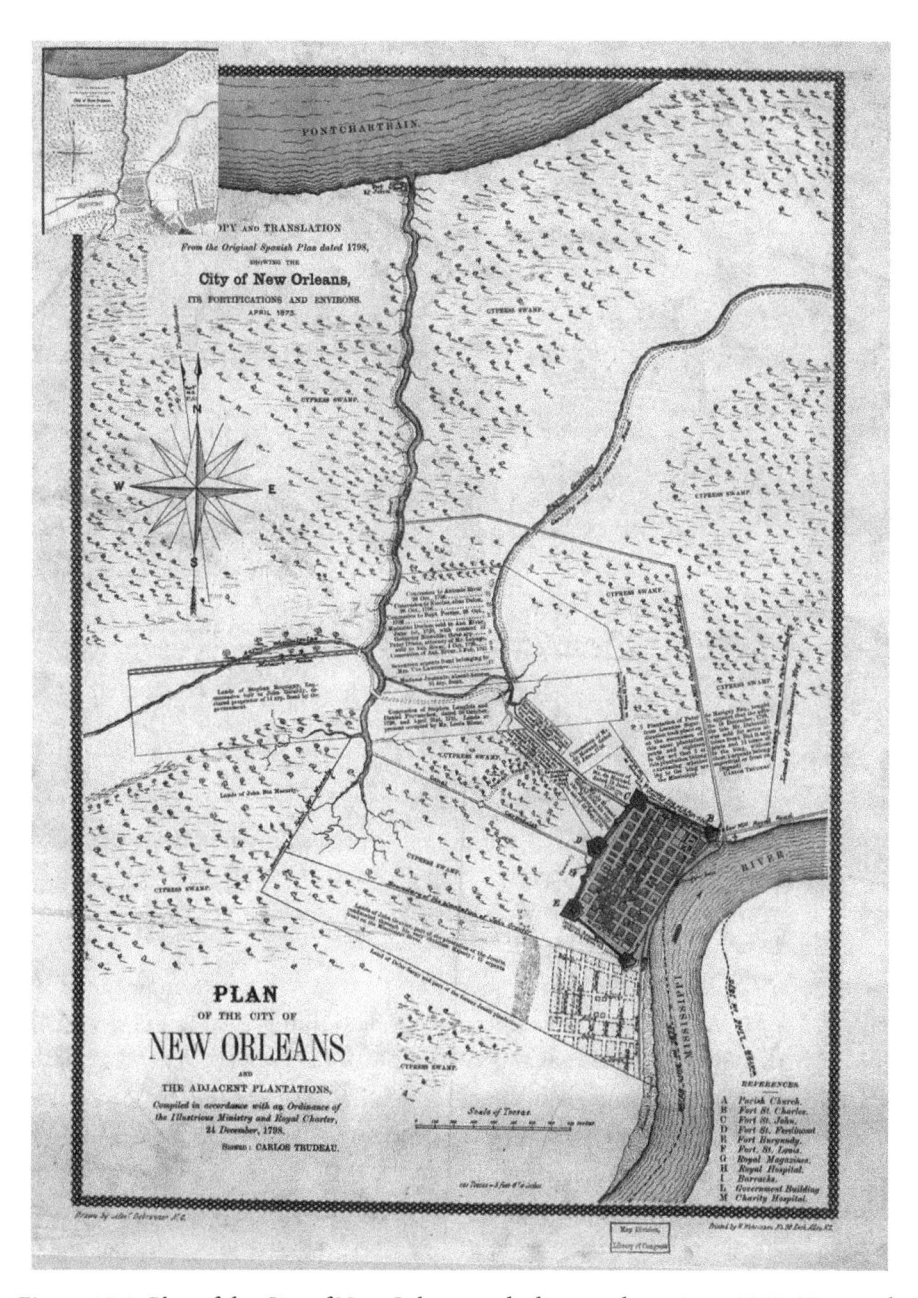

Figure 15.1 Plan of the City of New Orleans and adjacent plantations, 1875. *Historical land holdings, including plantation boundaries as shown here, create awkward intersections and weirdly shaped properties and districts.* Credit: Library of Congress, Geography and Map Division.

patterns. The classic case of these segregated districts—they cannot really be called "neighborhoods"—occurred under European colonialism in Africa, India, and the Middle East. For example, separate districts built by the British in the 1920s and then after World War II in Nairobi, Cairo, and Zanzibar to relocate indigenous

Figure 15.2 Beguinage, Brugge, Belgium. *Separated urban districts, this one for a convent, can create peaceful, secluded enclaves in the heart of the city.*

populations appear like geometric aberrations in an otherwise indigenous urbanism. They have been interpreted as an act of "enframing" that ultimately failed. Not only was there no resident sense of ownership of the imposed schemes, but the spatial layout was often completely unsuitable. In Zanzibar, clear demarcations between street and house—motivated by the need for control—conflicted with local social customs that were much more open and fluid (Figure 15.3). In Kuwait, the imposed districts were a severe alteration of the traditional Kuwaiti pattern, with housing units now separated, on wide streets, with large setbacks, and inadequate amenities (Figure 15.4).[2]

If not relocated to separate districts, indigenous people occupied the "organic" high-density urbanism of narrow, winding streets, while colonialists built low-density grids that had the ability to accommodate monumental buildings. For example, in Pondicherry, India, the French built the Governor's House to "project their power across the sociocultural landscape." It was the gridded district that enabled land division for the purpose of showing off imperial might and exposing to the world how power was, rightly in their view, unequally distributed (Figure 15.5).[3] The *cordon sanitaire*—an open space separating indigenous settlement from that of the European colonialists—separated the districts in dramatic fashion, for example in New Delhi (Figure 15.6). The separation was labeled a "hygienic measure" to help

Figure 15.3 Zanzibar, Tanzania. *The act of enframing: geometric aberrations (left) in an otherwise indigenous urbanism (right).*

Figure 15.4 Kuwait City, Kuwait. *Imposed districts were a severe alteration of the traditional Kuwaiti pattern, with housing units now separated, on wide streets, with large setbacks, and inadequate amenities.*

stop the spread of malaria: the width of the open space was calculated as the maximum distance a mosquito could travel.

Examining the differences between wealthy and poor districts is revealing, and the divisions can be stark. Rich and poor districts in Mumbai show a particularly strong

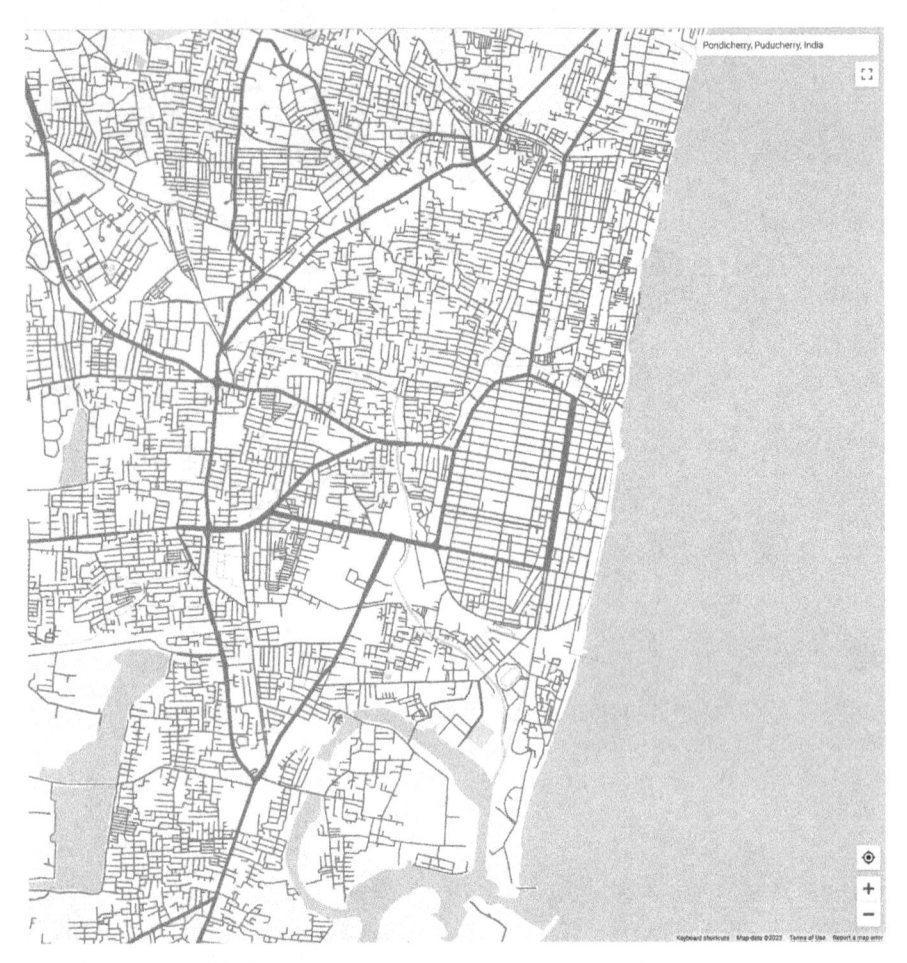

Figure 15.5 Pondicherry, Puducherry, India. *The gridded district proclaimed imperial might and unequal power.*

Figure 15.6 New Delhi, India. *An open space was used to separate indigenous settlement from that of the European colonialists. The separation was labeled a "hygienic measure" to help stop the spread of malaria: the width of the open space was calculated as the distance a mosquito could fly.*

Figure 15.7 Mumbai, India. *Rich and poor districts in Mumbai show a stark contrast, the rich surrounded by green and the poor tightly packed.*

contrast, the rich surrounded by green and the poor tightly packed (Figure 15.7). In the United States, wealthy districts at the periphery (in suburban mansions) reveal that access to open space and "green" is valued, while wealthy districts near the urban core reveal that access to cultural amenities is valued. If the wealthy find a way to create their own districts within the city, they can have access to both amenities and open space, while still maintaining exclusivity. This is an apt interpretation of two 19th-century enclaves formed along private, gated streets in St. Louis: Westmoreland and Portland Place (Figure 15.8). They were designed to literally exclude from their "line of sight" the realities of urban living, including both the land uses (factories) and the people (poor) that were deemed unpleasant.[4]

Urban renewal districts located in central cities emphasize their separateness by purposefully blocking connection with the surrounding street patterns of the city. Public housing projects in the United States were notorious for this maneuver. The projects were usually built in stark contrast with the surrounding grid, a visible declaration that the project didn't belong. The architecture was sterile and monotonous, which, because it contrasted with the surrounding character of older buildings, added to the sense of exclusion. This kind of radical spatial differentiation is not new—Renaissance and Baroque insertions of plazas were carved into the medieval fabric for the purpose of differentiation. But in those cases, the intention

Figure 15.8 Westmoreland Place and Portland Place, St. Louis, Missouri, USA. *Gated streets created wealthy districts in the heart of the city that excluded factories and workers from their line of sight.*

was to inspire awe. When the object is public housing, the created contrast reads like a public shunning.

Districts form around a city's assets—a waterfront or a group of historic buildings, for example. Waterfronts are primary assets, and how cities treat their waterfront districts can be telling. If they have been redeveloped as condos, it signals that residential developers and landowners have been prioritized. If now occupied by commerce or industrial development, it signals a different power structure, with job growth as a priority. If repurposed for public recreation, the public interest holds sway. Choices are contentious. Cleveland, Ohio's waterfront has grappled with a century of competing plans for its waterfront district, some geared more to public uses and some more to private development. In the absence of an adopted plan, Keating wrote, "the lakefront remains a place where priorities are unclear and frustration abounds among all of the concerned interest groups."[5]

Districts can be created by consolidating buildings devoted to a common purpose. A cluster of government buildings is commonly known as the "civic district." Planners have long debated the merits of grouping government buildings in civic districts vs. distributing government buildings throughout the city. Ancient Greek and Roman cities employed the former technique, where unified architectural groupings transitioned public buildings from being sacred and discrete sites to being part of an "esthetic whole." The advantage, according to Mumford, was that the district and the civic life it represented were "open and understandable at a glance." This had practical value for cosmopolitan cities full of visitors from distant lands. The ensemble of coherently designed public buildings signaled an "investment in the common life" that was readily evident, especially since many of these cities were small, often fewer than 30,000 inhabitants. The civic district stood out.[6]

But on the other hand, when ensembles of public or civic buildings are sorted and separated out into special districts, "like frosted pastries on a tray," their purification from the fabric of the city means that the civic function is removed from everyday life. Civic centers, many of which came out of the City Beautiful era, were, in fact, typically detached from daily life and human need, acquiring "an air of divorcement" where citizens were forced to "adjust themselves to the right formal arrangement." In this they were nothing like the Greek agora, or even the Roman forum, which were model settings for a civic life that combined civic and commercial functions (although in either instance, civic and religious activities always had priority over commercial ones). In places like Cleveland (Figure 15.9) or San Francisco, monumental buildings making up the civic center were more likely to be imposing than attracting, signaling "disdain rather than dignity," and keeping citizens "at arm's length."[7]

Jane Jacobs viewed this as a fundamental problem. People might find pride in such civic districts—certainly City Beautiful era planners viewed them as the essence of urban sophistication—but their separation meant that they didn't integrate with the everyday workings of the city. In addition, the areas around them tended to be characterless and bleak. Somehow, observed Jacobs, "when the fair became part of the city, it did not work like the fair." The iconic designs of these separated districts only added to the sense of disconnection. The design of Lincoln Center in New York City, a merger of modernist urbanism, garden cities, and the City Beautiful—the "Radiant Garden City Beautiful" as Jacobs disdainfully labeled it—made the area stand out like a "decontaminated" special cultural district (Figure 15.10). The purification aim of the civic center is no secret, as the dozens of civic center projects built in the first decade of the 1900s in the United States were simultaneously beautification and slum

Figure 15.9 Civic District, Cleveland, Ohio. *The monumental buildings might be more likely to be imposing than attracting, keeping citizens at arm's length.*

Figure 15.10 Lincoln Center, New York, New York, USA. Disconnected from what's around it, the Center stands out like a "decontaminated" special cultural district. Credit: Ajay Suresh from New York, NY, USA, CC BY 2.0 <https://creativecommons. org/licenses/by/2.0>, via Wikimedia Commons.

clearance projects. The civic center idea thus got swept up in the attempt to cleanse the public realm from the workaday world of cities.[8]

On the other hand, the consolidation of public functions into civic centers, centrally located, did have an efficiency advantage. In *Modern Civic Art* (1903), Robinson argued that the civic district ensured "the efficient, economical conduct of the city's business." And not unlike the Greek agora or the Roman forum, it might help advertise that the city took its civic function seriously. This was an important message in the early 20th-century American case, when the city seemed to be increasingly "lost in a wilderness of commercial structures." The civic district could stand as tangible evidence that Americans were capable of collaborating in the production of civic art and civic life. This was tempered, of course, since grouped public buildings arranged in a civic center expressed a system of order and unity that would only supplement, and always remain subordinate to, the industrial and commercial core of the city.[9]

If civic spaces and buildings were more dispersed throughout the city rather than sequestered, would this result in a better integration between civic and daily life, thus mitigating the impression that government is oblivious to its citizens? At least, more parts of the city would be exposed to the physical expression of civic life. And even with a dispersed arrangement, there are ways to provide some coherence, whereby discrete spaces in cities are "knit" together. In Brest, France, for example, a port city sponsored by Louis XIV (but significantly destroyed in World War II), government buildings were placed near each other, but they were not sequestered in a separate district (Figure 15.11). There was no need to employ absolutist planning and baroque diagonals to make the case that the ensemble was a government creation that was thoroughly in control of religious, administrative, and commercial

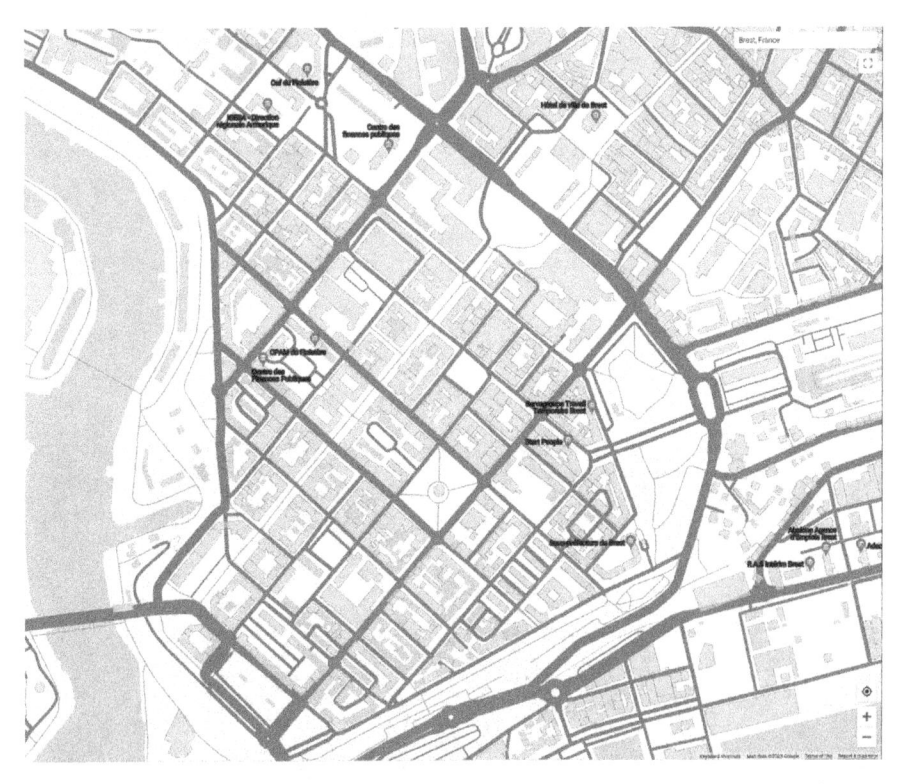

Figure 15.11 Brest, France. *Government buildings (labeled) are near each other, but not set in a separate district.*

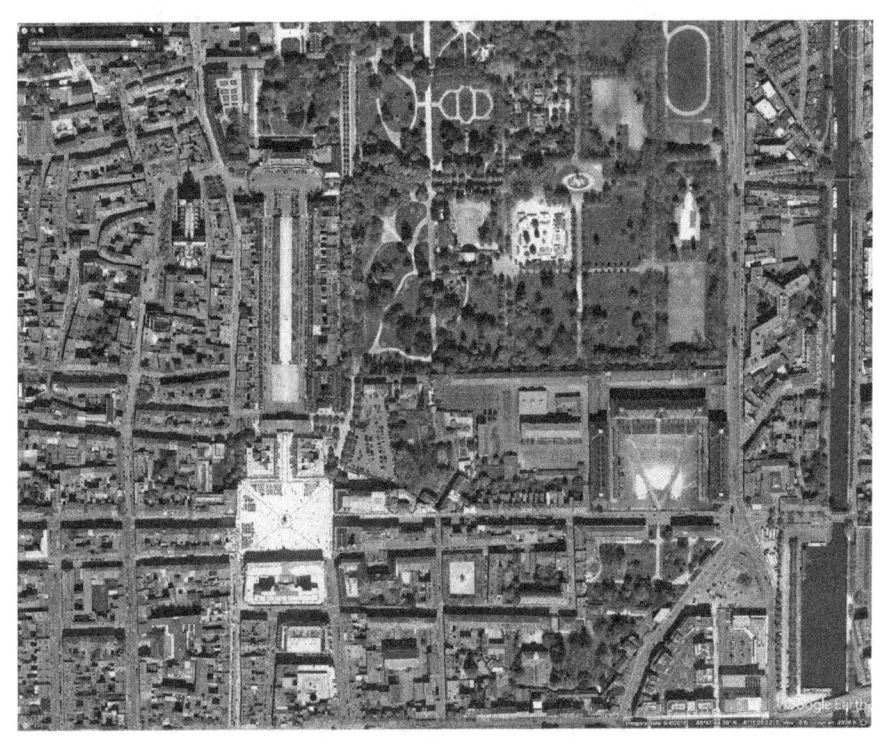

Figure 15.12 Nancy, France. *A sequence of spaces was used to bind together two parts of the town—medieval and Renaissance.*

interests. The basic method was to fit the collection of government buildings into the existing grid.

Districts of various kinds have been maintained by positioning related buildings and spaces in a coordinated sequence. A precursor of the approach was in Nancy, France, in the mid-18th century, where a sequence of spaces was used to bind together two parts of the town—medieval and Renaissance (Figure 15.12). The 19th-century "urban renewal" of Regent Street in London was also designed to create an ensemble, and successfully linked the Regent's Park development to the area around St. James Cathedral (Figure 15.13). Kostof

Figure 15.13 Regent Street, London, UK. *The 19th-century "urban renewal" of Regent Street in London was designed to create an ensemble.*

considered it a "masterful knitting together of new and existing streets" in a way that rejected Classical dictates and instead made "jogs and unmatched elevations" part of the design. Each street had its own axis. He labeled it, not pejoratively, "anti-Renaissance."[10]

But the sequence-and-dispersal approach can seem disjointed. Rasmussen considered Regent Street too mechanical and likened the ensemble to a "plumber connecting his pipes with fittings." It also seemed to facilitate movement through the city rather than arrival at a destination. And, unlike the Parisian boulevards that were based on the bulwarks that demarcated city and country at the outskirts, Regent Street was intended as a route straight out of town to the countryside. It wasn't about tidying up medieval irregularity, it was about "removal" to open land beyond the city.[11]

16

The Baroque

An urbanism of grandeur is called "baroque" in a generic sense, the "City Beautiful" in a more American sense, and "The Grand Manner" by Spiro Kostof. Each term has peculiarities of definition but the sentiments are similar. The focus is grandeur and uniformity, specifically classicism and neoclassicism, employed on a vast scale. With that, someone or something is being aggrandized—and by the same token, someone or something is being subordinated, since baroque planning's expression of order and control is only possible by way of squashing other ideas. "Order by way of repression of all plans but the planners," as Jacobs described it. Rasmussen thought this was necessary and he gave the despots a pass: "A country with any pretensions to importance simply had to have its splendid palace representing the power and culture of the state." The monarchy was merely developing the spatial signature of autocracy.[1]

The baroque employs symmetry in its expression of order, control, and majesty, although symmetry is not necessary for expressions of grandeur. The Acropolis had no insistence on symmetry, no effort to achieve a measured visual sequence, as in the baroque. Instead, structures atop the acropolis, like the Parthenon or the Temple of Athena Nike, were self-contained and equal, "not subordinate in any hierarchic kind of order," an independence that Mumford found "in no small degree symbolic."[2]

In Charleville, France, we see many of the elements of the baroque mode laid out: differentiation of minor and major streets, a prominent square (the Place Ducale) and subsidiary squares, careful attention to the facades of buildings lining the squares, and the placement of important buildings in relation to the axes of major streets as termination sites (Figure 16.1). These were the principles of the 16th-century Venetian architect Andrea Palladio, as detailed in his treatise *The Four Books of Architecture*. The same principles were applied to garden design.

The baroque is about sequence and vista and axis as opposed to centeredness. Trees planted in straight rows are used to enhance the effect, and perhaps mitigate a sense of alienation, since the baroque is prone to exaggeration. This is because expanse is needed to achieve the association with greatness—or fear and subordination. Monuments and their settings need to express triumphs, and "for the magic to work," as Kostof put it, "one needed room." Referring to the City Beautiful era boulevards of Chicago, Daniel Burnham believed there was "true glory in mere length" and that "scale is the all-important element in creating an agreeable form." To some observers, the subtext was control and submission.[3]

What Cities Say. Emily Talen, Oxford University Press. © Oxford University Press 2024. DOI: 10.1093/oso/9780197647769.003.0017

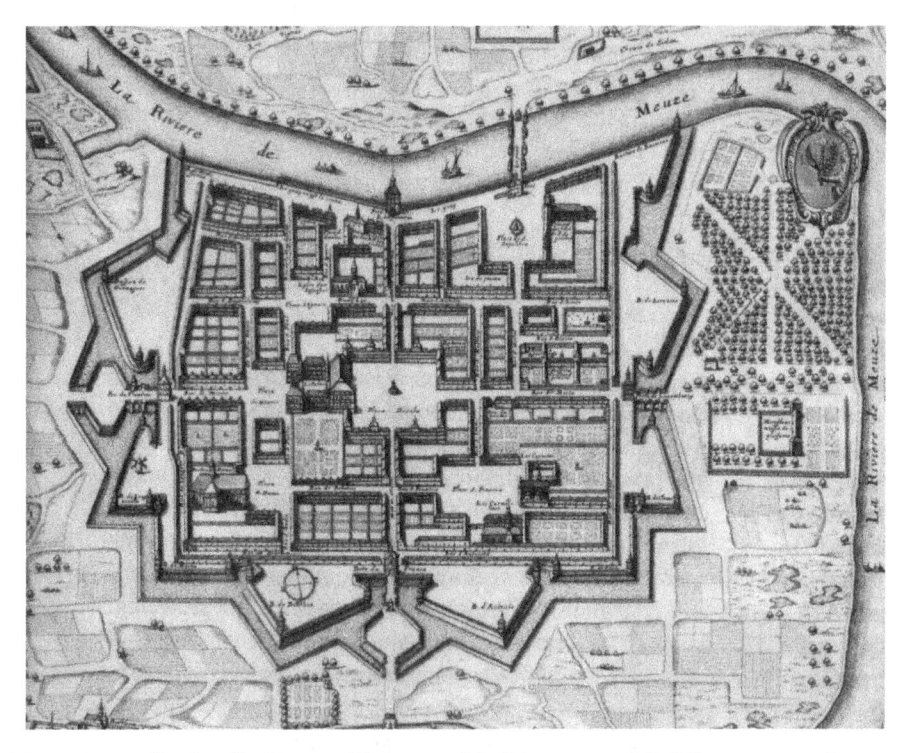

Figure 16.1 Charleville, France. *Elements of the baroque model: differentiation of minor and major streets, a prominent square and subsidiary squares, careful attention to building facades, and important buildings placed where major streets terminate.* Credit: Edme Moreau, Public domain, via Wikimedia Commons.

The baroque strategy of a strong central axis focuses attention on a singular idea, ranging from collective social life to a singular dominant authority. An example of the former case is Williamsburg, Virginia, where a dominant central axis provides a sense of collective identity—although, in violation of the conventional principles of baroque planning, the axis terminates on only one end. An example of a focus on a dominant authority is the Kartavya Path, originally "King's Way," the east-west axis of New Delhi, India (Figure 16.2). The western endpoint of the axis is what was the viceroy's house (at the other end, India Gate). The movement of machinery (tanks and other processional vehicles) along the axis terminated at "the prime moving power itself."[4]

In baroque pattern and form, space is vast but controlled. In the 17th century, this coincided with new monarchical authority. Space was measured, ordered, and meant to dominate and reflect state conquest and Absolute Rule. Straight lines, uniform facades, and wide streets fit into a coherent frame that controlled movement and space, and thus time. This reflected the state's subjugation and consolidation of territory—quite the opposite of medieval urbanism. Perspective drawing was useful, and perfect for despots like Louis XIV, since perspective drawing relates everything to one central point. The ruler wanted to know how the whole would look from his domain, and it was only from the king's bedroom windows that one

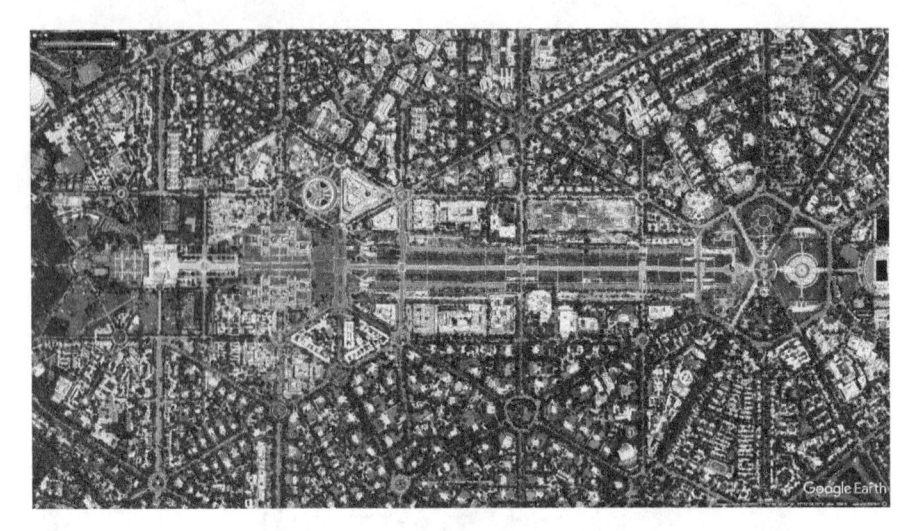

Figure 16.2 Kartavya Path, New Delhi, India. *A strong central axis focuses attention on a dominant authority, which, at the time of construction in the 1920s, was the viceroy's house.*

could comprehend the grandeur—and meaning. This power translated to dominance over nature, too. At Versailles, the geometric designs seen from overhead—the palace balconies—added an exclamation point to nature's subservience.

Kostof thought that the climactic phase of baroque planning occurred in 16th-century Europe. It paralleled new developments in science and culture, in which the view of the world shifted from being static and earth-centered to being infinite and sun-centered. This changed conception of space meant that urban objects could be altered to produce desired visual effects, a practice that mirrored the nascent world of illusion in theatrical performance. It was during the baroque period that concern for building placements and arrangements was elevated to its greatest extent. Rather than focusing solely on buildings as singular objects of beauty, buildings were placed in order to accentuate urban layouts.

But the baroque way of building cities is not limited to one time period. There are elements of baroque ideals in ancient cities, and the ideas emerge again during the Renaissance (the 15th and 16th centuries) with the advent of idealized cities and a concern for geometric perfection, perspective, and symmetry. When these ordered, grandiose plans come on the scene—whether in the 17th century in Europe, during the Third Empire in Paris, the City Beautiful era in the 1890s, or in the 20th-century urban renewal period—they signify the emergence of new economic and political powers. This prompted Mumford to ask, "[I]s it an accident that this aesthetic order," encountered in ancient Egypt and again in seventeenth-century Europe, "came into existence along with absolute monarchy and large-scale bureaucratic supervision"?[5] The unified architectural expression associated with the baroque seems to disparage the right of disagreement in the political process, or the right to resist subjugation.

Figure 16.3 Oroquieta City, Philippines. *Here baroque boulevards pull civic power away from the downtown and the seafront, which had traditionally formed the civic core.*

American civic improvements of the 1890s employed the baroque to reflect the sense of superiority and economic militarism that was taking place in American conquests around the globe at the time: American imperialism in Cuba, Puerto Rico, and the Philippines. In Oroquieta City in the Philippines, the Capitol complex built by Americans outside of the city used baroque elements to express domination. Three baroque boulevards pulled civic power away from the downtown and the seafront, places that had traditionally been the civic core (Figure 16.3).[6]

Spaces in the baroque are designed to elicit certain behaviors and feelings. The replanning of Rome, which started in the early 16th century, was an exceptional example (there was significant creative talent behind it, involving towering figures like Raphael, Bramante, Michelangelo, among others, and the political power of popes Julius II and Leo X). The Piazza Obliqua, in front of St. Peter's Basilica, symbolizes the arms of the Mother Church and is supposed to inspire "arrested" movement—a "brake" in the "main spatial thrust" leading toward the church (Figure 16.4). These spatial controls had been perfected even earlier in ancient Rome and then later in 18th-century France under autocratic regimes, which is why their employment in

Figure 16.4 Piazza Obliqua, St. Peter's Basilica, Rome, Italy. *Symbolizing the arms of the Mother Church, the space forces one to pause on their way to St. Peter's.*

Washington, DC, has always seemed inappropriate. It is an expression of political power, of absolutism, of the centralizing force of an authoritarian regime, be it a despot, a pope, or a government.[7]

With baroque plans, architecture and monument is the foreground, while the small, messy grind of everyday life is hidden away. The Palace at Versailles is one of the more extreme examples of monumental, controlled, ordered space standing in contrast to the everyday life of an adjacent town (Figure 16.5). A well-known French historian argued that because of this separation, the building of Versailles had "graver consequences than any of Louis XIV's wars or all of his wars put together." Yet despots recognized that if the town, through its architecture, mirrored the palace, then this could be a means of announcing to the world that the prince had extraordinary power. The trick was that the adjacent town had to be both worthy of the King and at the same time completely deferential. In Versailles' case, "dominance and dependence" were awkwardly put together, with the town "tucked away on either side of the central axis." New residential districts planned adjacent to palaces in 17th- and 18th-century Europe, such as at Kassel, Karlsruhe (Figure 16.6), and Mannheim (Figure 16.7) in Germany, included baroque elements like squares and avenues in a forced show of deference and submission to the court.[8]

The wide, orchestrated spaces of the baroque signal command and control, decisiveness, and a sense that there is an authority with the ability to immediately fix problems. This is exactly why the approach is attractive to despots and fascists who want to present the impression of control and certitude—straight lines rather than meandering indeterminacy. There is to be no incremental, organic urban growth involving multiple actors and plebeian decision makers. One downside, of course, is that the element of control in the baroque manner means that the cities and spaces it creates are not easily adapted or changed to fit different needs and inputs. It is an

Figure 16.5 Versailles, France. *Dominion over all: monumental, controlled, ordered space stands in stark contrast to the fluidity of nature and the everyday life of an adjacent town.*

Figure 16.6 Karlsruhe, Germany. *New residential districts planned adjacent to palaces included baroque elements like squares and avenues in a forced show of deference and submission to the court.*

all-at-the-same-time kind of idea about city-making: one concept and one way of doing things. Incremental change by many hands cannot be reconciled.

Is all this control a sign that there is an underlying social problem that needs to be covered up? Was the "perfected physical shell," as Mumford wrote, "the final expression of a frustrated and spiritually enfeebled civic organism"? In the American case, the baroque insistence on Beaux Arts classicism had a way of intensifying the opinion that the City Beautiful was more interested in facades than in underlying

Figure 16.7 Mannheim, Germany. *Like Karlsruhe, deference to the monarchy is reflected in town pattern and form.*

causes, in form without content, in satisfying business interests rather than social needs. It didn't help that baroque planners put uniforms on everything: nature (trees and hedges clipped to perfection), buildings, streets, places, and people. This regimentation would have been intolerable, writes Mumford, except for the "sexual exuberance and sensual ecstasy" on attendant fountains, architectural facades, and sculpture.[9]

Yet the baroque, although suited to a grand scale, is not scale-dependent, and can be implemented in small communities. There, the justification is that baroque elements instill elegance and culture in what would otherwise be a utilitarian frontier outpost or a boring grid town. This was especially important in the era of civic boosterism in the early 20th century, when there was a need to outshine other towns if one hoped to attract capital successfully. And what is wrong with a modestly scaled sense of formality?

But to some observers, baroque patterns in small places—Williamsburg, Virginia, or Letchworth and Port Sunlight in the UK, or Venice and Seaside in Florida (Figure 16.8)—seem pretentious. This can leave an especially awkward mark where the town is not fully developed. The pomp seems not to fit the circumstance. In the small city of Bawarda, Iran, the baroque grandiosity of the layout, devoid of any civic or public buildings, seems to have no reason for existing. The focus on "sheer design" without purpose becomes "theatricality" and emptiness.[10] There are many similar examples. In Sandusky, Ohio, grand diagonals go nowhere and terminate in open space rather than important building sites (Figure 16.9). The wide expanse of Hampstead Garden Suburb's central green is a baroque feature that seems out of place and appropriate for a much larger town (Figure 16.10). Or the opposite can happen. In Annapolis, baroque elements are squeezed in and the result seems distorted and out of sync (Figure 16.11).

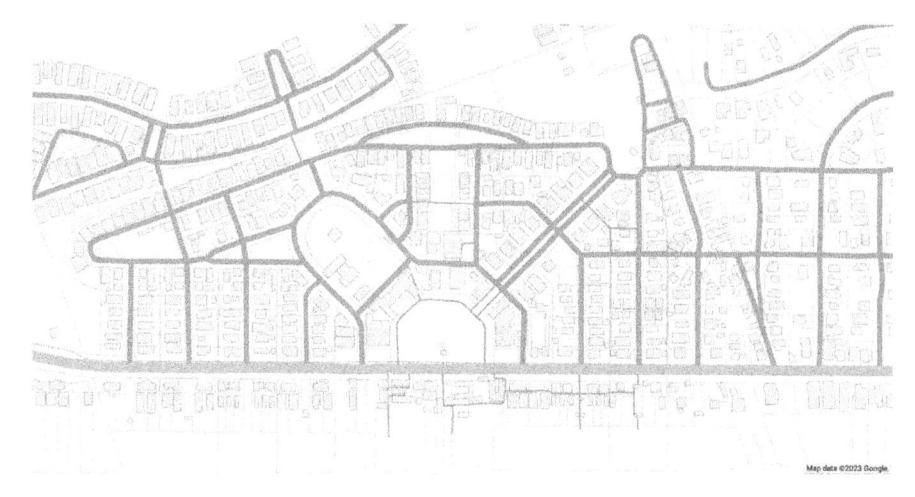

Figure 16.8 Seaside, Florida, USA. *Baroque patterns are found in small places.*

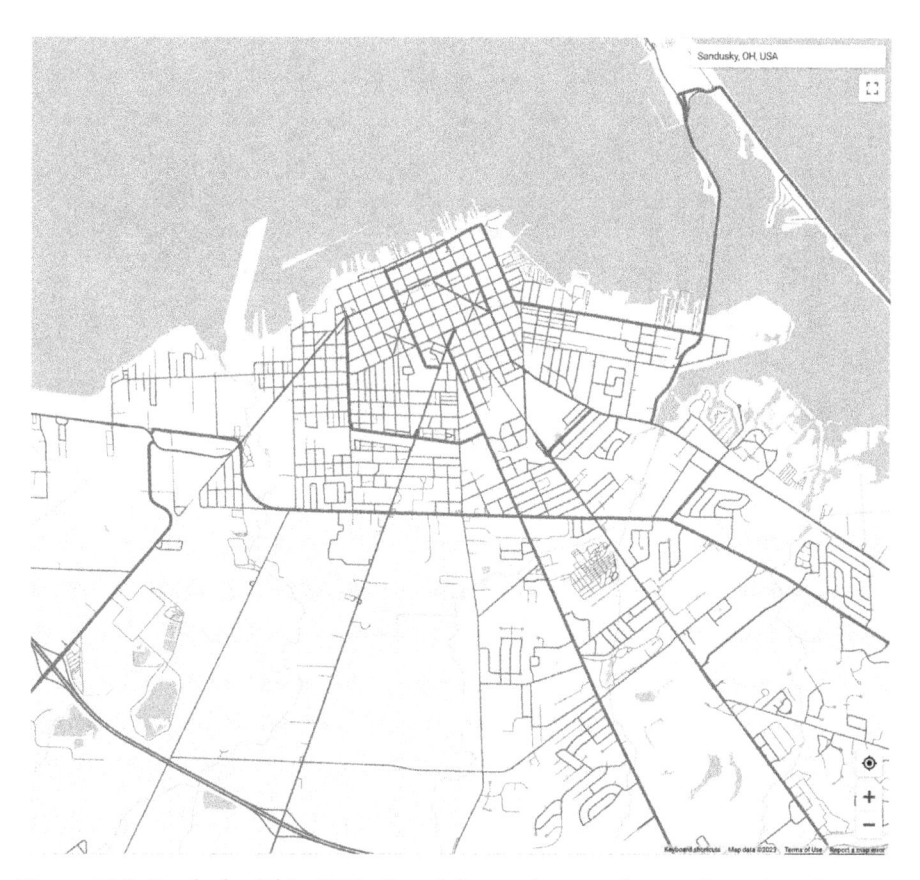

Figure 16.9 Sandusky, Ohio, USA. *Grand diagonals go nowhere and terminate in open space rather than important building sites.*

Figure 16.10 Hampstead Garden Suburb, near London, UK. *The wide expanse of the central green is a baroque element that seems out of place and appropriate for a much larger town.*

Figure 16.11 Annapolis, Maryland, USA. *Baroque elements are squeezed in, making the result seem distorted and out of sync.*

There are more positive associations to be made about the baroque, however. A city with boulevards, uniform classical facades, and grand public spaces can be interpreted as a city that believes enough in itself to invest in its own design. Boulevards and plazas provide a sense of long-term commitment and continuity. Raymond Unwin, from his early 20th-century perspective, thought that the baroque simply showed, in a positive way, "power and courage." Of course, there are ways for a city to be beautiful and awe-inspiring without needing to resort to top-down baroque-ism: witness the consonant, elegant 17th-century houses lining Amsterdam's canals, which inspired awe and a sense of grandeur and "belonged to the whole community." The effect was not the result of the dictates of an absolute monarch.[11]

Another charitable view of the baroque is that the order and uniformity it imposed provided a sense of orientation. In some cultures, such as Germany, baroque ordering fit a cultural and behavioral mindset that put a high value on regularizing one's behavior and adhering to the rules. Ordered plans were not compromising, but that suited the culture just fine. There is also the view that the grandiosity of the baroque, along with the big investments it requires, creates a culture of investment that is often needed to mitigate large-scale urban problems. Morris wondered whether London's avoidance of baroque form was actually a problem for it later, as the city now lacks "a comprehensible main route structure."[12]

If baroque plans are implemented by a benevolent dictator and improve citizen quality of life, perhaps the loss of individual agency can be forgiven. This was the narrative Robert Moses hoped people would accept. And, with the exclusion of instances where slave labor was involved, the massive public works projects of baroque planning amounted to a giant public employment program. There was generous spending involved. Haussmann's baroque rebuilding of Paris was said to employ a quarter of Paris's workforce. On the other hand, there is the problem of resilience: when funds run out, or there is an economic downturn, there is no built-in resiliency for ordinary citizens to carry on.[13]

Absent a dictator's benevolence, the valuation of baroque patterns and forms often requires disassociating the plan from the originator. This is "the lesson of the container," Mumford wrote: that it is possible to value certain designs "long after the tyrannous edits and the arbitrary acts of conquest passed into nothingness." Krier argued that nefarious associations can be reversed, that baroque symbolism can be inverted such that grand spaces provide settings for everyday life and thereby lend an elevated dignity to the otherwise mundane. Kostof doubted this was possible: "these compulsive shells from the Age of Absolutism, with their densely packed imagery and manipulative scale, betray their source with modern [obliquities]."[14] Perhaps the sense of awe that baroque cities originally intended has worn off, leaving the pedestrian feeling unanchored and isolated.

Yet there are cases where the vast scale of the baroque has been softened and humanized. Paris's boulevards are the result of monarchical control, but they are also tree-lined and full of pedestrian life and café culture—activity that the baroque boulevard provided a setting for. And although domination of nature was intended, it was an entirely different approach from the garden city or planned suburb, which involved retreat. In the baroque, landscaped elements were not separated out as remedial components to counter the grayness of the industrial city; rather, nature was brought into the city and made to align. This is not to say that the social purposes were very different—both the garden city and the baroque thought nature had the ability to cure social malaise. The difference is that landscape under baroque planning was used to celebrate and embellish the city, not escape from it.

17

Monumentalism

The baroque regularly employed monumental spaces and forms, but monumentalism occurs in many other contexts, and the quality of being expansive warrants its own interpretation. Hans Blumenfeld wrote that there were two kinds of monumentalism: one that "exalts" people because they identify themselves with the "strength and grandeur" of the built form, and an opposite one that "overawes" people who view it as "an alien and threatening force."[1] Either way, monumentalism is entirely relative: grandeur in one context can be diminutive in another.

In most cases, as with the baroque, the use of monumental spaces and forms is an indication of centralized power. A gigantic regional shopping mall and a grand boulevard lined with monumental buildings have in common a single (or at least centrally coordinated) source of capital to pull it off, whether private, public, or a combination (an interesting exception to the central power rule of monumentalism is Stonehenge—there is no indication that a singular authority was behind the unique arrangement of giant stone monuments). The sheer size of the endeavor means, at least, it is not easily ignored, although ironically, large size can limit access. In Stevenage New Town, the Town Centre is like a large shopping mall, and people can't get close to it (Figure 17.1).

The baroque relied on horizontal monumentalism, but vertical monumentalism is also effective. Power in the medieval city was by way of the tallest church spire or tower of a powerful family, for example. The Athenian Acropolis is a case of vertical monumentalism, rising up out of the rocks, "inducing a proper deliberation and humility in the ascending worshipper." This was a practice, Mumford points out, not unlike Washington, DC's Lincoln Memorial (although for the Acropolis, height was also a matter of defense). In the case of the Acropolis, fountains and delicate carvings on stelae preserved the human scale.[2]

There have been times in history when monumentalism has been especially dramatic. One is 16th-century Italy, when kings and popes transformed the fabric of medieval towns, straightening and widening streets and carving out large public open spaces. Rome's transformation included the Piazza del Popolo (Figure 17.2), the Via Sistina, the Piazza di Spagna, and Trinità dei Monti, the Capitol, and the forecourt to St. Peter's.[3] Politically, however, all this straightening and widening paid a price. A. E. J. Morris argued that Renaissance and later baroque plans were a prime cause of royal downfall. There is a commonly held theory that the British monarchy held on to power much longer than other European states due to its limited adoption of baroque monumentalism in London, at least for government

What Cities Say. Emily Talen, Oxford University Press. © Oxford University Press 2024. DOI: 10.1093/oso/9780197647769.003.0018

Figure 17.1 Stevenage Town Center, UK. *The "town center" is like a large shopping mall, and people can't get close to it.*

Figure 17.2 Piazza del Popolo, Rome, Italy. *The goose-footed (or patte d'oie, as geese have three toes) convergence of diagonals was part of Rome's dramatic transformation.*

purposes. It is symbolic that the political center of the UK, 10 Downing Street, is on a modest street in an unassuming townhouse.

Historically, monumental plans tended to originate with a small minority of powerful people intent on exerting a way of life on their subjects via over-sized buildings and expansive, straight streets. In cases where the monumental plan was overtly employed for submission, it was an act of violence. The Nazis claimed to use monumental spaces to "restore to each individual German his self-respect," but it was actually a way to intimidate people and enforce deference.[4] Urban design was weaponized and used as an instrument of Nazi propaganda. The idea was that if people could be awed by monumental spaces and buildings, they could overlook the hardships in their daily lives because, at least, the grandeur of the city was theirs. Never mind that this required submerging their own identities and freedoms.

It might be argued that monumental places can unite the citizenry. The Hellenistic city, with its arenas, stadia, and other forms of "impressive bigness," had the effect of treating "life itself as a spectacle," but at least "rich and poor, noble and low, were now united in that role."[5] Yet this is difficult to value in the face of an authoritarian figure like a king, in which case monumental plans express the desire of the king rather than the desires of the people. Grand spaces, whether vast plazas or wide avenues, are assertions of concentrated power, not collective power. People are bystanders rather than participants.

Monumentalism in the hands of a despot can reach absurd proportions, and one wonders what size might be trying to compensate for, such as loss of real power, or loss of confidence in the citizenry. In Pyongyang, North Korea, the gargantuan buildings, monuments and grand axes are an attempt to ensure that no one misses the point: power to "the people" under Juche ideology, but all hail the great leaders Kim Il-sung and Kim Jong-il (Figure 17.3). Beijing's Olympic Village, a vast assemblage of vanity projects, has been interpreted as a squelching display of state power and worker exploitation, a government seeking to use monumentalism as propaganda to rally a splintered citizenry around a "grand patriotic endeavor" (Figure 17.4). Monumentalism is used to pacify the masses and divert attention from human rights abuses as well as "evictions, tax increases, inflation, restricted civil liberties, and shrunken welfare programs."[6] This is how state-created monumentalism is often read: as power assertion, exploitation, and diversion.

Even in democratic contexts, monumentalism can seem too much. The Washington Mall is critiqued on this point, its width and length considered to be too far to draw meaningful connections between the buildings surrounding it. It is a plan of "magnificent distances" and thus its radials, not its underlying grid, dominate. One historian wrote that the Mall of Washington, the principal feature of the nation's capital, was "an element the Sun King himself would have admired." In fact, the connection is not particularly subtle: the position of the White House relative to the US Capitol mirrors that of the Trianon (Louis VIX's private residence) to the Palace at Versailles.[7]

But monumental scale might also convey a sense of optimism. Monumental spaces by definition leave "room for aggrandizement and embellishment," signaling a belief that the city has a future. Albert Speer argued that monumentality is characteristic of "quickly acquired wealth," an admirable quality in his view. For Stalin, it was the far-reaching vistas he created in Moscow that were a symbol of his far-reaching achievements.[8]

Dictators were especially fond of monumentalism in the form of a wide avenue. The Via dell'Impero in Rome was installed to ensure an unobstructed view of the

Figure 17.3 Triumphal Arch, Pyongyang, North Korea. *Gargantuan buildings, monuments, and grand axes attempt to ensure that no one misses the point: all hail the supreme leader.* Credit: David Stanley, CC BY 2.0 <https://creativecommons.org/licen ses/by/2.0>, via Wikimedia Commons.

Palazzo Venezia balcony, the seat of power of the Fascist Party and the place from which Mussolini bellowed out his tyrannical propaganda. Pointed toward the balcony, with the ancient Colosseum behind and imperial fora lining the avenue, pedestrians and vehicles became participants in "a carefully designed urban theatre piece" (Figure 17.5). But achieving this effect required massive displacement.

Figure 17.4 Beijing's Olympic Village. *Vanity projects and state power: the physical manifestation of a vast, exploitable workforce.*

Figure 17.5 Via dei Fori Imperiali, Rome, Italy. *Mussolini bellowed out his tyrannical propaganda from a balcony overlooking the wide avenue.*

The borgate romane were concrete housing slabs at Rome's periphery built to temporarily house people displaced by these stage sets. At the city center where the working class once lived, Mussolini's monumental public works decreased housing supply, increased land values, and made permanent the temporary displacement of people to the periphery. Places like Primavalle now stand as permanent symbols of the violence of Fascist monumentalism (Figure 17.6).[9]

Figure 17.6 Primavalle, Rome, Italy. *Concrete housing slabs at Rome's periphery, built to temporarily house people displaced by Mussolini, stand as symbols of the violence of Fascist monumentalism.*

Figure 17.7 Palace Square, St. Petersburg, Russia. *The most draconian imposition of monumentalism in modern history: spectacle and political theatre to legitimize the regime.* Credit: Villeke1, CC0, via Wikimedia Commons.

Marshall Berman thought St. Petersburg's imperial "modernization," begun in 1703, was the most draconian imposition of monumentalism in modern history. It turned the whole city into "a political theater," the everyday into "a spectacle," and it used art and geometry to "buttress and legitimize" the regime (Figure 17.7). Ordinary folks were exposed to some very ornate architecture, but behind the facades, poverty remained. The grandeur presented only a veneer of beauty and awe, the imposed spaces signaling an especially undemocratic way of life. As a practical

Figure 17.8 Tokyo Bay, Yokohama, Japan. *The megastructure reflects techno-optimism, but the entertainment district is isolated from the rest of the city.*

matter, these monumental open spaces enabled a lot more people to assemble and mill around together—but there was a risk to the exposure. The "anonymous multitudes" could turn into a swarm of enemies or a swarm of comrades—both with frenzied potential.[10]

Lately monumentalism has been pitched as a solution to global problems, from ecological disaster to economic stagnation. The Yokohama megastructure in Tokyo Bay reflects "techno-optimism" but also a belief, common to most megaprojects, in the ability to construct a perfect, totalizing environment (Figure 17.8). A "civic axis" of cultural facilities and open space is supposed to symbolize an "open society" that welcomes change, reflective of a new attitude about Japan's social structure. But in the end, it is really nothing more than a business and entertainment district isolated from the rest of the city.[11]

18

Urban Renewal

Urban renewal is a special case of monumentalism. The term refers to a mode of development that occurred in a specific time employing a specific design ideology: mid-20th-century modernism. "Urban renewal," however, if defined as large-scale, big-money projects intended to "renew" a "blighted" area, usually involving "public-private partnerships," is ongoing. Such projects involve a lot of capital and a lot of upheaval. As such, they symbolize centralized power and the belief that there are people in charge, such as architects and politicians, who know what's best for people and for city making.

Urban renewal in the mid-20th century, which happened globally but especially in Western, capitalist democracies, replaced the finer-grained texture of the 19th-century city with a much coarser form of urbanism—superblocks, wide roads, large buildings. The mega-forms are often so removed from history, local condition, and pedestrian scale that they are easy to pick out. The denial of history was not only expedient, but it reflected a newly emerging urban reality—social separation and a loss of connection with time, as well as a loss of connection to a city's unique local and regional culture, material, or building type. This fostered detachment, as not many people could be expected to cozy up to city development with no historical or cultural reference point. On the other hand, the detached, abstracted scheme was well suited to a highly organized mass society in which people are supposed to move like robots between points on a map, with highways serving as "channels" to move the population to and from districts as fast as possible, at least theoretically.

Cities the world over have plenty of remaining scars from the mid-20th-century urban renewal period. Cities are pockmarked with mega complexes, infrastructure, or perhaps a university, hospital, or some other large-scale corporate endeavor, in keeping with urban renewal's business-friendly, neoliberal, pro-growth political culture. Universities (such as Chicago's University of Illinois) demolished the homes of thousands of poor residents who did not have the means to attend the universities that displaced them (Figure 18.1). In the form of government-backed corporate complexes, urban renewal signifies a society that prioritizes high-rent, luxury apartment buildings and gleaming office towers, most likely with plenty of government largess and a high tolerance for political gamesmanship.

If there is demolition involved, which is often the case, urban renewal projects show that city leaders have no faith that smaller, bottom-up rehabilitation, rather than wholesale demolition, can be helpful for a place down on its luck. It signals a lack of patience for incremental change rendered by small-scale ownership, a

What Cities Say. Emily Talen, Oxford University Press. © Oxford University Press 2024. DOI: 10.1093/oso/9780197647769.003.0019

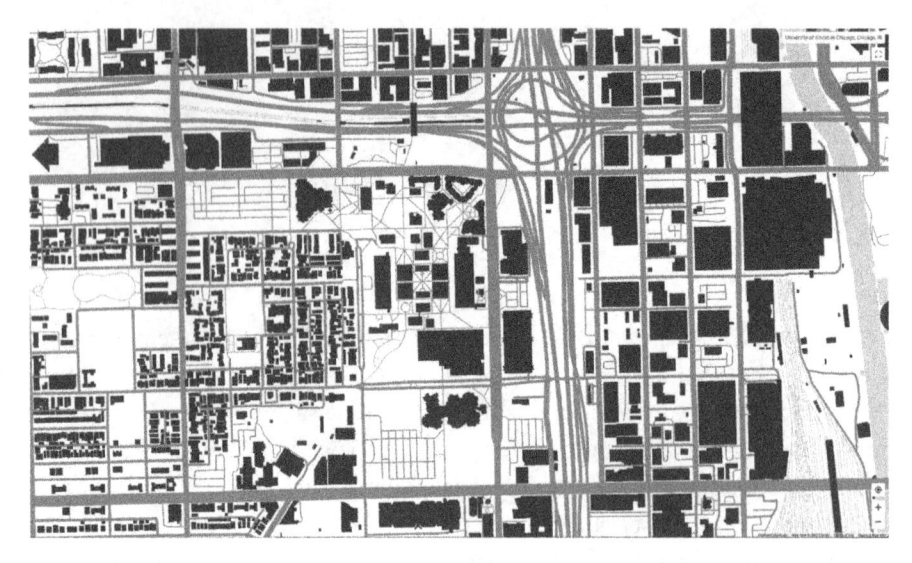

Figure 18.1 University of Illinois at Chicago, Chicago, Illinois, USA. *Government-funded urban renewal on Chicago's west side involved tearing down whole neighborhoods to make room for a university complex.*

disregard for local retailing, informal economies, and social capital. It has the imprint of powerful actors attempting to remake the city with the mindset that disinvested neighborhoods are incapable of self-improvement. Since individual adaptation does not play a role, urban renewal's megaprojects can never leverage the power of individual actions. Mumford's view about skyscrapers applies: "[they] wiped out the complex tissue of a thousand little and not so little urban activities."[1]

Big architectural projects have long been viewed as the antidote to what some perceive as chaos and disorder. When designed as a complete package, they give an impression of completeness, finality, order, and modernity. The ideology fit towering architects as well as towering dictators, so it is not surprising that a megaproject proponent like Le Corbusier would align himself with Mussolini. The "urban renewal" of Mussolini was devoted to monumentalizing, unencumbering, and reinstating the glories of ancient Rome, thereby hoping to affix the glory to himself and his Fascist regime. Such plans had little connection to the urbanism around them, signifying the urban renewal disdain for what came before—unless of course it was a structure symbolizing Roman grandeur.

Many spaces of urban renewal, like shopping malls, are now classified as "dead." At mid-20th century, malls were sometimes inserted in the middle of small to mid-sized cities in the hopes that the mall would rejuvenate a dead downtown. This usually didn't work. Successful at first, eventually the malls themselves accelerated the process of sucking life out of whatever remained of the downtown. Lincoln Square mall in Urbana, Illinois, is but one example. The city and the mall's private owner have been in a decades-long struggle to breathe life into the dying complex (Figure 18.2).

Figure 18.2 Lincoln Square, Urbana, Illinois, USA. *Meant to rejuvenate a struggling downtown, the mall itself has struggled with vacancy for decades.*

Figure 18.3 University Circle, Cleveland, Ohio. *Green spaces, water features, curving pathways and object architecture attempt to rebrand the city from dying rust belt town to technical hub with a bright future.*

Cleveland, Ohio's "University Circle" is an example of the "eds and meds" approach to urban renewal (Figure 18.3). The goal was not simply more room for facilities, but a method of rebranding the whole city from dying rust belt town to technical hub with a bright future. The complex was thus intended as a "bulwark" against perceived urban problems and a safe haven for suburbanites. Inserted green spaces with water features, curving pathways, and object architecture were not only supposed to "soften the hard edges" of the industrial city, but were thought of as a modern version of the green commons of a New England village or the cathedral square of a medieval town. But while university leaders thought the development was a "symbol of stability and quality" and the antidote to the surrounding "blight and decay," the green spaces and modern buildings seem sterile and unwelcoming. To maintain the image of stability, every experience is meant to be predicted, and the hyper-controlled complex looks, feels, and acts like a fortress.[2]

Urban renewal applied to public housing was about racial containment—the need to keep African Americans separate and apart from the existing city, cordoned off and controlled. James Baldwin famously said that the more appropriate term for "urban renewal" was "negro removal."[3] It was an effort to extend what W. E. B. Du Bois had labeled "the color line" into the heart of cities. The social damage was, and is, enormous. And, the insistence on open spaces around the housing towers invariably meant that public housing would be monumental—and therefore kept apart. Because of their size and surrounding open spaces, such projects suffered from what Stern and Massengale call "projectitis," which involved cutting off connections to surrounding neighborhoods. Perhaps large-scale housing projects did offer some degree of design coherence, which might translate to economies of scale and other efficiencies. The planner Clarence Stein thought that building housing in anything less than a coherently designed project was "pure waste." But for this mechanized efficiency to be realized, the building site needed to be wiped clean of any existing historical fabric.[4]

Another way urban renewal was leveraged to promote social separation was to construct large apartment complexes that physically blocked any possible connection between poor Black or Latino neighborhoods and wealthy White neighborhoods. Two examples in Chicago are legendary: Sandburg Village (Figure 18.4) and University Park (Figure 18.5). Both were middle-class apartment complexes that were purposefully constructed as buffers to "protect" adjoining wealthy areas from the encroachment of "blight." Sandburg Homes shielded the Gold Coast, University Park shielded the University of Chicago.

Highways have been another especially destructive feature of urban renewal. There was no secret that the idea was to facilitate the ability of White middle-class residents to quickly travel in and out of the city and not have to pay attention to the neighborhoods they were traversing through, which were invariably harmed by the increase in traffic, noise, and fumes. Transportation planners recommended clearance of "great segments of the close-in city" in exchange for highways that could provide services "on a regional basis." A modernist, tabula rasa design ethic, and popular metaphors characterizing urban neighborhoods as both "dying" and "ripe," created a perfect climate for widespread, often politically motivated demolition.[5]

Mumford makes an interesting point about the relationship between important civic spaces and the circulation pattern around them. If arteries needed for heavy traffic circulation are kept to the periphery, like the Grand Canal on the periphery

Figure 18.4 Sandburg Village, Chicago, Illinois, USA. *Large apartment complexes were constructed to physically buffer wealthy areas from the encroachment of "blight."*

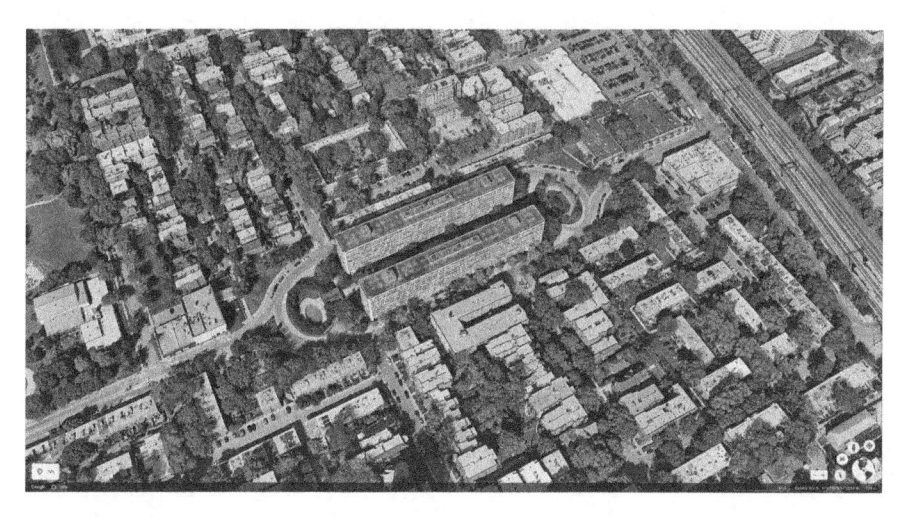

Figure 18.5 University Park, Chicago, Illinois, USA. *The linear apartment complex was built to buffer the University of Chicago from the adjacent neighborhood, mostly populated with African-Americans.*

of Venice, a city's civic spaces are respected. Heavy traffic never approaches "the delicate interior organs of the city." Access is maintained "through frequent minor arteries and capillaries."[6] Highways linking downtowns to suburbs showed no such respect.

At mid-20th century, highways exemplified technological "progress," the embodiment of modernity, an invisible force rendered in asphalt, and not to be stopped.

Figure 18.6 Robert F. Kennedy and Hell Gate Bridges, New York, New York, USA. *Bridges and tunnels create a "space-time" merger only grasped via movement.*

Figure 18.7 Long Island Expressway, New York, New York, USA. *The elevated highway that rips through Queens helped residents escape from the "junkyards" that cities were thought to have become.*

Siegfried Giedion argued in *Space, Time and Architecture* that this brand of progress should be embraced. Unlike the static nature of a beautiful plaza or garden, the beauty of modern infrastructure—highways and assorted bridges and tunnels that created a unified flow—revealed a "space-time" merger that could only be grasped via movement—that is, by driving. As Marshall Berman later observed, to travel over the Triborough (now Robert F. Kennedy) Bridge in New York City was to enter "a new 'space-time continuum,' one that leaves the modern metropolis behind" (Figure 18.6)[7]

Conceived thusly, urban renewal projects were a kind of savior that helped residents escape from the "junkyards" that cities had become. The Long Island Expressway shows it well. The elevated highway, a Robert Moses project from the 1950s, rips through Queens, showing "ferocious contempt for all natural and human life," focused only on maximizing the "sheer quantity" of moving vehicles (Figure 18.7). Berman postulates that the grim reality of the concrete and steel urbanism that the project created was responsible for the severing of ties between the art world and the world of city-making. The postwar urban renewal environments that were being created were not environments that any artist could draw inspiration from, so the art world withdrew. Artists and writers were forced to rely on their own "inner space," since there could be no inspiration found in the everyday urban forms of modernism.[8]

19

Uniformity

Any city or town can be interpreted for its degree of sameness, regularity, symmetry, or uniformity, for example, identical houses on identical lots or identical gridded blocks composed of identical streets. Uniformity in a city is often thought dull and incapable of competing with nature, since nature provides abundant diversity. "In a city," as one early 19th-century critic put it, "variety is essential to beauty."[1] Uniformity is also thought to be the opposite of distinctiveness, and without the latter, it is worth asking whether a place can still be cared about.

On the other hand, there is a place for uniformity. Diversity will only be palatable, it could be argued, if it exists within a framework that provides coherence, which usually means some degree of uniformity. The City Beautiful, for example, rested on the idea that stylistic variability needed a "language" to allow any variation to work successfully in an urban context.

But when uniformity occurs on a vast scale, for example at Levittown, New York, it signals production building: housing as commodity that can be cheaply constructed and easily bought and sold (Figure 19.1). On the plus side, it was a method able to satisfy "the acquisitive urge" of a booming middle class. After World War II, housing production was transformed into an industry, with standardized parts, labor, and processes. But this efficiency and uniformity of housing production on a mass scale was to be realized by private capitalists only. Politicians and developers worried that if control of housing design transferred from private interests to government-backed housing projects, socialism would surely follow.[2]

The uniformity associated with mass-scale production can be bleak. In Levittown, concern for community spaces and artful groupings of human-scaled apartment buildings (which occurred in planned suburbs like Chatham Village or Radburn) was all but forgotten in favor of churning out single-family houses at record speed. Over time, variety was introduced in incremental ways: small additions, bespoke landscaping, diverse house colors. But the quest for production efficiency undermined what was considered a key advantage of planned developments in general: that they are capable of design quality and attention to detail. Levittown was instead the physical expression of Whyte's "Org Man"—someone whose life and thoughts are controlled by the "organization" rather than by any personal thoughts or drives.[3]

There are more charitable ways to read a place like Levittown. Might the square miles of essentially homogeneous homes foster social connection and communitarianism? Is uniformity a more comfortable and manageable setting for everyday life,

What Cities Say. Emily Talen, Oxford University Press. © Oxford University Press 2024. DOI: 10.1093/oso/9780197647769.003.0020

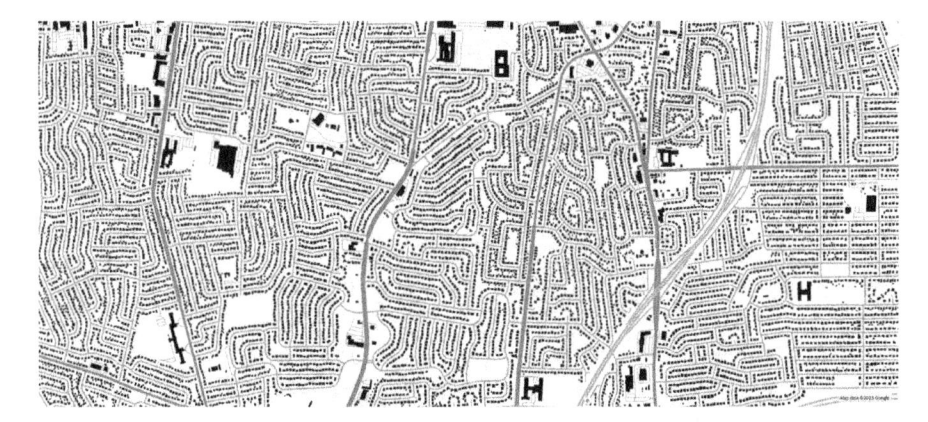

Figure 19.1 Levittown, New York, USA. *Housing as commodity translated to uniformity and production building, cheaply constructed and easily bought and sold.*

as compared to cities composed of housing extremes where inequality, rendered in physical form, creates an ever-present reminder of one's place in the world?

Uniformity is common with all housing types. Private developers and financiers, realizing the efficiencies and profits to be made, transferred Ford's mass-production techniques to the construction of garden apartment complexes, for example. This was unlikely to turn out well in terms of design quality, as there was usually a total lack of spatial definition. One example is Buckingham Village, Virginia. Gallion and Eisner observed that rows of identical garden apartment buildings were showing the "strong habit of the single lot" applied to larger buildings on larger lots (Figure 19.2). At least apartment building uniformity applied on a large scale was said to create a "metonymic logic" whereby tenants in small apartment units could see themselves as being parts of a whole. According to Lefebvre, the expanded and uniform scale of the apartment complex functioned as a kind of compensation for the "pathetically" small size of the living quarters.[4]

Uniformity has also been used to mask—and protect—an underlying social diversity. In ancient cities, like Athens, rich and poor lived side by side and their houses were indistinguishable from the exterior. Later this was employed as a socialistic device, whereby modest worker homes might be placed in a building that looked like a palace. An example is the 19th-century French phalanstère the Familistère de Guise (Figure 19.3). Also in the 19th century, Port Sunlight's "street of mansions" was intended to disguise large from modest dwelling sizes. The country manor was actually an apartment building. In another example, Amsterdam Zuid's perimeter blocks are four-story, traditional row housing blocks with internal green spaces that, with their uniform facades, are intended to hide social differences (Figure 19.4). Kostof argued that this was later eroded at the hands of architects who felt compelled to apply their own individualized, idiosyncratic designs.[5]

A possible problem with the uniformity approach to masking social difference is that it could be interpreted as an attempt to hide a city's social inequality.

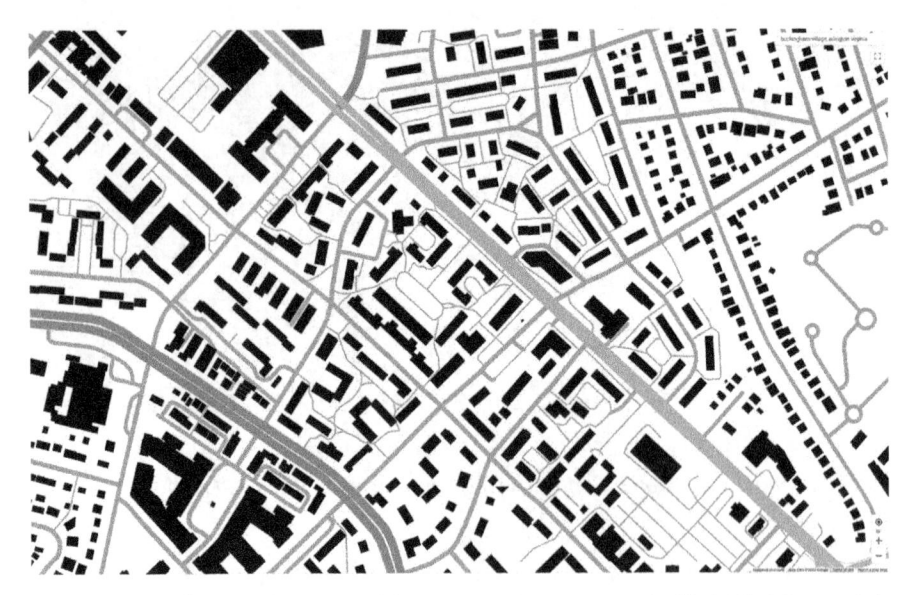

Figure 19.2 Buckingham Village, Arlington, Virginia, USA. *The "habit" of the single lot was applied to rows of identical garden apartment buildings (center of image).*

Figure 19.3 Familistère de Guise, France. *The central pavilion of the phalanstère housed workers in a building that looked like a palace.* Credit: Velvet, CC BY-SA 3.0 <https://creativecommons.org/licenses/by-sa/3.0>, via Wikimedia Commons.

Figure 19.4 Amsterdam Zuid, the Netherlands. *The town's "street of mansions" was intended to disguise large from modest dwelling sizes.*

Renaissance cities have been critiqued on this basis. The uniformity of classicism is thought to show "a lack of respect for the social conditions of a submissive population."[6] And in reality, the intent was a unifying aesthetic that could be readily understood, not uniformity for the altruistic purpose of minimizing social difference.

There are other possible positive readings of uniformity, particularly in an urban, rather than suburban, context. Private homes with the same frontage, for example housing in Mannheim built according to strict laws in the early 18th century, "make the whole street appear one house," which is a lesson in collective city-making (although to critics, also a lesson in regimentation, loss of liberty, and extreme conformity). In Barcelona, the equalizing intent of the grid was strengthened by uniform building height and by the fact that building height and street width were the same (Figure 19.5). Buildings were thus kept "subordinate to the hegemony of the urban realm." But at the city's fringes, architecture began to "trump urbanism," which some thought resulted in a degraded urban environment.[7]

Street grids are exemplars of uniformity, facilitating an even division and distribution of land. When the Huguenots fled France in the 17th century and settled in Germany and the Netherlands (and other Protestant-welcoming countries), their towns were platted out in equal, gridded land divisions, and, according to Kostof, "unequivocally the sameness was meant to express the social equality of all inhabitants." This interpretation is also applied to the Mormon grid, with its equal division of land reserved for the inhabitants of the City of Zion (e.g., Salt Lake City). In Barcelona, the squared blocks blanket a uniform grid across 10 square miles, regarded as an expression of "equality of rights and interests" and of "justice itself."[8]

If the grid also has uniform building setbacks, this is considered an important benefit for pedestrian life. Absent this uniformity, it might be hard to "read" a grid from the pedestrian's point of view. Williamsburg, Virginia, is an example where the

Figure 19.5 Barcelona, Spain. *The equalizing intent of the grid is strengthened by uniform building height and street width.*

Figure 19.6 Williamsburg, Virginia, USA. *Uniform setback distance made the grid more readable.*

town code (from 1699) stipulated uniform setback distance and frontage, which made the grid more readable (Figure 19.6). The grid of the model industrial village Saltaire is thought to succeed because of its uniformity, which included the "arcuated rhythm of the ground-story windows and doors" that helped soften the grid and "[conduct] the eye easily along the street" (Figure 19.7). Of course, if there is no building uniformity imposed on a grid, as in the case of Manhattan, the grid's "two-dimensional discipline" is capable of unleashing "undreamt-of freedom for three-dimensional anarchy."[9]

Uniformity can also help elevate a selected element, or person, in the city—the reverse of equalizing. This is why despots wanted uniformity for everything except their own domain. For domination to succeed, building heights and densities had

Figure 19.7 Saltaire, Shipley, UK. *The grid of the model industrial village: where some see the benefits of readability, others see stifling repetition.*

to be uniform so that whatever was being lauded—a castle, for example—could be easily recognized. The approach could apply to civic structures as well. However, the strategy proved difficult to sustain. Industrialization and modern technologies like the elevator and the automobile, combined with economic realities about land value, made maintenance of suppressed height and strict uniformity increasingly unrealistic.

Housing activist Catherine Bauer was a big believer in architectural uniformity as a way to solve housing problems. The International Style would set the standard: "[standardized] parts, instead of creating dull uniformity, become a positive force in creating a uniform whole."[10] Collectivism expressed in uniform style was thought to be ultimately liberating for the individual. Ironically, however, well into the 20th century in many parts of the Western world, it was Beaux Arts classicism, not modernism, that was selected as most appropriately communicating order and uniformity. Classicism was appealing because it was considered adaptable. Adhering to classical order also had the significant advantage of giving even the most mediocre architect a frame to work with, thus helping to ensure higher quality architecture.

Washington, DC, adopted a uniform classical order, and it is regularly critiqued because of it. Gallion and Eisner labeled Washington's adherence to classical architecture "hollow and unnatural." The commercial city, "warped into the pattern of streets," was considered "equally artificial." By constraining the commercial enterprise of Washington and constructing a National Mall that severely separated the city, its commercial function became disconnected and contrived. The city tried to strike a compromise between the classical and the commercial, but uniformity

Figure 19.8 Federal Triangle, Washington, DC, USA. *The cluster of coordinated neoclassical office buildings from the 1930s was perhaps the last major City Beautiful venture in the United States.*

seemed to become an object unto itself, abstracted from human need or purpose. Incorporating wide straight avenues and boulevards with uniform frontages only further subsumed individual building character and function. Federal Triangle in Washington, DC, that cluster of neoclassical office buildings from the 1930s, was perhaps the last major City Beautiful venture in the United States (Figure 19.8). Is it coordinated architecture, or a case of Imperial Rome imposed on a democracy?[11]

Whether classical or modern, can uniformity, or more specifically symmetry, go "a long step toward cementing together the [city's] heterogeneous elements," as Daniel Burnham claimed? The industrial city was viewed by reformers as confused and formless, a product of greed and a love of expansion at any cost. Symmetry was the antidote, evident in Chicago's City Beautiful era plans, for example where Ida B. Wells Drive (formerly Congress Parkway) terminates at Buckingham Fountain (Figure 19.9). Burnham and Bennett wrote that a city without symmetry was "barbarism" and "a crime against good taste that could never be atoned for."[12]

One possible defense of this seemingly arrogant adherence to symmetry and over-concern for visual uniformity over other needs (like housing) is that it was conceived as a way of making sure that commercialism—which most big cities embraced—was kept in check. In the end, however, the strategy didn't hold. The goals were inherently contradictory: civic beauty as both a rationale for commerce and a critique of commerce. Cities like Detroit eventually capitulated, their civic institutions—the art museum and the public library—placed outside of downtown. The supremacy of the commercial sector had won.[13]

Mumford contrasted the uniformity of the modern city with the pliability of the medieval city. Towns with a uniform style were guilty of "arbitrarily freezing the historic process at a given moment," valuing "uniformity more than universality,

Figure 19.9 Buckingham Fountain, Chicago, Illinois, USA. *City Beautiful symmetry as the antidote to the chaos of the industrial city.*

and visible power more than the invisible processes of life." Skyscrapers, which tended toward uniformity, were especially ill-suited to a multifarious human existence. From a money perspective this made sense, since uniformity is the very quality that makes the tall building commercially valuable and easily replicated. But the skyscraper's formulaic, uniform quality detaches it from "the complexities of human association." Humans and their relationships are heterogeneous. Should their settlements reflect that, or stand in defiant opposition?[14]

This question stands out wherever uniformity has been taken too far, or when there is an overly rigid adherence to symmetry. This is what Sir Patrick Abercrombie thought of the identical churches built during the Renaissance on either side of the street in the Piazza del Popolo in Rome. In similar spirit, Sitte railed against the love of symmetry, which he thought was propagated by those "least cultivated." All that was needed was proportion. But people seemed not to know that proportion and symmetry were one and the same—proportion being, simply, "an agreeable relationship to the eye."[15]

20

Variation

It's easy to spot city patterns and forms devoted to social sameness. Suburbs of only one housing type, public housing clearly marked and sequestered, gated communities, land use segregation in general—these patterns can be interpreted as fostering segregated social worlds. But there are instances where diversity is a valid interpretation: a variety of housing types in the same neighborhood, varied lot and block sizes, a mix of public spaces, or variegated movement paths to provide circulatory diversity, from street to alley to pathway. Perhaps a great variety of forms and patterns means there is a lot of churning going on: population moving in and out, each group leaving its mark.

The medieval town, with its compactness and human scale, is still, in its modern existence, a tightly knit, contiguous urban fabric that harbors a great variety of materials, facades, and rooflines. Well-distributed commerce added variety; there were central marketplaces, but commerce and trade took place in every part of the town: "the entire medieval city was a market," noted Saalman. It is because of this variety that Ruskin and Morris revered the medieval town so much—it was an urban form that was nonstandardized. Irregularity, they believed, meant creativity, and this, in turn, meant that urbanism was closer in structure and in meaning to nature.[1]

Early 20th-century social reformers tried to counteract uniformity. In the 19th century, construction of identical and cheap housing coincided with industrialization, arriving in the form of bye-law row housing. The lack of variety was seen as a form of oppression. Henrietta Barnett, an early 20th-century housing reformer, interpreted identical housing as undermining humanity. She put her faith in diversity, arguing that variegation in housing type and style could turn the "buried potentialities" of human taste and initiative "into facts."[2]

Places like Hampstead Garden Suburb were built on this principle. Assorted architecture and frontage type, culs-de-sac and closes, nonorthogonal street intersections, winding roads—these elements were combined to leave the impression that the community had as much diversity as nature. Varied block arrangements and layout patterns were explicitly for the purpose of integrating a range of income levels and social backgrounds—"the whole rainbow of human existence plainly visible." Yorkship Garden Village, built during World War I in Camden, New Jersey, was similarly variegated, incorporating diverse lot sizes and housing types, and grouping buildings in a variety of ways (Figure 20.1). Even Riverside, Illinois, can

What Cities Say. Emily Talen, Oxford University Press. © Oxford University Press 2024. DOI: 10.1093/oso/9780197647769.003.0021

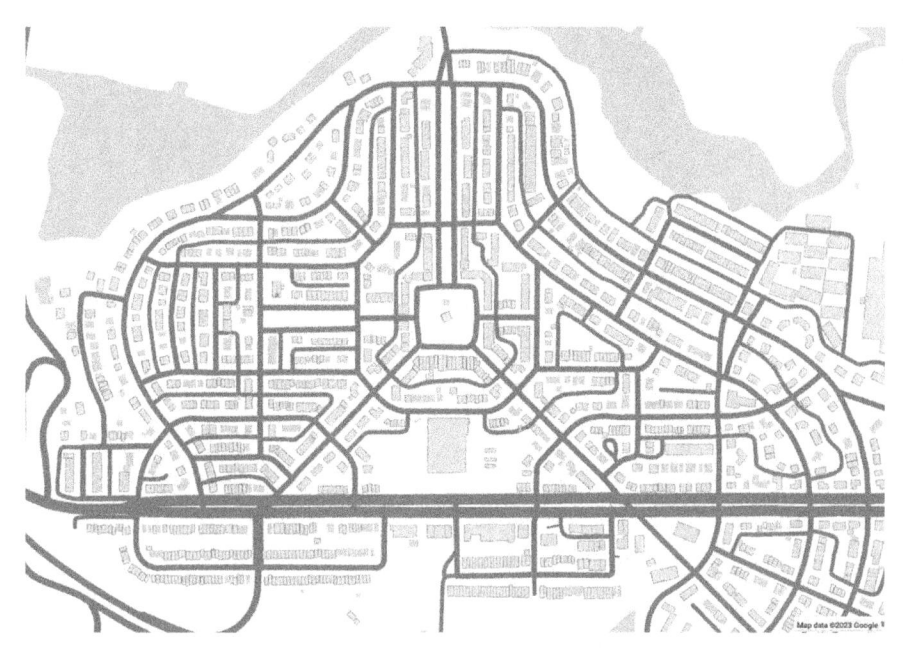

Figure 20.1 Yorkship Garden Village, Camden, New Jersey, USA. *Diverse lot sizes and housing types were for the purpose of integrating a range of income levels and social backgrounds.*

be interpreted as supporting some measure of diversity. It has smaller lots near the train station, exactly for the purpose of providing a place in the otherwise wealthy suburb for people of "modest means."[3] And Ridley Park in Philadelphia included lots both big and small, which was intentionally meant to mix income levels (Figure 20.2). The difficulty with all of these examples is that they were built as unified, complete places in one short time period, so diversity, not being a product of gradual accretion, seemed contrived.

Scale is an essential consideration when evaluating diversity. Is the uniformity block by block, or district by district? The larger scale of places built since the mid-20th century, in function of cars, is more conducive to separation than integration. But before cars, when urbanism was smaller scale, spatial (and social) separation was not so effortless. As a result, neighborhoods were highly mixed economically, religiously, occupationally, and, in larger cities, ethnically. Social distance was kept in other, nonspatial ways, such as through dress and social morays.

This fine-grained social variation has been documented for ancient cities, medieval cities, 15th-century Florence, 17th-century London, and 18th-century Paris, to give just a few examples. In 17th-century London, "Macro-segregation, the location of different social groups in different parts of town, was hardly the rule; meso-segregation—that is, 'around the corner' segregation—was far more common." Homogeneous blocks in the 17th-century Dutch city of Alkmaar were so small that no predominantly rich block was more than a half mile from a predominantly poor

Figure 20.2 Ridley Park, Philadelphia, Pennsylvania, USA. *Lots in a variety of sizes were meant to mix income levels.*

one, and most were within a 5-minute walk of each other. English cities had a "cellular" social composition, but "the poorest of the poor" were housed "only a few steps away from the self-employed shopkeeper and the small employer."[4] This has changed dramatically. In contemporary cities and suburbs, larger distances separate neighborhoods that are easily distinguished by finely tuned price points.

21

Sprawl

To properly interpret sprawl, it is important to make a distinction between the planned suburb, "garden" or otherwise, and suburbia as an amorphous blob—nevertheless intentional—spreading out over the landscape. The latter is simply termed "sprawl," although drawing a clear distinction between sprawl and a planned suburb is not always easy.

The distinction between sprawl and suburb is not based on timing. In either case the evolution can be lot-by-lot rather than via a singular, all-at-once plan. The railroad suburb, for example, would never be labeled "sprawl," but it often developed incrementally. But it started with a strong node—a station—around which the suburb developed, and eventually cohered, creating a unity of design without a single plan or designer. With sprawl, in contrast, for example in places like Los Angeles or Houston, development is organized around freeways and widely spaced arterials, not a defining civic core capable of providing meaning and wholeness to the surrounding milieu (Figure 21.1). The result is decentralization without a congealing node, culturally depleted.

Fishman argues that modern, post-1945 sprawl is fundamentally different from the planned suburb because with sprawl the home-work separation ceased to be a motivating factor. Sprawl might be organized into what Fishman calls a "techno-burb," a new form of decentralization that welcomes industry and commerce and seeks to combine—albeit ineffectively via the automobile—work and residence. As Fishman characterizes the technoburb, it is not only "an ugly and wasteful pseudo-city, too spread out to be efficient, too superficial to create a true culture," but its detachment from the central city is "profoundly antiurban as suburbia never had been."[1] The result is neither urban, rural, nor suburban in the original sense. It is instead the near opposite of the original idea of a planned suburb. It is planned sprawl, lacking any coordinated design, but nevertheless calculated.

Sprawl is best defined by what it is not. For one thing, there are no communal principles in its design, which contrasts sharply with the planned suburb. Riverside, descending from the Puritan New England township pattern, incorporates a green "commons" in the center of its blocks. At Bournville, the early model industrial village that was later a model for planned suburbs, private houses and gardens were carefully arranged "as cohesive elements, supplementing each other wherever possible." The maintenance of privacy was thus subtle, not demonstrative. The Mormons used a technique in which houses were grouped but no two house facades fronted each other directly across the street. The ultimate aim was not privacy but "group

What Cities Say. Emily Talen, Oxford University Press. © Oxford University Press 2024. DOI: 10.1093/oso/9780197647769.003.0022

Figure 21.1 Los Angeles, California, USA. *Development is organized around freeways rather than a civic core capable of providing coherence.*

Figure 21.2 Houston, Texas, USA. *Sprawl embraces commerce in big box form, which, disconnected from urbanism, struggles to remain viable.*

interest over personal interest." Such a pattern had the added benefit of exposure to light and air, and prevention of the spread of fire—but it was accomplished without compromising community as a fundamental basis of settlement.[2]

Also unlike the planned suburb, sprawl does not put limits on commerce. It moves in the opposite direction, embracing corporate commerce on a mass scale. This can be destructive: for every new big box store created, an existing retailer is cannibalized because the retailing of a region is fixed (Figure 21.2). Sprawl's

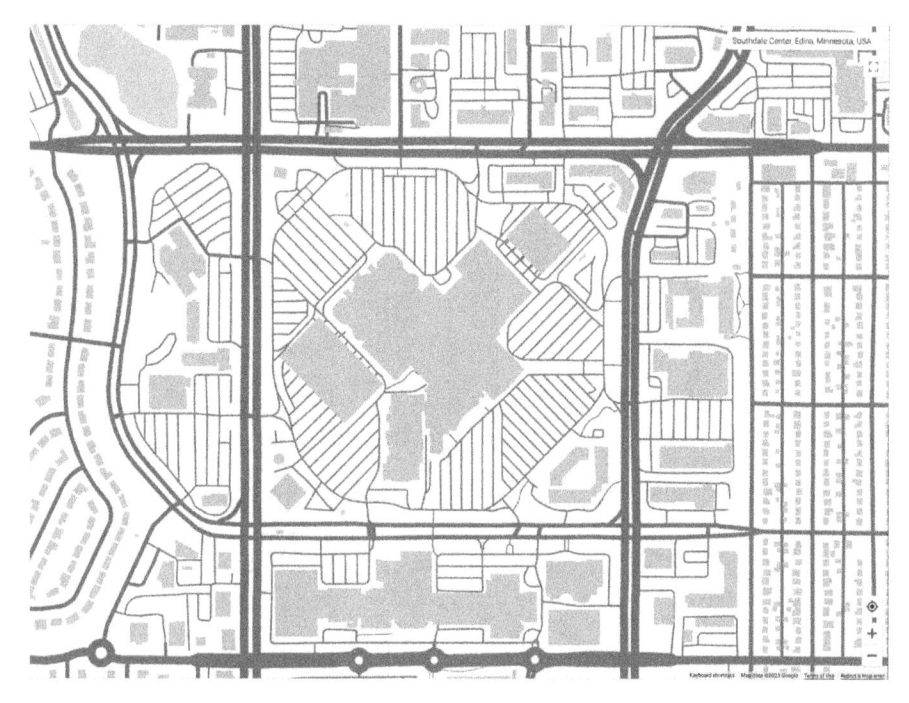

Figure 21.3 Southdale Center, Edina, Minnesota, USA. *In the mall, social life is detached from the outside world; women and children are thought to be empowered via consumption.*

shopping mall, therefore, is developed at the expense of main street. On top of that, sprawl's shopping malls are based on the "creation of consumer demand" rather than its reduction, a fact that puts it at odds with planned communities that explicitly sought "noncommercial cooperative bliss."[3]

Sprawl's focus on consumption is a form of exclusion. Although at first the shopping mall was expected to provide settings for social connection in suburbia since it lacked other collective space, sociality is strangely guarded. Southdale, Minnesota, a Victor Gruen mall that includes housing, is a prototypical example of how social life could be literally contained via parking lots and encircling roads (Figure 21.3). The idea was to be completely detached from the outside world, and certainly from the nearest city. Within this insulated world, women and teenagers were to be empowered via consumption, but never via their own production. Malls were feminized spaces, stoking the "power" of women to spend and consume, rather than produce.[4]

Except for the malls, which are detached and car-dependent, the residential areas of sprawl lack integrated amenities or services. This signals an attitude that the daily needs of residents are not much of a concern. It also sends a message that the future is irrelevant, since there is no place for children to go, or places to work in, once they grow up. The "centerless suburb" of Druid Hills outside Atlanta communicates this attitude (Figure 21.4).[5]

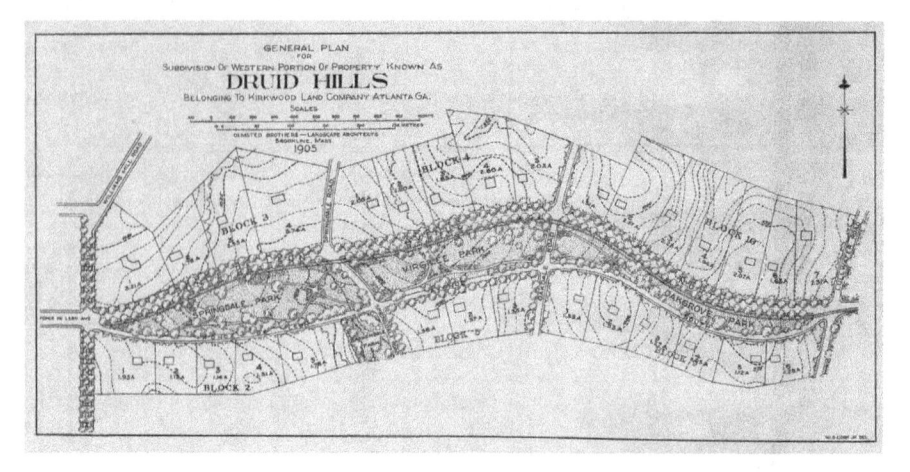

Figure 21.4 Druid Hills, Atlanta, Georgia, USA. *The centerless suburb. With no place for children to go when they grow up, the message is that the future is irrelevant.* Credit: United States Department of the Interior, National Park Service, Frederick Law Olmsted National Historic Site.

Sprawl is said to be inorganic. Whereas the planned suburb aligns with the "organic" theory of human settlement—that is, that cities or suburbs are organisms in the sense that there are limits to their growth, beyond which they cease to function—sprawl has no inherent limitation. The homogeneity of sprawl with its interminable, standardized product of miles of houses with only the slightest variation signals that the landscape is boundless. So, while both the planned suburb and sprawl might both be interpreted as evidence of giving up on the city, at least the planned suburb might claim to be attempting to develop organically.

Surveying the sprawl surrounding most American cities, what reads is not bourgeois utopia for an elite, but a version of suburbia universalized for the masses, enabled by the car, subsidized by freeways, and driven solely by profit-making. It shows a highly developed ability to cut corners and maximize profit by streamlining the production process. There is an attitude of excess and waste: overly generous lot sizes and redundant road building. Housing tracts, and the houses within them, are large and eat up the landscape with no sense of constraint. The excess is particularly American (although China is catching up). In comparison, Japanese cities also have many single-family houses, but the size of house and lot are kept small to prevent the city from spreading out excessively.

When low-density, American style sprawl is placed in foreign lands—for example, a suburban military base next to a dense city in Japan—it reveals a quest to make life familiar for the American military. Ostensibly, this is done with no hint of interest in indigenous patterns and forms. This is not without consequences. The exported suburban morphology of Misawa Air Base in northern Japan, complete with land-consumptive big box stores (which also feed the American appetite for consumption in general), and other forms of waste and domination exacerbate hostile feelings toward Americans (Figure 21.5).[6]

Figure 21.5 Misawa, Japan. *Exported American-style suburban morphology, complete with land-consumptive big box stores, exacerbates hostile feelings toward Americans.*

Sprawl has a much wider extent than a planned suburb and isn't really "sub" anything—it dominates the landscape and dwarfs whatever urban core it might be attached to. There is a sense of survivalism in this dispersion. Victor Gruen argued the need to spread the population out to make it "less vulnerable to bombing attacks," and he was happy to meet the commercial needs of sprawl by consolidating shopping in the form of malls.[7] When the COVID-19 pandemic hit, there was some concern that fear of contagion would create a new impetus for sprawl. But sprawl has its own inertia.

Sprawl is composed of housing developments rather than neighborhoods. With low densities, excessive open space, and separated buildings, defining neighborhoods in more traditional ways such as through a neighborhood center or a defined public realm is unlikely. And because sprawl has such a loose definition of public space, whatever spatial structure might exist is based on open land rather than built forms. What this means for neighborhood delineation is that the basis of definition, in the absence of spatial definition, often amounts to legal lines drawn on a map.[8]

The vastness of sprawl at the outskirts of major cities exposes the power dynamics at play. The main players are the banking, construction, and real estate sectors, kept afloat through government subsidy and tax breaks that mostly benefit White and wealthy Americans. Real Estate Investment Trusts (REITs) buy and sell sprawl components on Wall Street and there is no vested interest, and no caring about, what kinds of places are being pieced together. "Extreme speculation" eats

Figure 21.6 Casa Grande, outside of Phoenix, Arizona. *Planned sprawl in Casa Grande shows the result of speculative building gone bust.*

investment without paying any return, which Hayden likened to "alligator" behavior. This can go badly. In the planned sprawl of Casa Grande outside of Phoenix, for example, it is easy to see the physical result of speculative building gone bust (Figure 21.6).[9]

Sprawl also differs from growth via urban extension. Extensions have long been part of the historical record, enacted to relieve pressure on the city and its high land values. In earlier eras, for example in the Netherlands in the 16th century, cities extended in a circular ring around the city. Extension depended on municipal authority and funding to lengthen canals, reclaim land, and prepare building sites. Piecemeal suburban growth was therefore not possible. Towns grew compactly, but not in a stifling way. There was plenty of open space because of the numerous canals necessary for drainage and navigation.[10]

A defining feature of sprawl is separation—of buildings, functions, and spaces. Joseph Stübben, writing in 1890, recognized the problem of separation, pointing out the many advantages of attached buildings ("building in blocks"). They required less ground, were better suited for business purposes, cost less to build, made heating easier, and were safer because only the front of the building was accessible. "It would therefore be folly to make detached building the rule in cities," he wrote.[11]

Some might think of sprawl as an embodiment of freedom. The open space of suburbia gives it a veneer of adaptability and leeway to make changes and move things around—the opposite of constraint. In theory, standing alone, untethered to any neighbors, isolated buildings can do whatever they want, which would seem to engender freedom. But the irony is that the geographic spread of sprawl is often the opposite of freedom. Instead, the disarray imposes significant burdens because of the increased distances required to access what is needed for daily life. This is probably why Le Corbusier rejected the single-family house and proclaimed its inhabitants "slaves."[12]

The randomness of sprawl also has a pretense of individuation, as if people created sprawl by operating in a rule-free libertarian dream. Gottdiener noted the strange paradox produced: that sprawl could look so disordered when the objective was solely about profit. The randomness happens because there is no guiding vision, no sense of what the area—only loosely conceived as a city or town—is supposed to be or why it should exist. Formulating such a vision would be incongruous since the point of sprawl is individual realization of one's own bespoke version of suburban life, where one is free to drive here and there to piece that realization together. This makes for some pretty confused settlement patterns. Rather than a gradual increase in intensity of land use from periphery to center, the urbanization of rural lands unfolds in a haphazard way. In Las Vegas, the subdivisions are as disorienting as the casinos, although presumably, the residents of Las Vegas sprawl are accustomed to "spatial confusion" (Figure 21.7). In the casino, disorientation is a deliberate tactic.[13]

Filling the vacuum of a place devoid of a congealing public realm (which might be capable of holding the disarray together), sprawl is the outcome of rules about parking, drainage, and street width. Frederick and Mehta note that since suburban land is therefore "organized by purpose," the experience is "selective, single-variable, and destination-centric." The experience of cities, on the other hand, is "continuous, oblique, and incidental." In the sprawl case, people walk perpendicular, car to door. Each destination has its own purpose. In cities, people walk parallel rather than perpendicular, and destinations are experienced "all-at-once rather than one-at-a-time."[14] The difference has obvious implications for social and economic connectivity and interdependence.

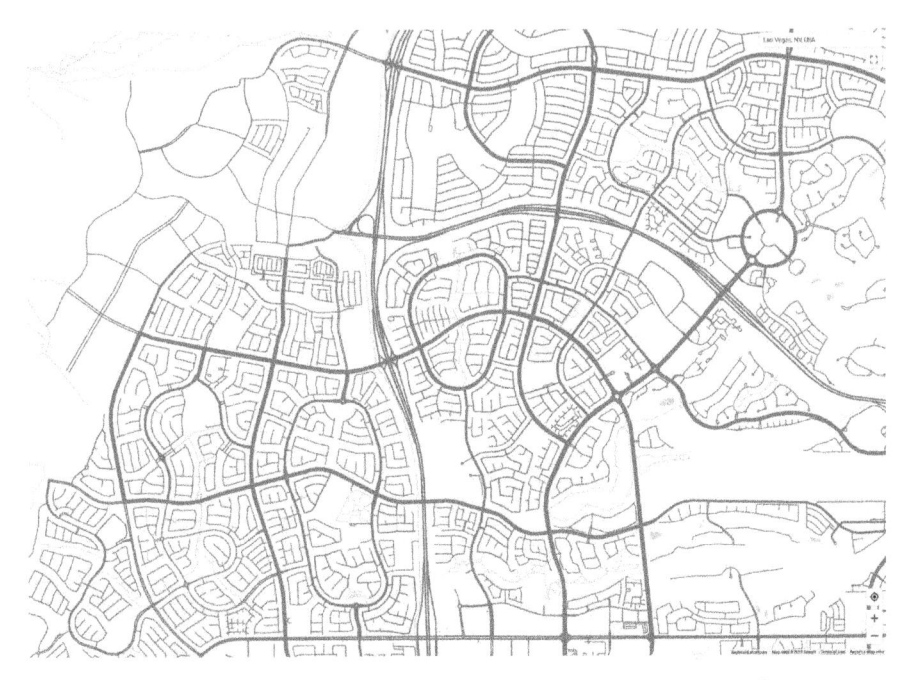

Figure 21.7 Las Vegas, Nevada, USA. *Subdivisions are as disorienting as the casinos.*

Like any suburban context, sprawl reads loudly of escape, especially escape from the urban poor, which is ironic because many sprawling suburbs are, increasingly, poor. The single-family house on its own lot, a building type meant to be owned, is increasingly rented. But in the detached and disorienting world of sprawl, residents might think of themselves as absolved from needing to care about the social and economic problems of the city.

Escape and exclusion are why many have argued that sprawl has a high moral cost. Aspirations of social equity are thrown to the wind, privatism and consumption are valorized, and political culture is greatly weakened. Sprawl is a physical form antithetical to citizen engagement, climate change activism, or social equality. In general, sprawl represents an escape from collective life; houses are set on private lots in an effort to assert seclusion. Kunstler's description of Atlanta is apt: the form of the city creeping outward in a ring of edge cities is "a dynamic efflorescence of money, power, and personal freedom, like a pulsating slime mold," expressing an attitude that "the outside doesn't matter" (Figure 21.8).[15]

Not everyone agrees with this characterization, of course. The urban planner Melvin Webber viewed the same sprawl as a natural outcome of technical evolution.

Figure 21.8 Atlanta, Georgia, USA. *Sprawl represents an attitude that the outside, and collective life, don't matter; houses are set on private lots to assert seclusion.*

He argued that the way to read Los Angeles' sprawl is as a "non-place" urban realm, an expression of people connecting and communicating technologically, in which case place is irrelevant. If there is superior communication—via the internet, or via highways—that level of interaction might foster the same density of interaction as any physical form of density—maybe even more. Form and content are separate and independent.[16]

But what about the homogeneity that this technology enables? While many settlement patterns and forms, sprawl or otherwise, can be accused of enabling homogeneity, homogeneity at the periphery is a special problem. There, mass-produced products are distributed over a large, mass-produced space, which tends to reduce culture to the lowest common denominator. What emerges, Fishman argues, is "crass conformity" and a "crucial loss of texture." The low density of sprawl, in other words, translates to a lack of cultural diversity, since there is only enough critical mass to sustain a single culture.

In addition, spread across so many square miles, whatever cultural diversity that might exist is not something experienced spontaneously, walking down the street. Because of the low density and spread, social contact is easily avoided or tends to be prearranged via the car. There is no opportunity for chance encounters or random social interaction. Mumford argued that this lack of ability to spontaneously interact not only negates the possibility of collective action but produces "silent conformity" in society. Sprawl, then, can be read as "the favored home of a new kind of absolutism." This is not to say that the planned suburb was ever the champion of spontaneous social interaction. In fact, social separation was invented there, in part because it was necessary for ensuring the feeling that one was experiencing a pastoral life. To carry the illusion, houses would be set back 30 feet or more from the sidewalk; at Bedford Park in London, the views from each sideyard were designed to look right through "from street to street."[17]

Sprawl's individualism feeds into the West's fear of socialism. Writing in 1919, US Secretary of Labor William B. Wilson summed up the sentiment aptly: "the man who owns his own home is the least susceptible to the so-called Bolshevist doctrines and is about the last man to join in the industrial disturbances fomented by the radical agitators." But the homeowner could still be counted on to be nationalistic. In Germany in the 1880s and 1890s, the single-family house was believed to be conducive not only to a "happy family life" but to "an encouragement to thrift, residential stability, self-improvement, and acceptance of the existing social order." Germans saw the rural, single-family home as not only the basis of individual responsibility, but the key to "national might" because it stoked a protective impulse of one's house and home.[18]

Of course, sprawl is not rendered only in single-family form. The phenomenon of "dense sprawl" is the worst of all worlds: people clustered but without amenities and usable open space, and dependent on their cars. The "townhouses" of sprawl are apartments without towns. People are forced to live densely without any of the usual compensations.

22

Grids

Grids, or orthogonal street patterns, are an orderly framework around which cities evolve over time, and thus grids are versatile. According to the urban planner Hans Blumenfeld, the original function of the grid was to divide land for plowing.[1] The fact that the grid became a common basis for planning cities speaks to its adaptability: the original purpose changed entirely.

Kostof thought highly of grids because, he wrote, they are unpretentious and uncontrived. Societies can make of the grid what they want because grids are practical and opportune. They are a blank slate that can anchor and organize, and their regularity is either strengthened or weakened by how buildings line them. The grid's regularity provides the ability to elevate the prominence of particular sites or buildings: special uses or buildings can readily stand out against the grid's homogeneity. A good example of this is in the Mormon grid: the dominance of the Temple was made possible by the gridded, homogeneous, and subordinated layout of the rest of the town.

Grids are enlisted to neaten and "modernize" places that have a more irregular pattern. Thus the Romans "tidied up" Germanic settlements, and princes regularized medieval settlements during the Renaissance. Sometimes the best that could be done to tidy things up would be to attach a regularized extension to an otherwise irregular settlement. This created a new socioeconomic organization—from the fine-grained mixing of land uses in the non-gridded medieval city, to segmented order in the Renaissance city. One example of this appendage approach is seen in Massa Marittima in central Italy. The gridded addition contrasts dramatically with the adjacent medieval irregularity. By the late 16th century, the regularization had created elite residential districts, separate from areas of production or governance (Figure 22.1).[2]

The imprint of a grid often starts with land platting—laying out streets and dividing up land into blocks and parcels. It is an ancient practice, done either by pacing off land in relation to natural features, or by formal surveying using instruments (surveying with instruments was practiced even in ancient Roman cities). In some places, times, and cultures, land was surveyed in speculative fashion, laying down a pattern of streets and blocks before any human settlement was even imminent. In this way, Jefferson's survey that gridded much of the United States was an explicit reminder that, according to Americans, property was there for the claiming—and a source of American liberty.

Where grids are laid down in such a way that there is no responsiveness to the landscape or topography, that is a clue that the grid was meant to adhere to some

What Cities Say. Emily Talen, Oxford University Press. © Oxford University Press 2024. DOI: 10.1093/oso/9780197647769.003.0023

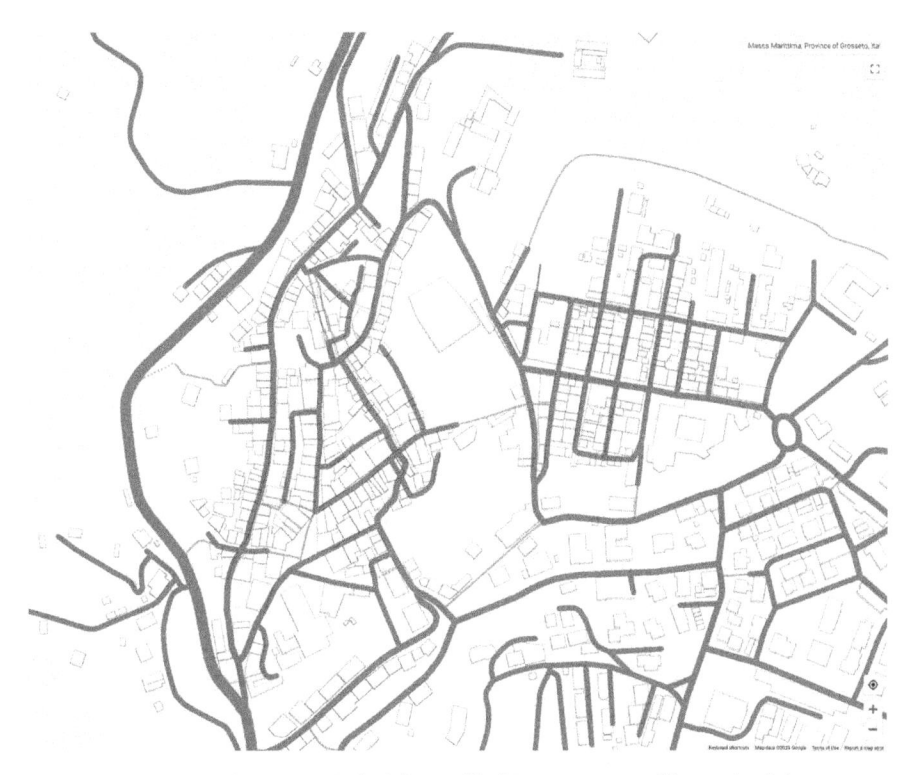

Figure 22.1 Massa Marittima, Italy. *The gridded Renaissance addition (right) contrasts dramatically with the adjacent medieval irregularity.*

sort of higher truth. Hippodamus, the Greek city planner, espoused this principle and thought of the grid as reflecting universal law and a "fixed unalterable order" in the universe. J. B. Jackson identified three sources for gridded truth in the American case: "the Bible, the Constitution, [and] the writings of Thomas Paine or Locke [or] Newton" (the divine importance of gridded regularity is extolled in the Bible in the books Isaiah, Ezekiel, and Revelation). The original nine-square grid of New Haven, Connecticut, shows the biblical interpretation. Since truth had been "revealed in the cosmological order," there was no need to adjust to the environment.[3]

Mormon town planning, unsparingly gridded, was guided by biblical reference that equated the City of God with, in addition to order and regularity, the need to dominate nature. Mormon grid design was ideological but simple, with strict geometric proportions, derived from descriptions of cities in the Bible (in Numbers 35 and Leviticus 25). Streets were extremely wide (132 feet), lined with half-acre lots and houses set back 25 feet. Certain centrally located blocks were designated for churches and public buildings. The simple egalitarianism of these "Cities of Zion" was directed at shunning the sinful ways of American society, and preparing for a new social and religious order.[4] It is somewhat ironic that the form they chose was identical to the one seen as most befitting of commercialism.

The religious symbolism of the grid in ancient times was a theme explored in depth by Joseph Rykwert in *The Idea of a Town*. According to Rykwert, everything the ancients did city planning–wise was in mythical terms. The Roman castrum (military camp), a miniature diagram of the city of Rome, was laid out in a series of rituals and ceremonies linked to Roman deities. In India, an aesthetic manual called the Manasara from the first century BCE included religiously motivated grid designs for Hindu cities. The Manasara combined design theory with geometrically ordered mandalas; squares of particular sizes were assigned to different deities. Building these "magic diagrams" was an act of "bringing disordered existence into conformity" with natural laws of existence. Madurai, India, is cited as an example of these symbolic patterns at different scales: the cosmos as the basis of gridded order. The form is designed for rituals like processions.[5]

Chinese grids were based on the rules of feng shui, a "system of thoughts." Nine squares created a holy diagram, and grid organization played a role in leveraging energy forces to connect humans with their surroundings. Gridded cities were "microcosms of the universe"; locations of walls, gates, temples, courts, and markets were placed within the grid to fit the cosmological order. The fact that the grid held on long after these cosmic interpretations were taken seriously annoyed Mumford, who described the gridiron plan "as a kind of fossil of an earlier culture."[6]

Religious practice aside, the dominant purpose of this gridded platting was order: ensuring regularized, uniform, controllable growth. Right-angled streets in a grid pattern seemed to fit that goal best. The first-century architect and engineer Vitruvius, author of the widely read architectural treatise *De architectura* (which later inspired the Spanish *Laws of the Indies*), lauded these principles, extolling the virtues of "symmetry, perspective and proportion" in city pattern. Vitruvian principles of proportion and symmetry impacted gridded street layout for centuries. The ordering was often accumulative, whereby a "succession of grids" was added incrementally to form a contiguous urban fabric. At Turin, Italy, the original first-century grid, still intact, acted as an anchor for subsequent additions (Figure 22.2).[7]

In ancient cities, especially Roman, the spatial order of the grid fit military purposes especially well. Apparently, the order imposed on the military needed to have a physical counterpart in the mathematical discipline of the city: "the layout of the city became a mirror of the army's discipline, its ascetism, its monotony, and its lack of freedom." Even building exteriors resembled military uniforms. In one example, Valletta, the capital of Malta, a military engineer laid out the gridded town based on a trigonometric design scheme (Figure 22.3). Orthogonality was really the only option for "rational urban design" at the time, as gridded street platting was the only system known for calculating area, locating points precisely, and coordinating urban parts. It was only during the Renaissance, when surveying techniques advanced, that it became possible to plan out cities with irregular shapes.[8] However, if the intent of a city plan was rationality and order, right-angled streets and blocks continued to be the norm.

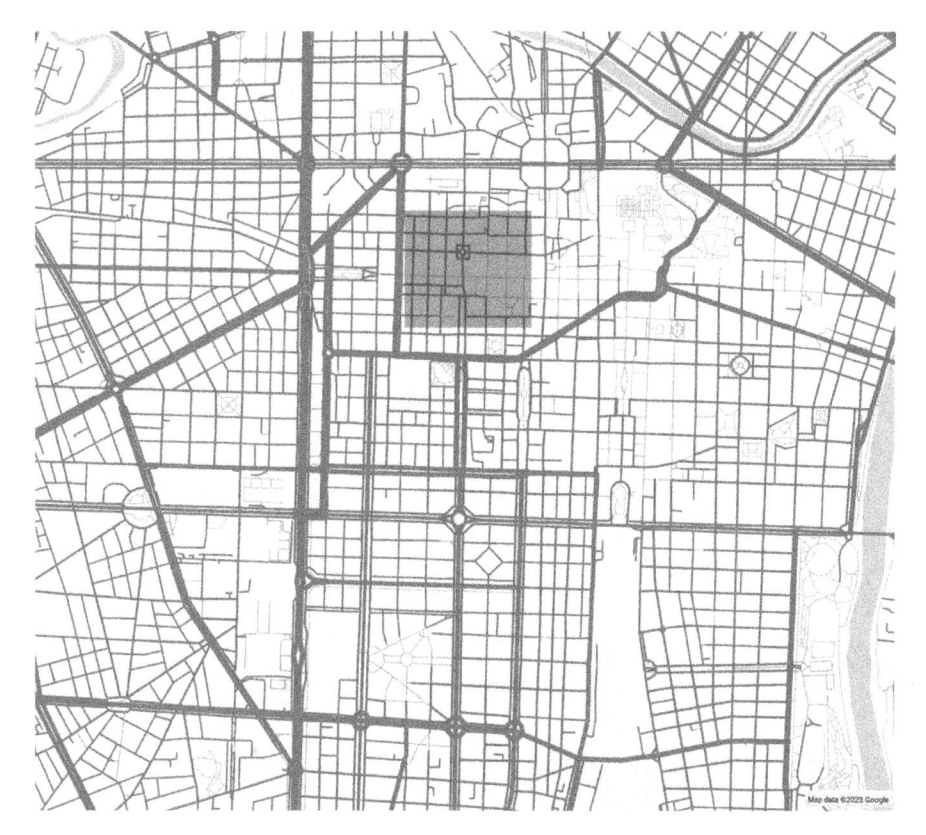

Figure 22.2 Turin, Italy. *The original first-century grid (shaded area) was an anchor for subsequent additions added incrementally.*

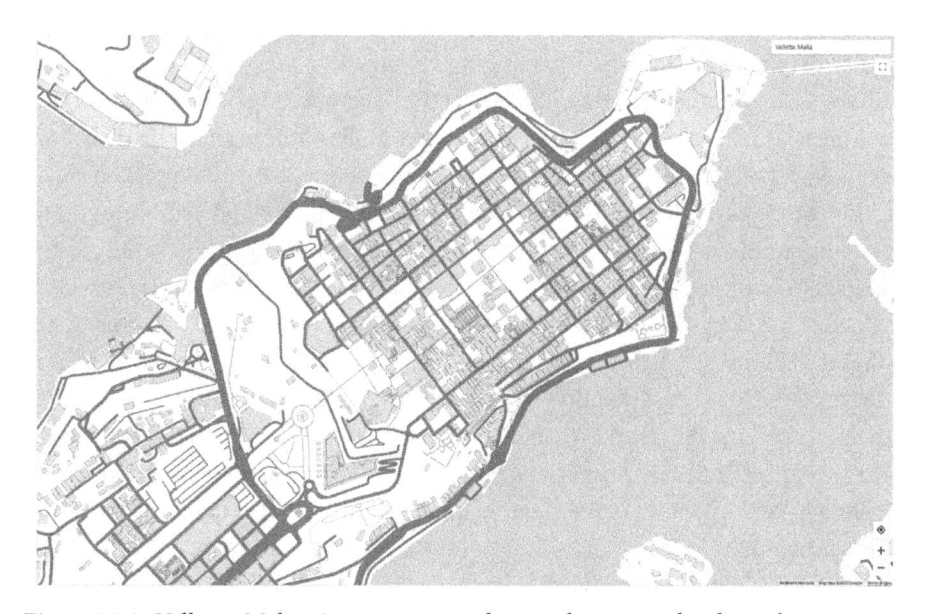

Figure 22.3 Valletta, Malta. *A trigonometric design scheme was the physical counterpart of Roman military discipline.*

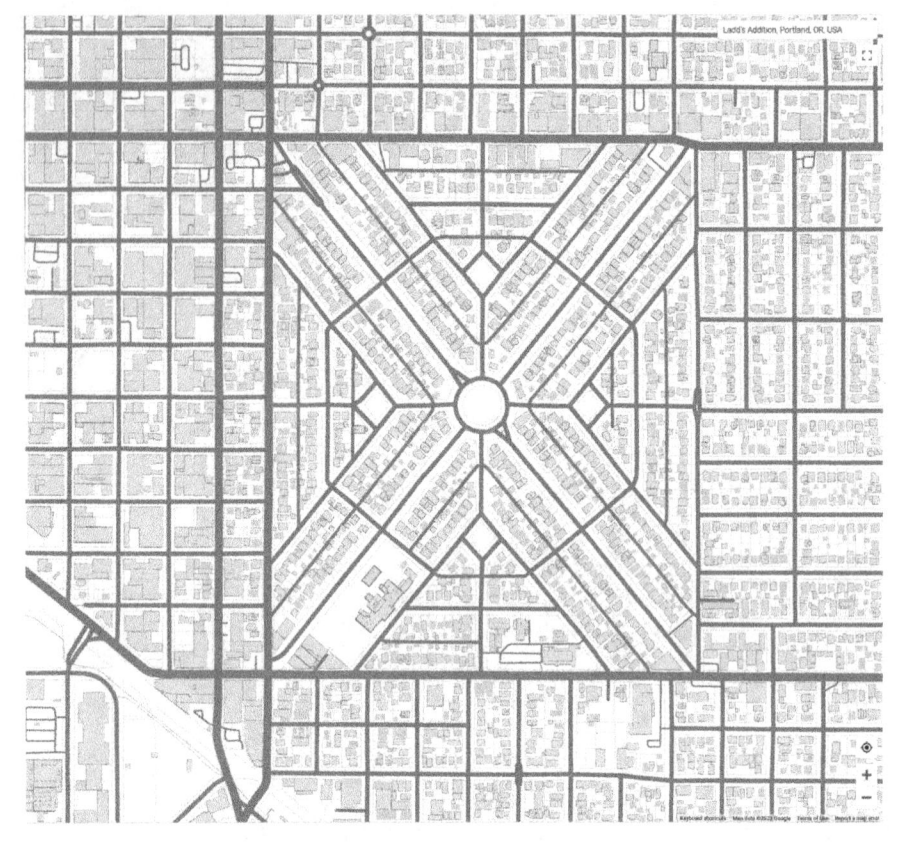

Figure 22.4 Ladd's Addition, Portland, Oregon, USA. *Neighborhood identity grafted onto a speculative grid: an insertion of creative spirit.*

If grids extend out into the surrounding countryside, they can have the effect of unifying, or at least integrating, the city and its surrounding territory. But if they have been laid down too exuberantly, if they are endless, they can create their "own brand of lostness." There are ways to mitigate the oppressive order: open space insertion, or a slight shifting of the grid to create a termination point. Grids are good at exposing contrasts, which can be introduced to create novelty or showcase creative design. For example, against an otherwise regular grid, the short diagonal streets in Williamsburg, Virginia, demarcate a "W" and an "M" for "William" and "Mary," the colony's 17th-century British rulers. Two other examples show the attempt to graft a sense of neighborhood identity onto a speculative grid: Ladd's Addition (1891) in Portland, Oregon (Figure 22.4), and the radial plan of Perryopolis, Pennsylvania (1814) (Figure 22.5). These special grids, both of which survive intact today, successfully produced "oases of the creative spirit within the larger desert of the checkerboard mentality."[9]

Another kind of special pattern is created when a grid is based on abstract principles. The mathematical formula used to structure the hierarchical block sizes at Grenade-sur-Garonne is an important, and uncommon, example (Figure 22.6). Another is Sabbioneta, in the Lombardy region of Italy, laid out in the late 16th

Figure 22.5 Perryopolis, Pennsylvania, USA. *A special grid creates distinction.*

Figure 22.6 Grenade-sur-Garonne, France. *The blocks surrounding the center of this bastide are hierarchically proportioned in three successive sizes.*

century (Figure 22.7). One architectural historian described it as a Mannerist plan, meaning that, for stylistic reasons, the grid was made deliberately asymmetrical and inharmonious. Freudenstadt is another mannerist grid, laid out in 1599 on the basis of a board game called Mühle (apparently the Duke was playing the game when the

Figure 22.7 Sabbioneta, Italy. *Under the influence of Mannerism, the grid was made deliberately asymmetrical and inharmonious.*

idea occurred to him). The special design meant that the church and city hall had to be placed at opposite corners of the square rather than adjacent, "contrary to all tradition" (Figure 22.8).[10]

Laying out a new colony based on the simple spatial order of a grid would be the best option if the terrain was unknown and the settlement needed to be fast and uncomplicated. This describes colonial settlement practice from the ancient Greeks onward. Clearly there has been a lack of imagination at times, as in the 16th-century gridded colonies of "New Spain," which can be read as plans by bureaucrats in Spain who knew nothing about the local terrain. The grids did communicate that someone or something was in control, and in that sense they were politically expedient. Control was quick and easy, and it might have made colonists feel at home.

But since the grid does not easily adapt and mold itself around environmental features, there is often no reflection in a grid, no notice at all, of the hills, coastlines, rivers, valleys, or any number of natural features the grid is laid upon. San Francisco's unrelaxed grid draped over the steep slopes of the city is one example. Streets are staircases rather than thoroughfares, which, it could be argued, is not necessarily a bad outcome. The ungridded street pattern of Riverside projects an air of being

Figure 22.8 Freudenstadt, Germany. *A mannerist grid laid out in 1599 on the basis of a board game called Mühle.*

highly responsive to the terrain, but the curvilinearity and organic block shapes are not in response to natural contours, and the whole pattern is disorienting. An example of true responsiveness is when development is made to run parallel to a natural feature like a river, with curvilinear secondary streets fitting into the upward slopes of the river bank. Magdeburg on the Elbe fits this pattern (Figure 22.9).

The grid is a pattern that is thought of as "rational." The fact that grids sprang up here and there in all places and time periods, without a conceptual linkage among them, attests to some kind of innate human predisposition toward gridded form. Mumford asserts that gridded cities were common in Ionia as early as the seventh century BCE (well before Hippodamus who, though he didn't invent the grid, can at least be credited with popularizing them). Many centuries later, it was the focus on rationality that led modernist architect Le Corbusier to opt for the grid rather than a medieval street pattern, which he denigrated as the "pack-donkey's way."[11]

Part of the grid's rationality is that the grid helps people orient themselves. Historically, orientation and familiarity were important in foreign lands, or in places filled with strangers. This is one reason the American grid was admired by foreign visitors, who could not only find their way much more easily than in the seemingly random street pattern found in European cities, but it appealed to their sense that America was a modern place guided by rationality, efficiency, and

Figure 22.9 Magdeburg, Germany. *On the river Elbe, streets run parallel to the river.*

science. Mumford wondered whether all the ordered perfection of the grid came "at the expense of life," meaning that the quest for urban order likely extended to an insidious quest for social order.[12]

Grids were often squares, but they could also be elongated rectangles. Elongation occurs when the goal is to maximize the number of buildings, and especially shop owners, with street frontage—creating what Kostof called an "urban framework suitable for a merchant economy." This pattern might make use of the so-called burgage plot, a long, narrow lot where the narrow side of the lot fronted the street (the skinny lots along Main Street in Pembroke, Wales, are a good example; Figure 22.10). Long lots maximize access to a linear resource, like a street or a waterway (access to water produced the long lots of New Orleans). Another motivation for rectangles as opposed to squares is that square blocks are more challenging to build on, since the lots created by squares tend to limit the available building types. Sometimes mews and alleys were inserted in the leftover spaces. In New Orleans, lots were inserted at the center of square blocks, but that still made for awkward building sites.[13]

Jefferson gridded a huge swath of the United States in 1785, creating a basis for land division that later produced the gridded streets and blocks of American cities. We see the imprint of Jefferson's grid in cities like Chicago, and in the many railroad towns platted throughout the middle and western states in the 19th century. And yet, Jefferson's platting of the West was really only a continuation of the "rectilinear urban habits" of American urbanism that were well established before him. The application of Jefferson's grid across the unsettled territories of the United States seemed a logical extension of the grid culture of US town planning.[14]

Jefferson's grid was large scale, and cities subdivided it to create a much finer mesh. Now, a tighter grid with smaller blocks—a function of how close together the streets are—is thought to be advantageous because it provides a greater level of

Figure 22.10 Pembroke, Wales, UK. *Long, skinny lots maximize access to a linear resource: the street.*

connectivity. Grids are routes to destinations, and once attached to a street system, a destination is no longer just a place, it is part of a network that connects it to whatever else is on the network. These networks have different levels of connectedness, reflecting different ideals about the importance of access and closeness. If the network is a grid, it prioritizes connection and access over other goals, like protection, security, or the emulation of nature.

And yet, despite the high connectivity, grids do not always offer the most direct routes between destinations, which in many cases might be a diagonal line rather than via an orthogonal pattern. Grids require zigzagging through town rather than taking a straight "as the crow flies" route. This might be fine if the grid is part of a network that includes plenty of services and facilities to walk to.

Short, gridded blocks, perhaps less than 275 feet on one side or the length walked in one or two minutes, are considered better than long ones for pedestrians, simply because pedestrians will have an easier time walking through the city if blocks are kept small. Portland, Oregon, is revered for its short blocks (Figure 22.11). Short blocks are not only good for exploration, but they are also considered "friendlier." Short blocks provide more route choices.[15]

There are at least two caveats to the notion that small grids are better than large ones. First, some blocks need to be sized bigger to accommodate larger structures; cities need to make room for important civic buildings. Second, smaller blocks translate to more streets, which is good for commerce but not for the problem of excessive pavement and infrastructure, both of which increase costs.

But short blocks on tight grids seem to do a better job of dispersing economic activity. One reason is that there is an association between small blocks and multiple ownership (as opposed to singular ownership), of both parcels and storefronts. If there is one monolithic block with a big box store taking up street frontage and

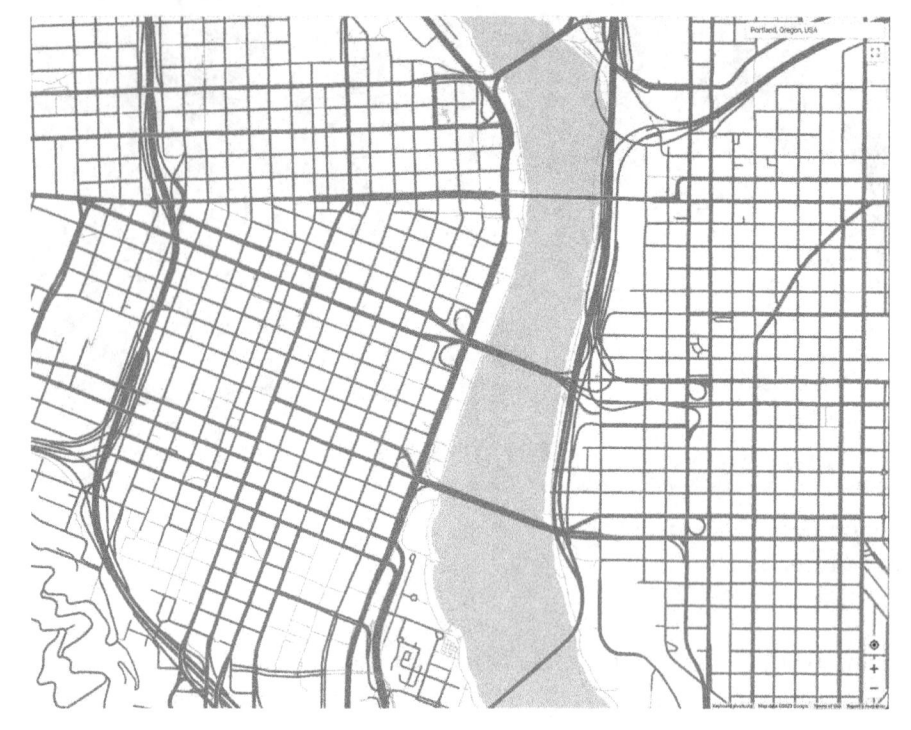

Figure 22.11 Portland, Oregon, USA. *The city is revered for its short, square blocks.*

offering only one entry, made possible by a large grid, that could translate to fewer businesses, fewer experiences, and less interest for the pedestrian. Small blocks on a tight grid also keep egos in check. Manhattan's relatively small square grid is said to constrain "totalitarian intervention" by making the small square block, as Koolhaas put it, the "maximum unit of urbanistic Ego."[16]

Grids express multiple purposes that at times can seem contradictory: both egalitarianism and profit claim to be a primary purpose. Grant dissected the various attributions to summarize that grids might be about "diffusing power, centralizing power or globalizing power." It's certainly true that equal land division does not result in social equality, if defined in terms of equal land ownership. But there are other ways of drawing the connection between the grid and equality. For example, the egalitarianism of the grid could stem from the fact that all parts of the city are unified through their adherence to a common pattern. In ancient Greece, the unifying structure of the grid showed that "all parts of the city, whether private or public, were subject to a common law, imposed by the public will." And, if the gridded streets, blocks, and lots extended outward from a public space, for example in gridded town squares like Savannah's, a kind of unity could be created by connecting private dwellings to the public square. There was still individual ownership, but attached to the collective grid, it was also communal. The grid is thus capable of acting like a "collective umbilical cord" to join "proud, individual houses." In Savannah, the merger was accomplished through the repetition of gridded wards with central common spaces, where the grid balanced "individual aspirations with a larger communal order."[17] In the 18th century, it was a communal order necessary for survival.

Jefferson wanted a modest grid for the US capital as a way of expressing equality, or at least, the opposite of centralized authority. Certainly the baroque elements superimposed on Washington's grid provide an explicit reminder of the incongruity between gridded egalitarianism and authoritarian control. The grid introduced in Tehran in the 1930s in a quest to modernize the city was equalizing in another way: it "unified the city by equally distributing the lack of spatial identity" (Figure 22.12).[18]

Grids can provide cultural continuity in the face of radically different building form. New Haven, Connecticut, is an interesting case. Its low-intensity grid, from 1812, resembled a modest New England village (Figure 22.13a). The open space of the streets was dwarfed by the open land in the blocks dotted with detached structures. By the mid-20th century, the streets of the grid played a much more significant role in terms of providing breaks in the dense build-out (Figure 22.13b). Thus, despite the density change, the grid stayed consistent and provided continuity. A Buras put it, the grid expressed a "multigenerational time horizon reflecting the community's institutionalized commitment to itself beyond the duration of its initial settling."[19]

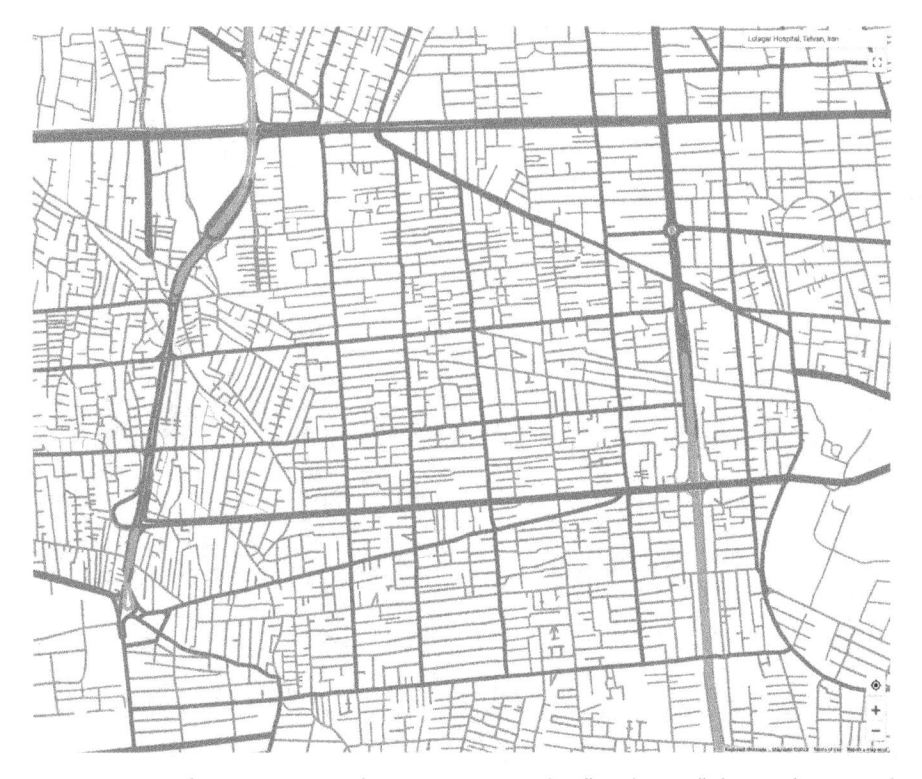

Figure 22.12 Tehran, Iran. *A grid was superimposed to "modernize" the city, but spatial identity was lost in the process.*

Another aspect of egalitarianism is simply that the grid is easy to lay out, and so anyone can do it. If one wanted to design a city with intermittent public spaces, one simply reserved some of the grid's blocks for that purpose. The grid makes space differentiation easy: places for public buildings and open spaces, easily inserted into the regular grid, can break the monotony (the neglect of this kind of "functional differentiation" inserted to break up the grid is what gave the 19th century "endless grid" of places like Manhattan a bad rap[20]). In addition, an evenly patterned grid is non-hierarchical, which means it can disperse bad things (e.g., traffic) and good things (e.g., amenities) evenly. This makes the burden of traffic and the benefit of access more equalized.

But while gridded uniformity can seem conducive to equality, it is also capable of generating the opposite condition. In the colonies of ancient Greece, for example, a uniform grid was thought to be a mechanism for privileging the ruling class, whereby the first settlers arriving at a newly platted site were allocated "hereditary

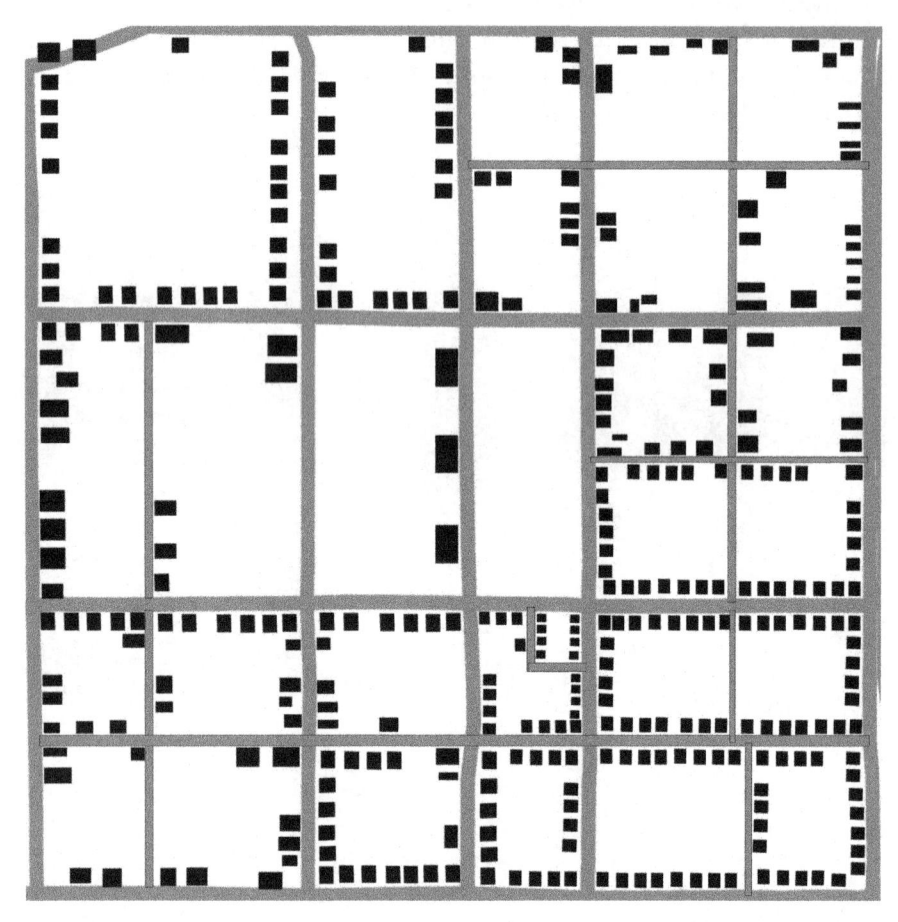

Figure 22.13a New Haven, Connecticut, USA, 1812 (above) vs. 2023 (below). *Despite a radical density change between 1812 and the present day, the grid stayed consistent and provided continuity.* Drawn after Gallion and Eisner, *The Urban Pattern.*

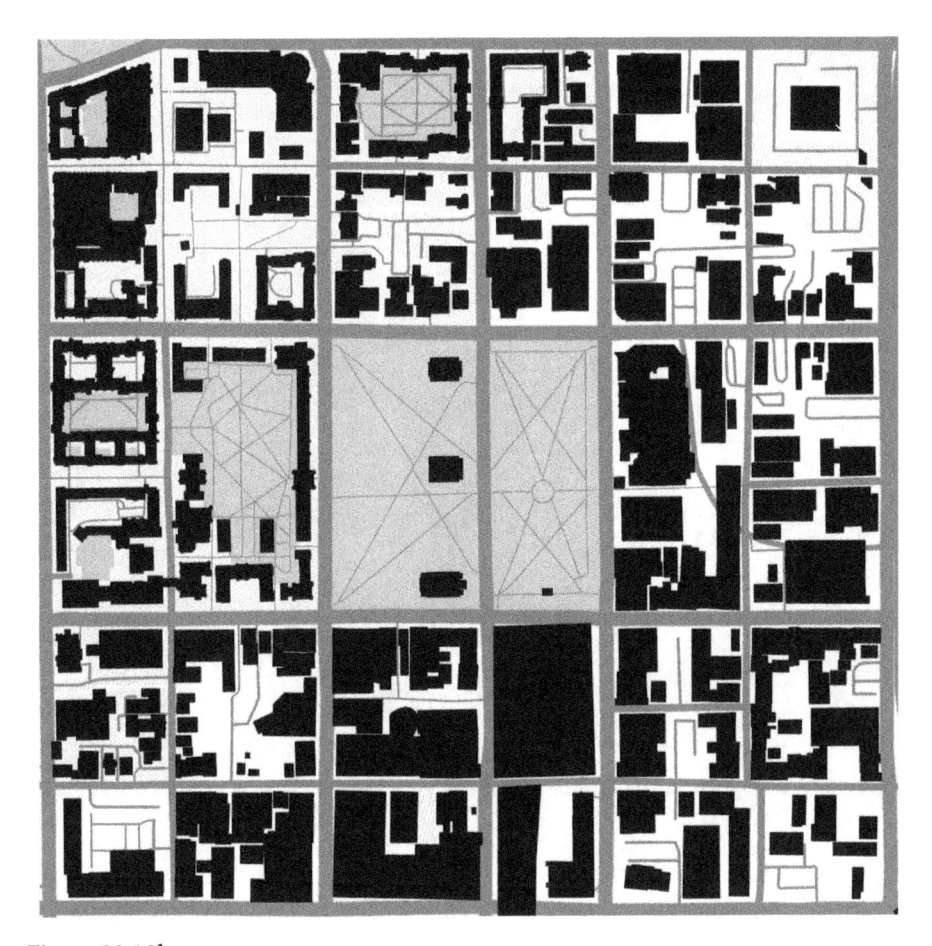

Figure 22.13b

estates" that they then had the power to subdivide. Barcelona's equal grid was similarly compromised; much higher densities and block coverages than anticipated not only "distorted" the egalitarian grid, but the middle and upper classes took over, "banishing" industrial workers to the city's much grittier industrial periphery or to "rundown houses" in the older sections of the urban core. The grid can also use block size variation to express social dominance. In Nagoya, Japan, the size of a block a person lived on was an easy way to gauge social status (Figure 22.14).[21]

There are also many examples of the grid turning into exploitation. The gridded urban pattern of the Swedish empire imposed throughout the Baltic region in the 17th century was of fortresses intended to correct nature and civilize what was thought to be an uncultured population. For townspeople previously living in a more non-orthogonal urbanism, an imposed grid might instill a sense that they were now being protected, which in turn might make inhabitants grateful—but also subjugated.

Gridded city form, with its perfect proportionality and measurement, was sometimes considered the only appropriate framework for "high" culture. Mullin linked

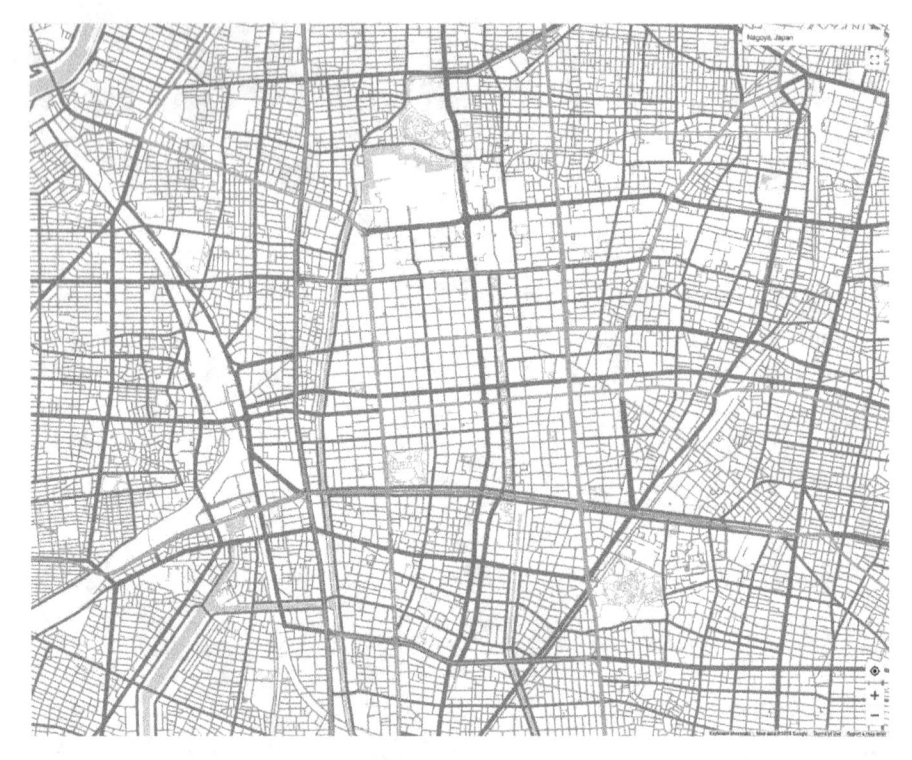

Figure 22.14 Nagoya, Japan. *Gridded block size variation was used to express social status.*

gridded city form to Christianity's desire to conquer nature and "reinstate Man's power over the elements." There is no straight line in nature, the thinking goes, so imposing it on the land shows dominance—even more so if the straight lines are regularized. The subjugation might be cultural, as at Lisbon, where the grid was imposed to express "the will of the state," since the grid was culturally alien. Or it might be more about the conquest of nature, as in New Orleans, where "engineering tactics" disrupted hydrological processes and imposed straight lines and right angles "utterly absent in nature."[22]

The grid was blamed for sanctioning oppressive forms of housing in the 19th century, as cities sought to house industrial workers. One example is the gridded, uniform street and lot pattern associated with 19th-century "bye-law" housing in England, where "unified rows of repetitive design" created dismal conditions. The bye-law street resulted from the 1872–1875 Public Health Acts and gave speculative developers an excuse to institute "a standardized formula of broad straight streets and monotonous rows of near-identical houses." In Berlin, gigantic blocks that were supposed to include internal courtyards and green space were instead covered over with five-story Mietskasernen (apartment buildings) "and damned the grid, in the eyes of a new generation of urbanists," for having enabled a "perfect matrix of slum landlords and abusive congestion" (Figure 22.15).[23]

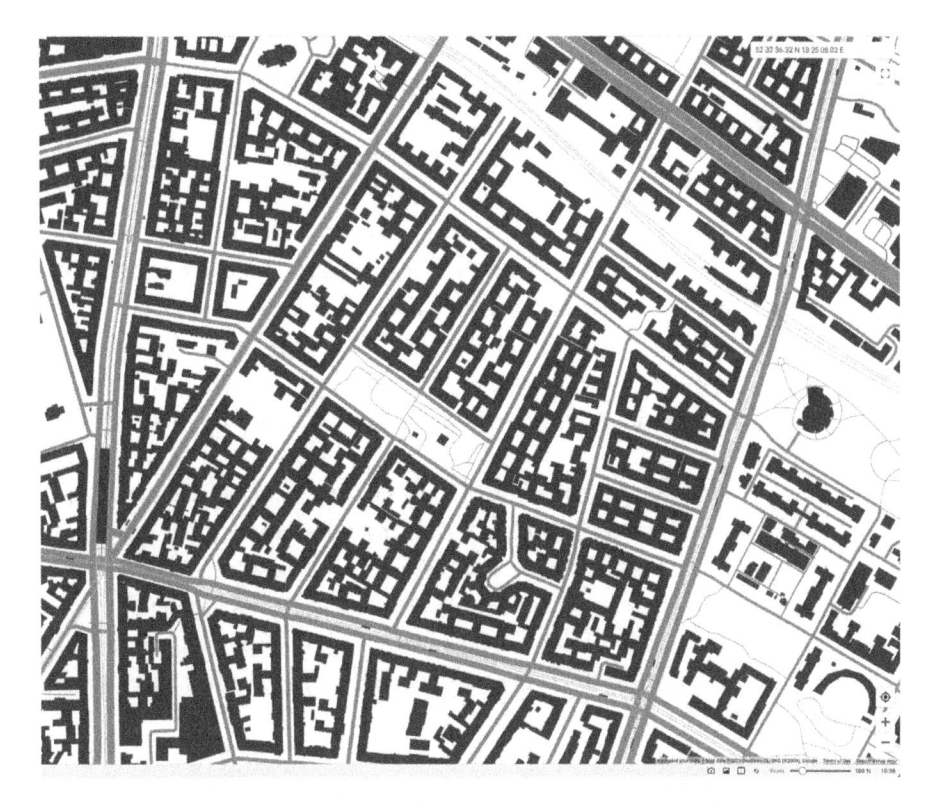

Figure 22.15 Berlin, Germany. *Large blocks, which lessened the need for streets, were supposed to include internal courtyards, but instead resulted in overbuilding. Many blamed the grid.*

Orthogonality has always been thought of as being best for business. Gutkind interpreted the Dutch grid of the 17th century as an example of "democratic egalitarianism," but Kostof argued it was more a matter of "pragmatic bourgeois mercantilist culture." Prior to industrialized capitalism, the profit objective applied specifically to merchants. Patterns other than a grid, like diagonals and monumental formality, were basically "irrelevant" in Dutch culture at the time. What mattered was frontage. In cities like Amsterdam, even canals became an extension of the grid, since they had the ability to extend the commercial value of a port further inland.[24]

The grid was a pattern well suited to capitalism: grids supported the efficient buying and selling of land. Under 19th-century capitalism, land value, which had always been based on building frontage, was now a matter of land square footage, which the grid facilitated. Grids were the instrument needed to maximize saleable lots, where lot depth could be controlled and regularized. However, it is important to keep in mind that efficiency in land sales is a late addition to the list of motives underlying the grid pattern, since property markets were not even in existence during much of the grid's history. It was only in the 19th century that the social value of land was dropped, and the unimproved grid became the basis of 19th-century expansion focused exclusively on land speculation and consumption.

Gridded, Western land platting in the United States was a notorious exercise in town planning devoid of concern about civic life, railroad companies being the "worst offenders." In large cities, the grid procured an attitude of boundless and centerless urbanism, with no natural boundaries for neighborhoods, and "no point from which city dwellers could define their own vicinity visually and socially against the endless metropolitan complex." In the non-hierarchical, large-format grid of a city like Los Angeles, the endless grid had the effect of weakening a centralized civic core, especially since LA's economy was so dependent on suburban real estate development.[25]

But as Mumford pointed out, the irony is that, far from being efficient, strict grids could be "spectacular in their inefficiency and waste" because of their rigid adherence to right angles and the tendency to avoid pattern variegation—a standardized street grid with standardized street widths would blanket all development no matter what was fronting the street. This could result in streets that were unnecessarily frequent and wide in places that didn't need that amount of pavement, such as residential neighborhoods.[26]

A famous case of rigid grid-based expansion motivated by land speculation is New York City's 1811 grid for Manhattan, still in place. The platting commission did not attempt to hide the rigidity. The grid would be the basis of "strait sided, and right angled houses" which would be "the most cheap to build, and the most convenient to live in." It is an explicit example of the connection between city plan, development efficiency, and profit motive. The plan makes no provision for natural features or service alleys because that might decrease the amount of land that could be bought and sold. There are too few sites for civic spaces and public buildings and too few north-south avenues. On the plus side, part of the focus on efficiency was to maximize the number of people with access to surrounding rivers, which was accomplished by keeping gridded lots very small. Shipping access was intended to be unobstructed (New York was a maritime city, and "shipping was part of the cityscape").[27]

At least the Manhattan grid covered the full length of the city. In other American cities, such as Chicago, individually platted grids created a patchwork of speculative development that crisscrossed the landscape (Figure 22.16). Individual land developers marked their territory for quick lot selling, and in this way, the grid became an essential enabler of capitalist greed, stoking a "gambling ethos" where the city could be treated like a game board on which one could wager on a lot's future value. It did not speak of permanent attachment, but instead of profiteering.[28]

And yet, the grid is still interpreted as an equalizer, from the layout of the temporary Burning Man festival, to rapidly urbanizing global cities. It is a quest for an ordering framework, drawn from what has been the basis of city planning for millennia. It is considered a "bottom-up" development approach—all that people

Figure 22.16 North Side of Chicago, Illinois, USA. *Individually platted grids created a patchwork of speculative development that crisscrossed the landscape.*

need is a basic street grid atop water and sewer infrastructure, interspersed with open spaces, and beyond this framing, urbanism can proceed in laissez-faire fashion. Gridded cities might thus be thought of as a merger of individual freedom, in the form of one's own piece of property, with a sense of the collective via a gridded and networked web, draped over the land.[29]

23

Wide Streets

We think of wide streets in today's cities as the product of car traffic, but historically, wide streets were places in their own right. They were not created solely for the purpose of accommodating wheeled traffic—they were created as open, public spaces. There might have been additional utilitarian purposes, like air circulation and the need to create firebreaks, but wide streets were often thought of as a thing of beauty. As a German architectural treatise from 1744 put it: "The wider and more straight a street, the more beautiful it is." Wide streets did not have to be straight to be beautiful, of course. Olmsted and Vaux laid out Ocean Parkway in Brooklyn with multiple separated lanes and enough room for six rows of trees. It was meant to be a bucolic setting for stately country homes (although development pressures ultimately thwarted that idea).[1]

Mumford makes the case that it was the grid that elevated the street as something existing "in its own right, not as before a devious passage grudgingly left over between a more or less disordered heap of buildings."[2] Once it acquired these spatial rights, it was widened to accommodate the movement of people, especially processions, providing an essential public space at a time when parks or other public open spaces were nonexistent.

Ancient cities were purposefully laid out with wide, straight streets to allow greater airflow in the city, although Vitruvius, the first-century BCE Roman planner, argued that the system of straight streets was creating "cruel wind-tunnels."[3] However, under the theory of miasmic disease transmission (especially popular in the 19th century), wide streets were considered the key to public health. Following England's Public Health Act of 1875, wide, straight, long streets were deemed significantly healthier and a kind of "philosophy" about street design because of the light, air, cleanliness, and ease of circulation they allowed. Wide streets were thought to make sense especially in colder climates where solar exposure could be maximized, a nuance included in the *Laws of the Indies* (conversely, narrow streets made sense in hot climates).[4]

But there was a significant caveat to the increased light and air of a wide street: how would it benefit buildings not immediately fronting the wide streets? In the buildings lining the street, better airflow, and light, would only reach the front rooms of the buildings. So, while Berlin's notorious apartment blocks did insert wide streets around the city's massive blocks, in terms of providing light and air it was only those buildings directly on the street that benefited. And, if wide streets also meant that tall buildings were permitted to front them, this only further

What Cities Say. Emily Talen, Oxford University Press. © Oxford University Press 2024. DOI: 10.1093/oso/9780197647769.003.0024

diminished light and air to the internal parts of the block. Thus the idea that wide streets provided light and air was somewhat of an illusion—although it did seem to temporarily absolve municipal leaders.

The wide, straight street (because wide streets are usually also straight) was the language of reason. The mathematical precision of a straight street had a kind of unambiguous truth to it. But wide streets, like England's bye-law streets, were also infamous for the associated monotony of small identical row-houses often built on them (e.g., in Leeds; Figure 23.1). The houses were so cramped that the wide streets, at least, provided some form of outdoor space—but they were dehumanizing. As Creese observed, the bye-law streets "are so cold and impersonal, so sterile, that they appear to aggravate the loss of identity and personal locus which the town and factory had brought at the outset of the industrial revolution." Wide British streets were criticized for being "devoid of poetry," producing "a great loneliness" in contrast to the lively culture inside the home (full of "good music, English, French and German literature and pictures of noble men and heroic deeds").[5] Of course, if these oppressively sterile rows of buildings found themselves decades later in a central, amenity-rich location, they were perfectly capable of gentrifying.

But in other times and places, wide streets were not oppressive; they were instead the most important streets in town, especially where they intersected. In Roman cities, two wide streets crossed in the center of town creating an intersection that had symbolic value, as well as a lot of congestion (which was sometimes exactly the point). The two main streets were the *cardo*, which ran north/south (and often closer to one side of town) and the *decumanus*, which ran east and west. According to Rykwert's analysis, the intersection of these two wide streets was an alignment with the universe: the *cardo* followed the "axis of the sky," while the *decumanus* set "in line with the axis of the sun." Cities throughout Europe still

Figure 23.1 Leeds, UK. *The lack of variety in 19th-century bye-law housing, although placed on wide streets, was seen as a form of oppression.*

Figure 23.2 Poreč, Croatia. *The sacred intersection of the north/south* cardo *and the east/west* decumanus *can still be seen.*

exhibit the intersection of these two main streets, for example in Poreč, Croatia (Figure 23.2).

Near this sacred crossing the Roman forum, the center of public life, would be located, a space that combined religious and civic functions (it was a combination of the Greek acropolis and agora). The intersection created a setting for spiritual connection since, for the Roman, "the whole universe and its meaning could be spelt out of his civic institutions."[6] Verona, Italy, founded in 89 BCE is an example. There, the forum is on the intersection and the amphitheater (now the Verona Arena, still in use) was positioned just outside the city walls (no longer present) (Figure 23.3).

Centuries later, the wide, straight street would be called "avenue" if it was relatively short with terminated ends and a landscaped median, or "boulevard" if it was longer and had small side roads buffering sidewalks. These became the preferred spatial elements of baroque city plans. Mumford dubbed the wide avenue a "parade ground" for the display of power. The "unswerving line of march" added significantly to the display of military might (Mumford asked: "were not the ancient medieval streets of Paris one of the last refuges of urban liberties?"). Even outside military display, wide, straight through-streets were used to "keep under watch a restless population," a purpose recognized by Aristotle.[7] This applied to prisoner camps and garrisons, but also any settlement where leaders felt the need to keep surveillance, such as the barrio of Barceloneta in Barcelona, laid out in the 18th century (Figure 23.4).

Figure 23.3 Verona, Italy. *The forum was located at the main intersection of town, creating a setting for spiritual connection; the amphitheater was just outside the city walls.*

Figure 23.4 Barceloneta, a neighborhood of Barcelona, Spain. *Wide straight streets were used to keep a restless population under watch.*

The long, wide, straight street was the urban language of capital cities throughout Europe. Streets became settings for ceremony and power displays. Straight and expansive streets connecting monumental places were a natural fit for authority and control, as they presupposed "an unentangled decision-making process."[8] They showed the populace that the ruling authority had the necessary power to get things done.

And yet wide, long streets were usually alienating and lacked human scale. Mumford was especially unimpressed with streets that were too long, observing that from a distance, wide, long avenues are "no more formidable than a horizontal factory unit, built for the straight line assembly of puppets." Long avenues were a "diminishing glass," and the central figure, despot or king, became increasingly small and "soon reached his political vanishing point." Camillo Sitte thought that any excessively long straight street, even one beautifully adorned, was unnatural and caused boredom and mental fatigue. Triggs set a rule: a street of "monumental character" should have a ratio of breadth to width of not more than 1 to 25, which usually meant that a wide street should not be longer than three-quarters of a mile "as beyond this the eye is unable to distinguish the focal point in which such streets should generally terminate."[9]

If not for displays of military might or despotic power, wide avenues could just as easily be for the display of money and commerce: places like Michigan Avenue in Chicago or Park Avenue in New York (Figure 23.5). The United States over-zoned its avenues for commercial uses in the misguided hope that doing so

Figure 23.5 Park Avenue, New York City, New York, USA. *Wide avenues work well for the display of wealth.* Credit: midweekpost, CC BY 2.0 <https://creativecommons.org/licenses/by/2.0>, via Wikimedia Commons

would increase tax revenues. Indeed the wide, straight avenue pulled commerce alongside it, as commerce yearned to be close to traffic. But since the amount of commerce strung along miles of avenue could never be supported, the strategy created vast stretches of vacancy. Neighborhood-based commerce, with its neighborhood-serving functionality, was depleted in the process. The effect of this practice was to remove commerce as a social connector and center of neighborhood activity, and instead make commerce a linear activity focused on the car, with little connection to the surrounding neighborhood. It is a form very different from a shopping district embedded in a neighborhood, such as the one in Radburn, New Jersey.

Wide, straight streets also hasten movement and "the conquest of space" for wheeled traffic, creating a significant burden for crossing pedestrians. They signify a desire to get somewhere fast, speed having a certain thrill. Historically, this meant that the avenue was the province of the wealthy, since they were the only ones with horses and carriages. And at a fast pace, the uniformity of building lines and facades became an asset, as the regimentation and regularity of the building line, cornice line, and roof line went well with speed. Moving too slowly along the wide avenue, with its uniform frontages, could be oppressively dull (although rows of street trees could help break the monotony). Uniform building facades meant that one acquired the same viewpoint at any given location along it. The perspective of the city, therefore, was not from multiple angles and viewpoints, but it was controlled from a single perspective. The design was "mathematically ordered" and "taken in standing still," comprehended in a single glance.[10]

Sometimes the streets and avenues would terminate with a prominent building. A monument at the end of the street supposedly rewarded the pedestrian walking along the otherwise monotonous straight street with its uniform frontage. As Abercrombie wrote, the goal was to keep the frontage buildings "plain" in order to "enhance the climax—private simplicity and public magnificence."[11]

But the frontage of a wide street was not always plain. In Vicenza, great palaces were built along the city's principal streets and, positioned this way, the "elegant prospect of a palace" was "in a way a tribute that great families felt obliged to pay to the community."[12] Perhaps these great palaces lining the street were an attempt to create an illusion of generalized well-being, since, with rampant disease, war, and other injustices, this was the only way to show visible improvement.

Wide straight streets contrast with the medieval city, whose narrow, crooked streets mean that the city is experienced bit by bit, in small parts and details (although even in the medieval period there were insertions of straight streets: divine beauty was ordered and geometrical). Meandering around Paris's Latin Quarter or the "organic" streets of Boston is thus very different from experiencing the city all at once from the perspective of a wide avenue. With narrow, winding streets the city is viewed from multiple angles (and in the case of a zigzagging ascent, like to the Acropolis, multiple levels). One implication is that the slow pace of

Figure 23.6 Kumasi, Ghana. *British colonialists imposed wide, straight streets, which were easier to maintain, but the result was social alienation.*

the meandering pedestrian requires variety at a more intricate scale. Thus there seems to be an association between street width and variety—of materials, forms, and even uses.[13]

Wide streets imposed in places not at all accustomed to them have been interpreted as an act of oppression. British colonialists who imposed wide, straight streets in Kumasi, Ghana, claimed it was for sanitary reasons because such streets were easier to maintain than irregular ones, but the result was social alienation (Figure 23.6).[14]

This is part of a long tradition of using wide streets for "renewal." Haussmann's Boulevard Saint-Michel cutting through the Paris's Latin Quarter in the 19th century was a precursor to highways cutting through urban neighborhoods throughout the United States in the 20th century. New, straight, and widened streets, along with the insertion of monumental buildings with attached squares, were common techniques used to "update" the old medieval city and eradicate "slums." In Ferrara, Italy, for example, the aim was to "link" the wide streets of new peripheral extensions to the "communication channels" of the medieval city, establishing a "social continuity" that connected "the old and the new sectors." But it required demolishing parts of the old city center (Figure 23.7).[15] When the goal of connection brings demolition, one has to consider what connectivity is being lost in the process. It is a question of scale: connectivity via wide streets connects at a much larger scale, and at the expense of, localized, neighborhood-based connectivity.

When overly wide streets appear in small towns they seem especially out of place. Initially there was a good reason: horses and wagons needed wide streets to turn around. Were these widths also a symbol of progress, whereas narrow streets signified that the town had no intention of going places? Were wide streets meant to convey a belief in the town's future, such that the extra investment was warranted?

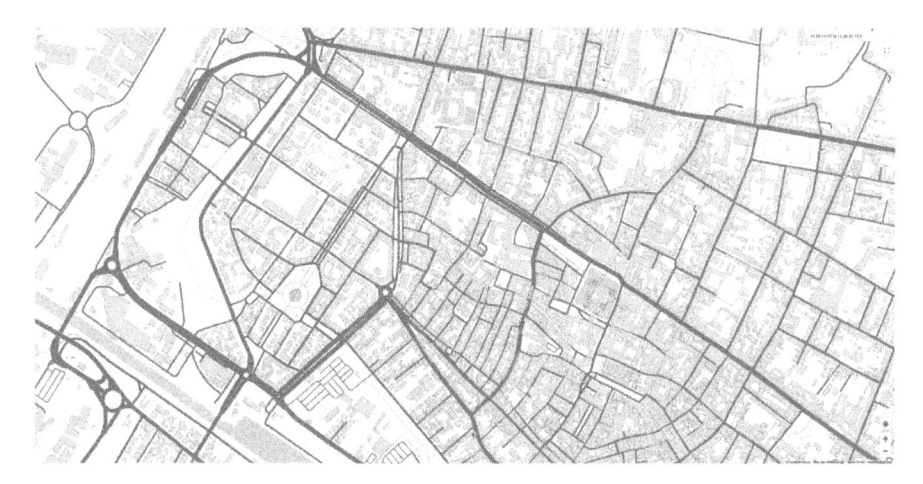

Figure 23.7 Ferrara, Italy. *Wide streets connected new peripheral extensions to the medieval core, but at the expense of localized, neighborhood-based connectivity.*

Or was the cost of pavement and upkeep increasingly less important?. In medieval times, it was the building owner who had to maintain the street in front of their building, which meant there was a cost saving if the street was kept narrow.[16] Loss of this relationship, between property owner and street maintenance, might have contributed to the modern city's love of the wide street.

24

Street Hierarchy

Hierarchy in the street pattern of cities is a common practice in both grids and non-grids. There are certain advantages. Without it, where all streets are equally sized, there can be no prioritization, no matching of street location and design to street function or purpose. On the other hand, hierarchy tends to create specialized streets that are mono-functional, which can be wasteful. Under modernism, specialized streets would curve and meander to service an isolated use, and other infrastructure would be obliged to follow the same indirect, wasteful pattern.

A criticism of baroque planning is that streets have no hierarchy: there is often no differentiation between streets that are supposed to carry traffic and streets that are meant to be residential. However, not everyone agrees that this is essential. Kevin Lynch thought that hierarchy in cities was all about dominance and social control, or for the suspect purpose of "indexing and cataloging." This impeded human interaction: there are no "'higher' and 'lower' functions in cities, or at least there should not be," Lynch wrote.[1]

Street hierarchy was a regular feature of ancient cities, such as in imperial China and Japan (e.g., Heijokyo/Nara, laid out in 710; Figure 24.1). Wide streets connected to a temple or palace, narrower streets were found within the residential sections, and the narrowest streets were reserved for alleys, the lowest in the hierarchy. But the correlation between width and importance has become ambiguous in the modern world. For example, it is unclear if highways, which are often very wide, are really what we would think of as our most valued thoroughfares.

Width is the most common way of establishing hierarchy. The classic 19th-century American railroad town—Chama, New Mexico, is one example (Figure 24.2)—had two principal roads—a main street for commercial establishments and an industrial street aligned with the railroad tracks, both of which were prioritized by being wide, typically 100 feet. These two dominant streets would either intersect or parallel each other. Cross streets were next in importance (80 feet), and residential streets (60 feet) were to be less traveled and more intimate.

Grids have been known to make use of hierarchy to reinforce a sense of order and to establish priority in a system that is otherwise uniform. Street hierarchy in a grid is found in the ancient cities of Mohenjo-Daro and Harappa, which are believed to be the earliest examples. The wider, longer or straighter the street, the more important. Typically, the width of commercial streets would be wider than residential streets. This is evident in ancient Greek cities like Priene. Alberti, writing in the

What Cities Say. Emily Talen, Oxford University Press. © Oxford University Press 2024. DOI: 10.1093/oso/9780197647769.003.0025

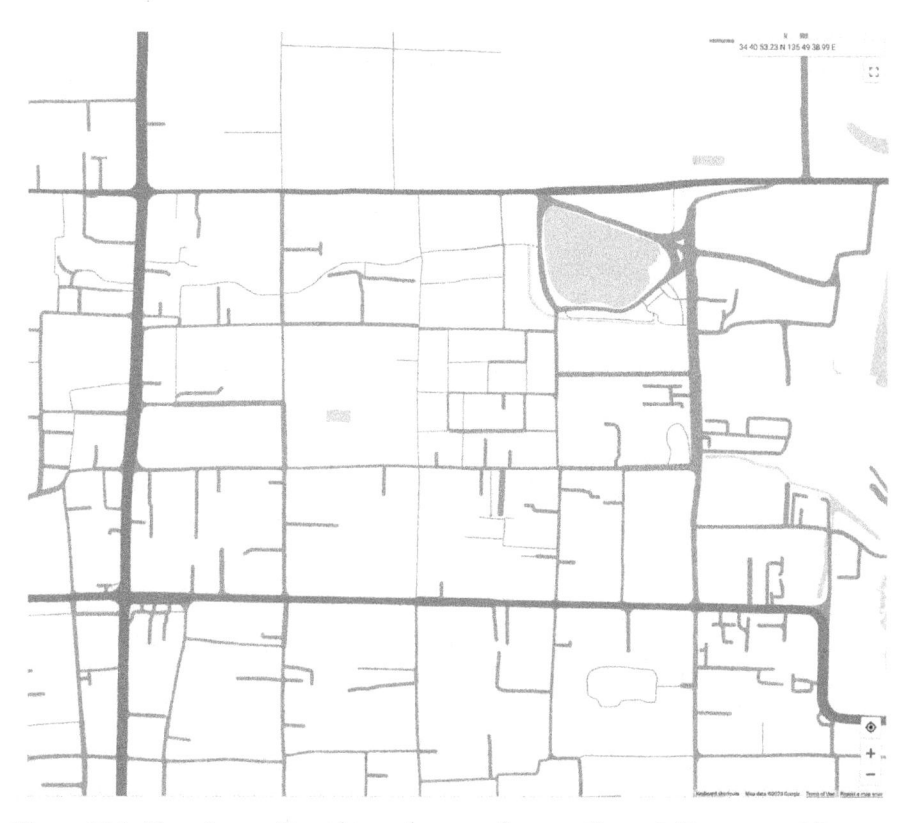

Figure 24.1 Nara, Japan. *Street hierarchy was a feature of imperial Japan, providing an unambiguous relationship between width and importance.*

Figure 24.2 Chama, New Mexico, USA. *Street width in the 19th-century American railroad town was used to establish dominance for commerce and industry.*

15th century, articulated the reasoning: "orderly arrangement of streets, squares, and buildings" should be "according to their dignity and their function." Variation in width, straightness, and length was a way of reflecting this dignity.[2]

Another approach to establishing hierarchy within a grid is to have two dominant streets intersect at right angles to create a focal point (this was not really an option when the two dominant streets ran parallel). As discussed in the chapter on "Grids," in the Roman castrum (military encampment), there might be two axes that crossed in the center (or just off-center), at which point there was often a public square. The Roman cross-axis can still be seen in Chester, UK (and in fact any town in England ending in "-chester" was originally a Roman camp, the term being derived from "castrum"). The crossing of two central axes was later interpreted as a Christian cross by the monk Lucian (Figure 24.3).[3]

Hierarchy is present in curvilinear street systems too. What might emerge is a hierarchy based on irregularity—long vs. short streets, through-streets vs. dead-ends. Different kinds of uses might naturally associate with this variation—through-streets attract more traffic and thus commercial use, while short streets are quieter and attract housing. Absent any kind of street hierarchy in a curvilinear system, the experience can seem disorienting.

Radburn, New Jersey, was famous for installing street hierarchy in what came to be known as the "Radburn Pattern"—cul-de-sac local streets that gave access only to residences, emptying into "collectors" that carried through-traffic. Although Radburn was specifically built with cars in mind (a "town for the motor age"), the street hierarchy it employed was devoted to shielding people from cars. Streets were not multifunctional; each type served one purpose.

The cul-de-sac is at the lower end of street hierarchy, which doesn't make it less consequential. It is ubiquitous, connecting to a housing family tree that includes

Figure 24.3 Chester, UK. *Street hierarchy involving the Roman cross-axis can still be seen.*

bungalow courts, religious and camping compounds, Arabian cities, and worker housing in Los Angeles. Metaphorically, houses around a cul-de-sac are like a "flattened building," where the street, because of how it functions, is the equivalent of an entrance hall or a staircase, or the elevator of a condominium. The cul-de-sac thus benefits from being treated like private property: no one would expect an entrance hall, staircase, or elevator in a building to function like public space.[4]

Doug Allen said that there are two types of streets: those that form blocks, in which case public space is visible and blocks can be added on, and those that are dendritic or tree-like, in which case public space can be hidden and adding on is difficult. The street patterns of suburbia are the latter: dendritic, curved, and intrinsically hierarchical. It is a pattern believed to be responsive to the environment— unlike the strict grid—because it can adjust itself to the terrain. However, although pedestrian paths can be inserted to make the street network more interconnected and continuous (as at Radburn), there is no opportunity to disperse or vary one's route, as routes are directed and predefined. Neither is there a dispersing web for cars, making traffic congestion inevitable. This is a problem with dendritic street patterns in general: not only do they funnel traffic onto a few unlucky streets, but they lengthen trips and eliminate the ability to take alternate routes. In the late 1920s, this was not a concern; the priority was to accommodate speed.[5]

The traditional Islamic street pattern is also built on hierarchy, but unlike in the American suburb, the hierarchy is not in service to cars. The relationship between self-contained neighborhoods (mahallehs) nested within a larger urban realm is "negotiated" by a hierarchical system of private courtyard, leading to semi-private alley or cul-de-sac, to pedestrian network, to wider public street, to the public bazaar. There is an unambiguous understanding of how space is controlled—what

Figure 24.4 Fes el Bali, Fez, Morocco. *The Fes el Bali medina reads like a solid mass, with paths and open spaces carved right into it.*

space is private and what is not. Through-streets, which are few, are used as social dividers. The interior of each neighborhood is compact, quiet, and protected, with narrow passages that shield the neighborhood from the heavier traffic of outsiders, a form that is an important source of protection. Circulation is not made easy, which provides additional protection in the event of disputes between family clans. And although it is a hierarchical street pattern based on fear of strangers and enemies, whereby through-streets are minimized, the connectivity is high. Viewed as a whole, the Fes el Bali medina in Fez, Morocco, reads like a solid mass with paths and open spaces carved right into it (Figure 24.4).[6]

25

Curved and Irregular Streets

Curvilinear and circular patterns have at times in history been thought to be god-like, the forms most associated with nature and the divine. Right angles and straight lines are not "natural." Curvilinearity is also believed to be more responsive to nature. Curves, for example, and the long blocks they usually create, are better at negotiating slopes.

Kostof termed curvilinear and irregular street forms the "planned organic," stressing the point that irregularity does not mean unplanned. There are examples in all time periods and in all places. The Acropolis of ancient Athens is one example, where curves, in tandem with variation in street width, produce an impressive approach to, and view of, the Parthenon sitting atop. The street pattern of medieval towns is another instance. During the Middle Ages, streets aimed for cathedral spires in whatever was the shortest way possible, which produced irregularity. In China, houses rather than streets were the primary organizing element of cities, and since the front door had to face south because of the rules of feng shui, the result was an "unsystematic and mazelike" street pattern. In the 20th century, curvilinear streets were a feature of planned suburbs—and, somewhat ironically, a curved street came to be seen is an indicator that the street was actually planned rather than randomly laid out. As a result, lots on curved streets were thought to sell at a higher price.[1]

Street curvilinearity was a matter of safety. Vitruvius, writing in the first century BCE, argued that there should be no "acute angles" because that "protects the attacker more than the attacked." If resilient means protected, then by this logic, grids are not particularly resilient. In the case of the medieval city, curves signified protection—the labyrinth of curvilinear streets surrounding the core shielded it from intruders. The absence of "system and orientation" was "prized as a means of defense in case the enemy penetrated the outer wall."[2]

Curvilinearity and complexity in the street patterns of residential areas, from ancient cities and medieval times to now, comprise another kind of planned disorientation. They can produce highly variable and potentially awkward lot and block sizes as well as strange intersections, incapable of being spatially defined. Nantucket provides an example (Figure 25.1).

Suburban curvilinearity plays a role in maintaining fantasies about living in "nature," as well as instilling a sense of "leisure, contemplativeness, and happy

What Cities Say. Emily Talen, Oxford University Press. © Oxford University Press 2024. DOI: 10.1093/oso/9780197647769.003.0026

Figure 25.1 Nantucket, Massachusetts, USA. *Curvilinearity and complexity in the street pattern produces highly variable and awkward lot and block sizes—but also character.*

tranquility." Non-angled meant peaceful: the purpose of curving streets in Olmsted and Vaux's meandering roads through Central Park in New York City was peace and rustic calm. Gridded, straight streets, according to Olmsted, expressed "eagerness to press forward, without looking to the right or left." Design-wise, the contrast between Chicago's grid and the suburban sinuosity surrounding it couldn't be more pronounced.[3]

Sometimes curved disconnection deliberately limits access points, which is the opposite objective of gridded connectivity. As Frederick and Mehta summarized it, "suburban streets collect; urban streets interconnect." Modern suburbs embraced the goal through curvilinearity, which came in the form of dead-end streets and culs-de-sac. The drawback is that the system of collectors means more traffic and more congestion on collector streets, as opposed to dispersion in a grid. Worse, the disconnection of suburban street patterns is likely to invoke "defensive instincts" where there is no obvious means of egress.[4]

In the medieval case, non-angled and non-straight streets were believed to be good for protection, but the evolution, as compared to suburban form, was different. One difference was timing: the curvilinearity and irregularity of medieval towns was the result of gradual, though purposeful, development. With an incremental approach, medieval cities simply didn't need to go through the contortions and expense involved in creating straight streets, which in some eras might have been necessary for wheeled traffic or to create space for military processions. Later, straight streets facilitated water and sewer lines as well as land parceling for easy real estate transactions. None of this mattered for medieval towns.

We think of straight streets in modern cities as being best for pedestrians, but curvilinear streets had advantages for pedestrians too. The practical curves of the medieval street pattern were adaptations to site conditions, but they were also built to create, as Alberti observed, changing vistas for the pedestrian. Mumford agreed, adding that "the slow curve is the natural line of a footwalker." And, curving streets that connected the center marketplace to the city gates were not just pathways out of town, they were linear marketplaces. A curving main street could be expanded at some location to create a marketplace so that traffic could get past, clearly visible in Munich's Marienplatz (Figure 25.2).[5]

Even though curves cannot be interpreted as unplanned, in some circumstances they can give the impression of freedom and lack of top-down control, especially in contrast with the strict orthogonal pattern of the gridded city. Lacking top-down control, a curve evokes the feeling that the street has evolved "naturally," where

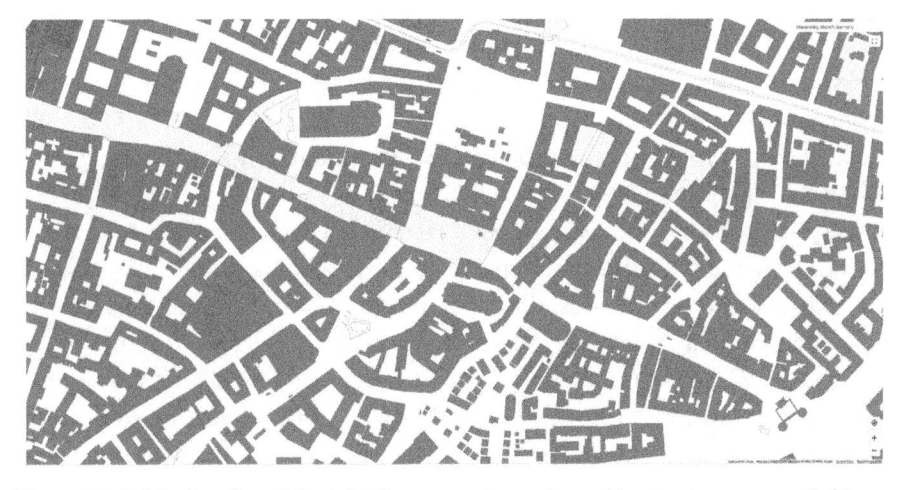

Figure 25.2 Marienplatz, Munich, Germany. *A curving main street was expanded to create a marketplace where traffic could get past.*

Figure 25.3 Bath, England. *Enclosure does not require straightness.*

humans have been free to discover their own route from place to place and not be constrained to take an engineered, gridded, and therefore less direct route. Curved streets might also be thought of as providing a sense of mystery, whereas straight streets are simply boring and uncreative. Three-dimensional form enhances the feeling. Curves lined with a colonnade, according to Rasmussen, lend "splendour and depth," for example the colonnade around the Piazza di S. Pietro in Rome. Or curves are lined with houses as at Bath, England (Figure 25.3), or parts of 19th-century Regent Street in London. Usually, however, curvilinearity correlates with a lack of spatial definition, since buildings tend to be set back. If the street pattern is irregular or curved, as at Greenbelt, Maryland, spatial definition can still occur—and help define the irregularly shaped public realm—but only if the buildings meet the streets (Figure 25.4).[6]

Straight streets have sometimes been interpreted as mechanized and lacking in character, and curvilinear streets are considered the antidote. The influential 19th-century urbanist Camillo Sitte espoused this view and thought that the gridding of America via Jefferson showed a definite lack of culture. But if curvilinearity is set within large suburban tracts with identical houses on identical lots—places like Levittown—curvilinearity is in service to conformity. Suburbia is critiqued on exactly this basis—that despite the attempt to mimic nature with "organic," curvilinear streets, the repetition equates with sterility and cultural depletion.

Figure 25.4 Greenbelt, Maryland, USA. *Spatial definition can still occur with curvilinearity, but it's difficult if the buildings don't meet the street.*

Merging gridded with curvilinear street patterns offers a reprieve. The merger has produced cities capable of combining open space and urban connectivity, for example at Bath. Amsterdam's 17th-century baroque planning was an integration of curvilinear growth along canals merged with the orthogonal grid—organic and inorganic combined, such that there is open area (along the canals) but also internal connectivity.

Curved streets were more capable than straight streets when the goal was to be "picturesque," involving the creation of "street pictures." Curvature made streets appear shorter, which helped. The concern with creating linked vistas, which could only be appreciated from the pedestrian perspective, was something that emerged out of the 15th century: from painting, to stage scenes, to garden design, to urban ensembles. The practice was of special interest to social reformers in the late 19th and early 20th centuries, who championed the "visual delights" of cities from the pedestrian's point of view, and raptured over the "exciting volumetrics of old European towns."[7]

Curves re-emerged later in the 20th century not as a means of visual delight but as a modern inspiration aimed at facilitating movement. Although Le Corbusier took the value of a straight line to extremes and denounced anything curved as "ruinous, difficult and dangerous" and in fact "paralyzing,"[8] modernists also wanted to maximize flow, which for car travel meant curves. Especially valued were elevated or submerged highways that could flow and curve unimpeded.

Somewhat paradoxically, integrating curves into an existing urban street network could, in some cases, be a device for calming traffic down and limiting the ability of a road to be used as a through-street. This was the intent of Patrick Geddes's street

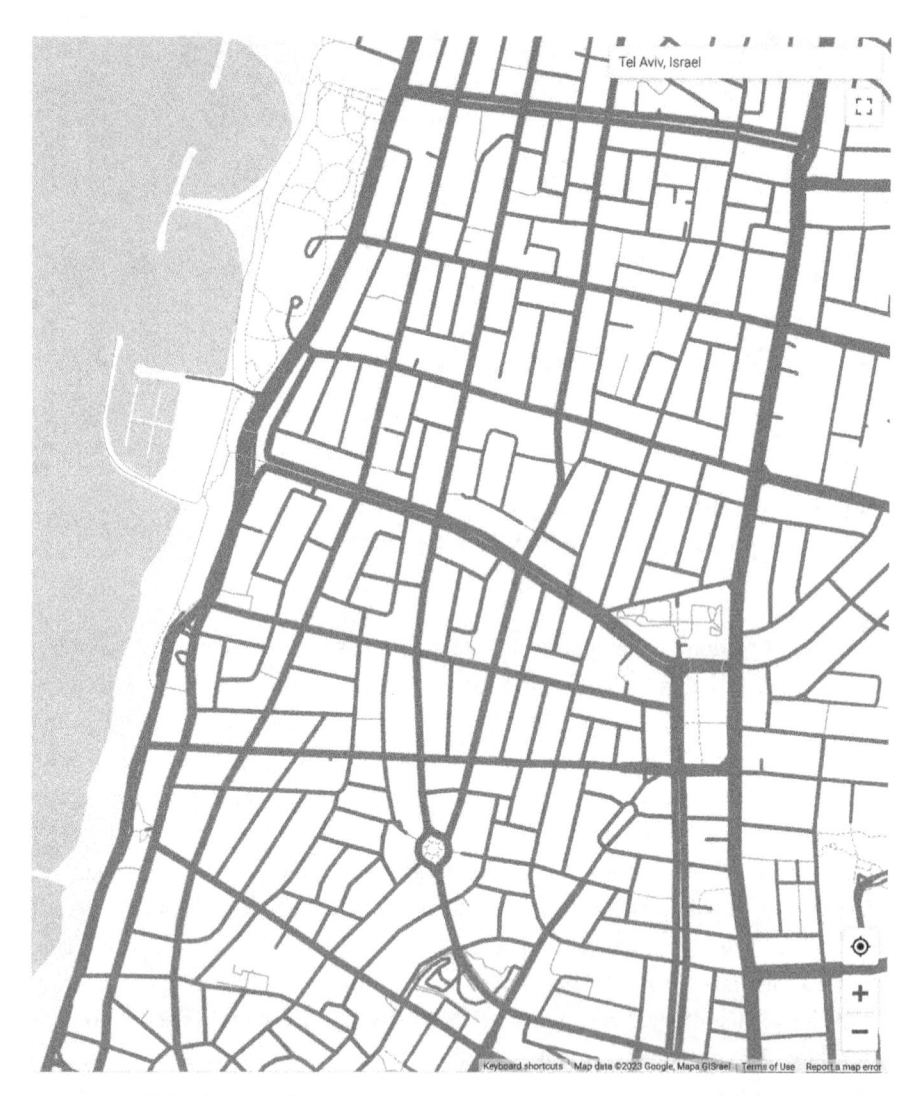

Figure 25.5 Tel Aviv, Israel. *Curving streets were integrated into an existing street network as a traffic calming strategy.*

system in Tel Aviv (Figure 25.5). Curves slowed cars down, and non-right angles in general were deemed safer. Relatedly, the intention of Wythenshawe's wallpaper-inspired hexagon blocks was to create soft intersections that would be safer because drivers would have a better view of oncoming traffic (Figure 25.6). Of course, in low-density suburban contexts, winding streets and soft intersections are probably only safer because of the low traffic volume. Curvilinearity in the context of sprawl usually translates to wastefulness—meandering, indirect routes that increase asphalt coverage for no practical reason.

If curves go full circle, it suggests a desire to focus internally, perhaps with an emphasis on social connection and even unity. Two 18th-century examples of

Figure 25.6 Wythenshawe, Manchester, UK. *Wallpaper-inspired hexagon blocks created soft intersections that were thought to be safer for drivers.*

Figure 25.7 San Gregorio da Sassola, Rome, Italy. *An oval community was an Enlightenment declaration of the importance of communal orientation.*

Figure 25.8 Grand Hornu, Belgium. *Housing arranged around an oval suggests a desire to focus internally.*

Figure 25.9 Nördlingen, Germany. *The circular form was thought to inspire a desire to be community-oriented.*

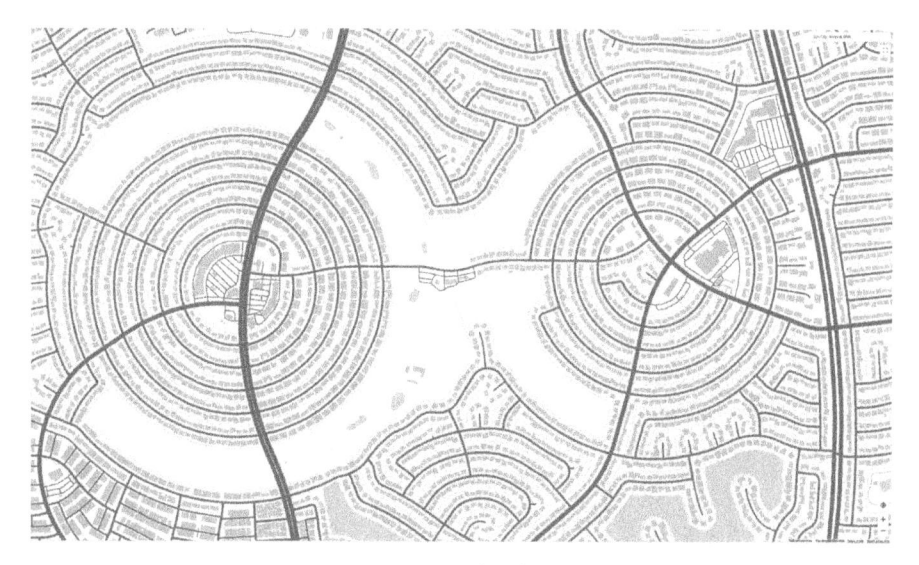

Figure 25.10 Sun City, Arizona, USA. *A model of circular insularity.*

housing arranged along an oval street, facing inward, are an Enlightenment declaration of the importance of communal orientation, rationality, good government,
and "noble sentiments of social harmony" in the worker's colony: San Gregorio da
Sassola near Rome (Figure 25.7), and Grand Hornu in Belgium (Figure 25.8). The
Nazis also admired circular communities, for example Nördlingen, believing that
the form inspired a desire to be community-oriented, whereas, in contrast, "rows
of houses resulted in social indifference" (Figure 25.9). Blumenfeld argued that if
a city viewed itself as mostly a fortress, then a circular form was its best bet.[9] That
is perhaps an apt description of Arizona's Sun City, a model of circular insularity
(Figure 25.10).

26

Boulevards and Avenues

The boulevard is most associated with the rebuilding of Paris under Napoleon III and Baron von Haussmann in the mid-19th century, after which it was transplanted around the globe. In modern cities, the boulevard, which is landscaped, played the role of bringing green space into the city. But the term has a complicated history. "Boulevard" was first used in France in the 14th century as a military term for "city wall." Three centuries later, the definition had changed, and it meant a promenade at the edge of European cities atop the old defensive 17th-century earthen ramparts (which, a century earlier, had replaced stone walls). As such, the boulevard began life as a demarcation between the city and the country.[1]

Avenues started out differently, as they were straight roads that cut through the countryside, contrasting sharply with nature's irregularity. The term comes from "venir," a French verb meaning to come or to arrive. However, according to Kostof, by the latter 19th century the difference between "boulevard" and "avenue" had become negligible. In the United States, the distinction held on a bit longer, as planners in the early 20th century were trying to distinguish between streets for aesthetic and green purposes (boulevards) and streets devoted to handling traffic (avenues).[2] Although avenues do tend to be smaller than boulevards, both are essentially wide-open spaces cut through the city.

Boulevards and avenues are associated with destruction. This happened when they were used as devices to elevate a ruler, which usually involved inserting a wide road through existing urban fabric. Ratchadamnoen Avenue in Bangkok, for example, constructed in the early 20th century, is an avenue that connects an old palace with a new one, which had the effect of symbolically extending the monarch's influence (Figure 26.1). The wide avenue cut through the city, serving the purpose of promoting the ruler's image as a "modern monarch" capable of constructing a "modernized city." This quest, to modernize and gain influence by inserting a boulevard or avenue, is seen in all types of regimes, including fascist. Tirana, the capital of Albania, was subjected to boulevard treatment in the 1930s. The insertion of the wide boulevard in an otherwise modest place destroyed the "fragile texture" of the existing Islamic town (Figure 26.2).[3]

Boulevards and avenues provide a new kind of space for social contact. In European cities, they were usually built by blasting through dense, impoverished urbanism, creating new settings in which people could "see and be seen." In mid-19th-century Paris, the boulevards were lined with apartment buildings, which ensured that the social space of the boulevard would be well populated and lively.

What Cities Say. Emily Talen, Oxford University Press. © Oxford University Press 2024. DOI: 10.1093/oso/9780197647769.003.0027

Figure 26.1 Ratchadamnoen Avenue in Bangkok, Thailand. *The early 20th-century avenue connected an old palace with a new one, which had the effect of symbolically extending the monarch's influence.*

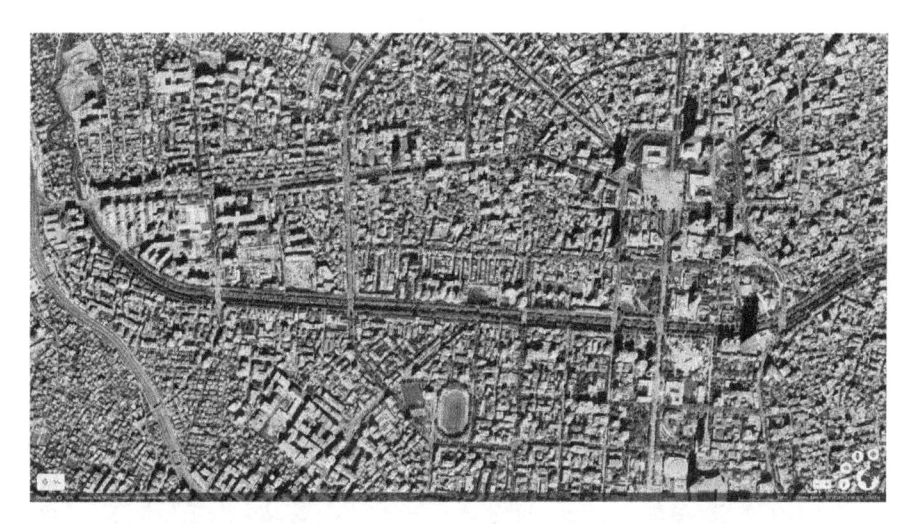

Figure 26.2 Tirana, Albania. *The capital was subjected to boulevard treatment in the 1930s, damaging the fragile texture of the existing Islamic town.*

The Parisian boulevard became an expression of "the union of middle-class values with authoritarian planning." An urbanism of stage sets and spectacle was no longer for the elites—it was now for the middle class.[4]

The boulevard also provided a setting for new types of behaviors. Communication in all forms was on display. Marshall Berman concluded that Paris's wide-open boulevards created "a new primal scene," a "boudoir in the making of modern love," where lovers could be "private in public." But not only was the boulevard the new locale of life and vitality, of people-watching and of theater, but it held all the power: the shops, cafes, and residences that lined the boulevard seemed to exist only for the streets, with everything in perpetual motion: movement "an end in itself."[5]

Socialist countries embraced the boulevard as a staged setting for the masses, but they might not have bargained for the exposure of class inequality that these open spaces provided. There could be no more hiding of the reality of class inequity. The poor could observe the rich and vice versa. The Nevsky Prospekt in St. Petersburg is an example, a main avenue lined with neoclassical buildings that became a showcase of modern consumerism (Figure 26.3). Classes intersected freely. And although the government could monitor behavior, the government could not dictate interactions. In fact, the street was the only venue available for "free" communication. However, the street's "aura of ebullient freedom," was superficial. The tsar's regime was tyrannical and Russian society was intensely stratified. Berman observed that this is how misery became fact. Social interaction was cursory, with people looking past each other. There was more inter-class exposure, but what social purpose was served, and who benefited?[6]

The boulevard was made for consumption. Françoise Choay argued that the reordering of Paris was essentially an attempt to give unity to, and make operative, a "huge consumer market" that had previously been disjointed. With the

Figure 26.3 Nevsky Prospekt, St. Petersburg, Russia, 1984. *The staged setting for the masses exposed class inequality and became a showcase of modern consumerism.* Credit: SteveInLeighton's Photos, CC BY-SA 2.0 <https://creativecommons.org/licenses/by-sa/2.0>.

newly inserted boulevards, Paris became "a metropolis unified by the fever of capitalism." The newly designed circulation and ventilation system, with houses subordinate to wide, straight streets, was part of the new unity. At least in Paris the consumption was within reach. In St. Petersburg, the imported wares that the boulevard showcased "concealed a dangerous lack of depth behind the brilliant façade," since Russia was far behind other Western countries in economic and technological terms.[7]

The Parisian boulevards also showed that the middle class was perfectly capable of urbanizing: the urban apartment house helped to successfully combine family life and the pleasures of urban culture. As Fishman observed, the French were helped by the fact that there was no Puritan tradition of needing to escape the city with its evil temptations.[8] Of course, it didn't hurt that the reconstruction of Paris amounted to a large-scale government stimulus that supported the construction of the urban apartment block to line and validate, in opulent fashion, so many miles of new boulevards. There was a social benefit, too. If the wealthy occupied side streets coming off of the boulevards, or perhaps on the second floor of a Parisian apartment building, and if poorer people occupied the attic floor under the mansard roof, apartments lining boulevards was a means of supporting social diversity.

Boulevards and avenues were conceived as new arteries for a better, more modern circulation system. They showed what modern urban living could be like. In US cities, urban apartment houses lining boulevards stand as a testament to the fact that it is possible to withstand a suburban exodus. And one does have to admit that all the attention paid to boulevards did, at least, mean that the public realm was being prioritized far above the private realm. This should be contrasted with modernists like Le Corbusier and Robert Moses who sought to replace the street entirely with a new urban structure that appreciated the "space-time continuum" of modernity, and in the process attempted to rip out the life—which had always taken place on the street—from the city.[9]

27

Radials, Rings, and Diagonals

In the radial-concentric street pattern, there are radial roads pointing to a center, and ring roads that circle around. Although there are ancient origins, the form became especially prominent when highway belts started to encircle cities in the mid-20th century. Zooming out, the pattern is readily seen in London (Figure 27.1).

The radial-concentric pattern has prehistoric roots. The form was thought to be the natural evolution of villages in Africa that started with a gathering of shelters around the residence of the chief. The area in front of the chief's residence became a civic space for ceremonies and public meetings, and there was a main road leading to it. Circular walls eventually became circular roads, and additional radials to the center were added.[1]

The major thoroughfares—the radials—point to something at the center of a city in need of aggrandizement, like a palace or government building. This is perhaps why the radial-concentric is thought to be "beloved by chieftains, emperors, priests and popes," or hierarchical societies in general. The architectural critic Christopher Tunnard, however, was willing to think of the "Metonian plan," as he called it, as a form of justice in some circumstances. He labeled Pope Sixtus' scheme in Rome, for example, a "democratic concession" and an upgrade for a populace trying to make a spiritual pilgrimage. With the new circular routes and radial connections, pilgrims were no longer forced to go from "church to church through tortuous and unsanitary side streets." If not a palace or seat of government, the center of a radial-concentric scheme could also be a marketplace, which might be interpreted as a case of the merchant class holding power.[2]

Broad avenues that push out from the center into the surrounding countryside is particularly common with capital cities—the avenues exert a gravitational pull on the surrounding region. The pattern has a long history in plans with a military focus. Imperial cities in Europe in the 13th and 14th centuries were circular for defensive reasons—circularity created the shortest distance between center and edge. Renaissance city plans would keep the center of a radial-concentric scheme open for military maneuvering, with the straight streets quickly linking center to surrounding gates and bastions. Earlier, before the installation of artillery, the connection between town gate and town center (a church plaza or market square) would have been more indirect, to confound an enemy who managed to enter the town.[3]

The radial-concentric pattern can be unwieldy. Awkward intersections and irregular block and lot shapes are created when orthogonal street systems are made to

What Cities Say. Emily Talen, Oxford University Press. © Oxford University Press 2024. DOI: 10.1093/oso/9780197647769.003.0028

Figure 27.1 London, UK. *In London's expandable radial-concentric highway system, radials point to the center and concentric roads circle around.*

intersect with surrounding radial streets and defensive walls (although interesting nodes and vistas might also be the result). A good example of where this happens is with the bastioned walls of a Renaissance city built for defense—Palmanova, Italy, for instance (Figure 27.2). The merging of patterns resulted in a radial-concentric street system that was likely to conflict with the everyday access needs of citizens.

In Detroit, remnants of a radial scheme peep out from the more recent collection of street patterns (Figure 27.3). Vestiges of "a baroque vision" are still seen amid a "jumble of grids." The attempt at grandiosity is a lasting imprint there, although the fact that the imprint is reduced to remnants is testament to the power of land speculation. Reps claimed that the mixture of grid and baroque street systems, which is widely known to create problems like odd lot shapes and acute angles (as in Washington, DC, or Indianapolis), was overcome in Detroit, where the two systems were better integrated.[4]

In the United States, radial-concentric patterns usually put commercial and political power at the center. The way to "read" a city like Chicago, then, is that, at least initially, a single predominant center possessed a strong gravitational pull, and all major transportation routes emanated from it. But now, the radial-concentric form is out of whack with the way life is conducted. The pattern suggests a dominate

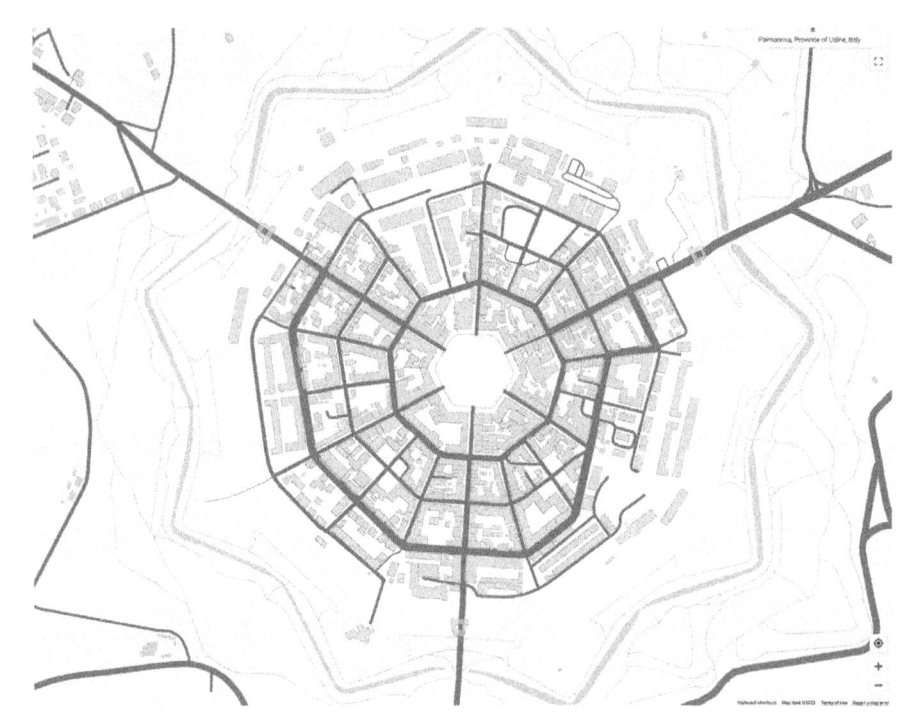

Figure 27.2 Palmanova, Italy. *Built for warfare, the radial-concentric street system conflicted with the everyday access needs of citizens.*

Figure 27.3 Detroit, Michigan, USA. *Vestiges of a baroque scheme are still evident, but the fact that they were reduced to remnants is testament to the power of land speculation.*

urban core, but the citizenry is not singularly focused on it. It is a historical relic, now representing a poor alignment between built form and contemporary life.

The radial-concentric pattern often failed to live up to its goals. It was supposed to be filled in with compact community nodes along the radials rather than creating an overly congested center. In between the nodes would be wedges of green space. The reality, however, was that the forces of free market capitalism could not be held to this pattern, and the green wedges transitioned into low-density sprawl. As for the radials, they became social dividers rather than connectors. One example is the "gash-like, overscaled thoroughfare" of Canal Street in New Orleans. It became a radial that served as "a geographical recognition of the armed truce between Creoles and Americans" (Figure 27.4)[5]

If straight roads are not part of a circular system, they are simply "diagonals." The diagonal was the shortest path between two points, and an element to be designed in its own right. A common use for the diagonal was to link focal points, for example in Washington, DC. Kevin Lynch wrote approvingly of the approach because it created an economical and "memorable" structure of "strong visual effects . . . without imposing control on every part." The downside was that the in-between areas were generally ignored as filler, with all the attention and money focused on the monuments that affirmed state authority and mostly glorified war and its heroes.[6]

The guiding principle of the diagonal was communication via improved circulation and the ability to geographically locate oneself: essentially, wayfinding. In Rome, diagonals cut through town to link basilicas. Sir Patrick Abercrombie called the practice "clear-headed logic in town-modernisation," an approach that "straightened up" centuries of "spasmodic" planning.[7] What was being designed

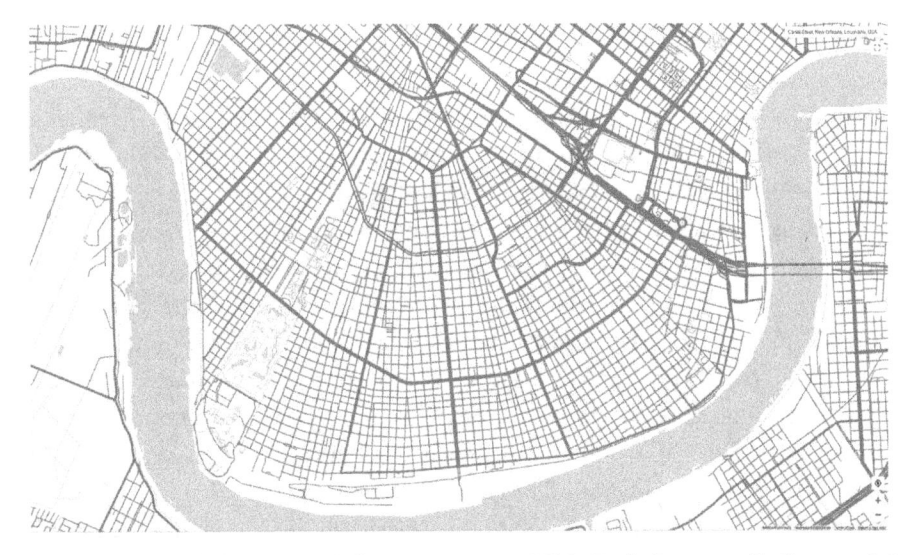

Figure 27.4 Canal Steet, New Orleans, Louisiana, USA. *Radials, especially if overscaled, became social dividers rather than connectors.*

Figure 27.5 Via de' Tornabuoni, Florence, Italy. *Diagonal streets cut through the meandering maze, straightening the link between churches and public buildings.*

was a movement system, not the least of which was a pilgrimage route to the Holy City. This not only facilitated processions but established Rome as an international city of "people in transit." In Florence, Italy, diagonals linked churches and public buildings (Figure 27.5).

Diagonals cutting through developed cities and towns is also an apt description of American railroads. Railroads reigned supreme and had enormous impact on city form, slicing through existing towns at will. The town of Galva, Illinois, was dutifully platted in Jeffersonian grid style, and later the railroad literally steam rolled diagonally through the heart of it, showing its dominance as well as its disregard for how it impacted the functionality of the town (Figure 27.6). At the time, townspeople most likely overlooked the disruption and welcomed the ability of the railroad to put their town on the map.

Sometimes diagonals were cut through the countryside to reach a termination point. Tallmadge, Ohio, laid out in 1807, has four diagonals that terminate at the village green where the town hall and church were located (Figure 27.7). This was to be the focus of all attention, practically and symbolically. But the town languished, and, absent more robust development and something significant to terminate into, the diagonals seem ill-suited. Now, the green and the preserved church and town hall are surrounded by a traffic circle with strip malls and fast-food joints.

Diagonals could be purely cosmetic, for the sole purpose of making a town look more interesting. In Martinborough, New Zealand, a 19th-century colonial outpost in need of land sales, property was sold from a "memorable image," a diagonal, based on the idea that a town with a diagonal was an easier sell (Figure 27.8). Private speculators were "looking for a point of difference" in the "colonial settlement industry," which was competitive, and a diagonal street lined with impressive building facades was one way to stand out.[8]

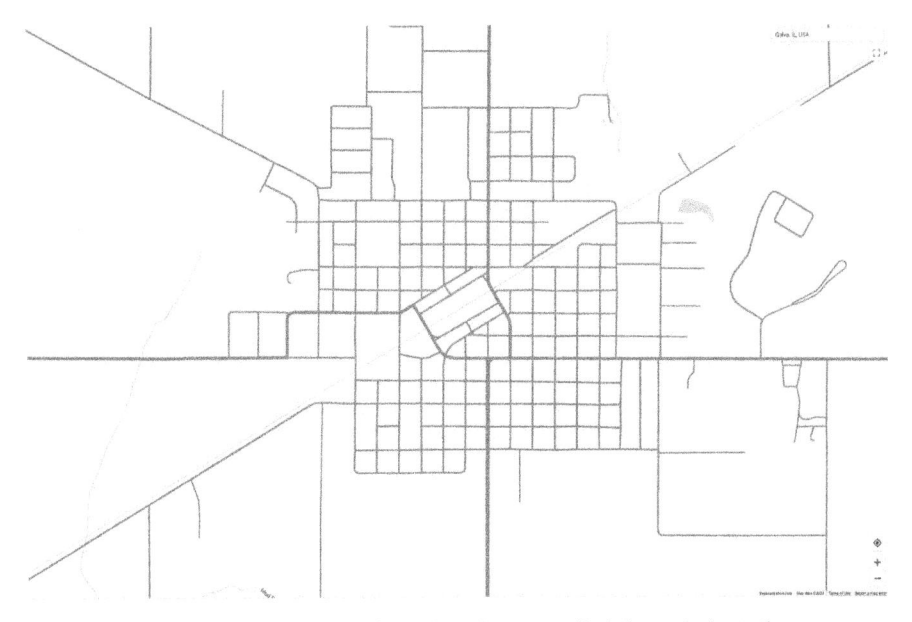

Figure 27.6 Galva, Illinois, USA. *The railroad steam rolled through the Jeffersonian grid, showing its dominance and its disregard for how it impacted the town.*

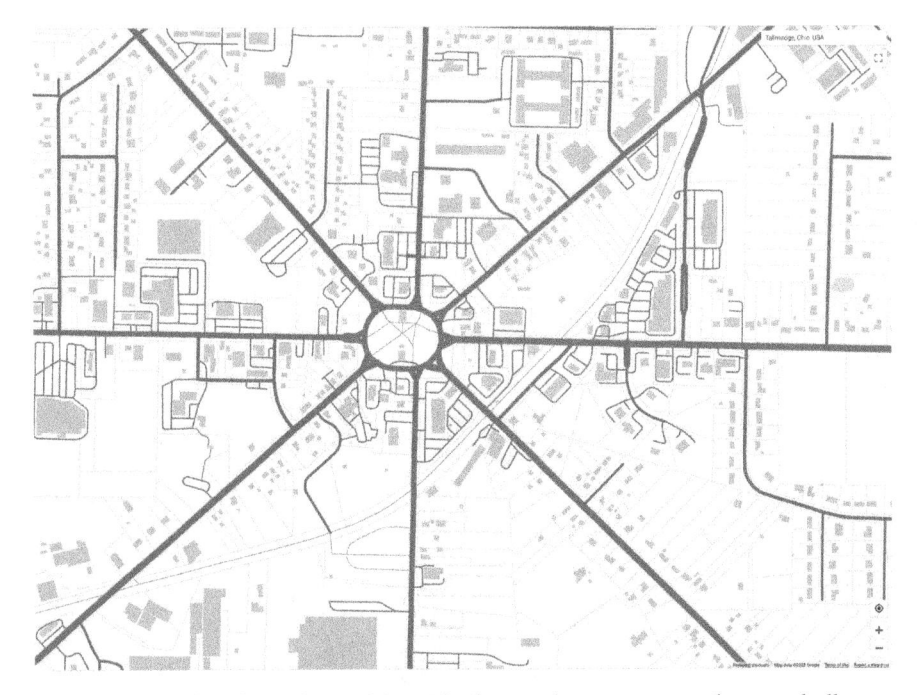

Figure 27.7 Tallmadge, Ohio, USA. *Eight diagonals terminate at the town hall, but its stature is diminished by the surrounding traffic circle with its strip malls and fast-food joints.*

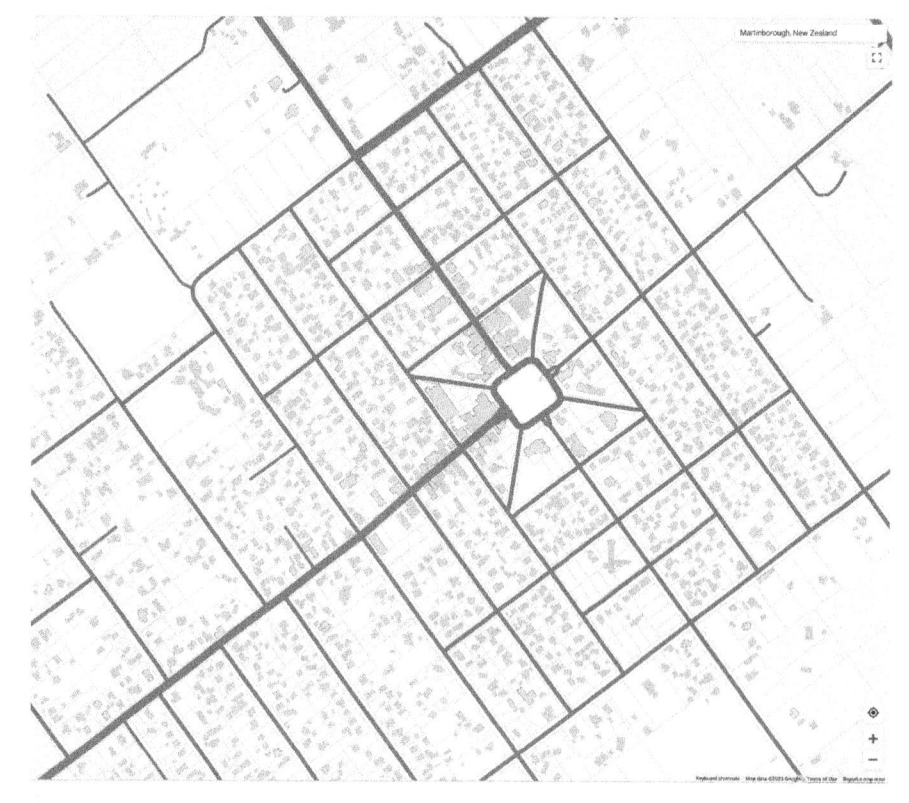

Figure 27.8 Martinborough, New Zealand. *Diagonal streets were used to "sell" the town.*

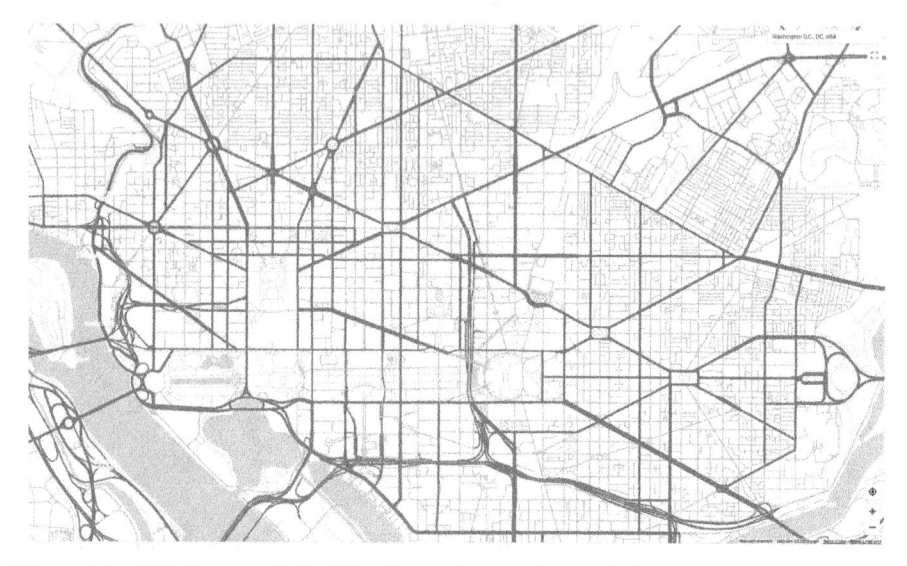

Figure 27.9 Washington DC, USA. *The exuberant diagonals help mesh the dynamic baroque aesthetic against the timidity of the subservient grid.*

Diagonals focus attention, but they also tend to consolidate rather than disperse traffic, and therefore usually generate too much of it. This can make the street unusable as a social space. Another downside is that the diagonal is associated with long expanses of frontage uniformity, which translates to a loss of neighborhood diversity and differentiation. Where there was once intimacy, the diagonal creates anonymity and spectacle.

But on the plus side, if the diagonal is juxtaposed with a gridded urban fabric, such as in Washington, DC, it meshes the "exuberant" and "dynamic" baroque aesthetic against the "timidity" of the subservient grid, a metaphor for the nation's ideals of "independence and unity" (Figure 27.9).[9]

28

Superblocks

Superblocks come in two main categories. One type combines existing city blocks to create one large superblock. Interior streets are closed to traffic and converted to public space. This describes Barcelona's superblocks—or "superilles" in Catalan—which consolidate up to nine contiguous blocks to transform streets and intersections into plazas and playgrounds. Streets are pedestrianized in a way that goes beyond the typical "pedestrian mall" created by closing a street. The pattern redefines mobility. Circulation and movement are no longer dominated by the automobile but are instead a mix of modes—walking, biking, transit. In the process, space is recovered for social needs. Japanese cities also have this brand of superblock, where streets are essentially "passive interspaces" between houses and blocks. The type was common in ancient Greek cities, too.[1]

But the second category of superblock, championed by modernists in the mid-20th century, is a different sort. It consists of blocks in which the buildings within them are unaligned with streets. Buildings are set in open land, untethered. There is no street frontage, per se. As streets do not function as the primary organizing element of urban form, their significance is seriously downgraded.

Modernists were enamored with this type of superblock because, first, they believed it opened up the city to "nature," and second, they wanted to break free of the dense, Manhattan-style grid, believing that it lacked freedom. Low lot coverage and exposure to open land outweighed any social connectivity benefit that a grid with small blocks might have provided, although early proponents did not think of green space as lessening social connectivity—far from it. In Letchworth Garden City, an early adopter, the superblock allowed buildings to relate to each other rather than to the street, which advocates believed would improve social connection.

But mostly the appeal of the superblock was that it would give apartment dwellers immediate access to green space—towers set in parks (the special case of the "tower in a park" is discussed in a separate chapter). While planned suburbs had always been steeped in greenery—houses set in parks—the important contribution of the superblock was that houses could front green space rather than the street. One very early example of this idea was the 1854 London suburb of St. Margarets. The interior linear park was shielded and protected from the "evils" of the city, while the houses served the function of "negotiating" between urban and rural domains.[2]

Stuyvesant Town–Peter Cooper Village in New York City has 11,200 residents on their own two superblocks, closed off by surrounding arterials, inwardly focused on their own green space, and definitely not a part of the Manhattan grid

What Cities Say. Emily Talen, Oxford University Press. © Oxford University Press 2024. DOI: 10.1093/oso/9780197647769.003.0029

Figure 28.1 Stuyvesant Town–Peter Cooper Village, Manhattan, New York, USA. *Inwardly focused on superblock green space is a peaceful—or ambiguous—district.*

(Figure 28.1). Critics might say that what this kind of loosening up of traditional urban streets and blocks did was to make the public realm ambiguous and indecipherable. Proponents might argue that Stuyvesant Town creates a peaceful district that is a welcomed contrast to the rigidity and chaos of Manhattan.

Apart from access to green space and the impression of freedom, it was not lost on city leaders that superblocks could save money: fewer streets meant lower land cost. The use of large blocks to lessen the need for street-building was a motivation behind Berlin's much-criticized 1862 extension plan (the Hobrecht plan), although planners claimed the objective was to provide flexibility. The superblocks resulted in dense apartment building construction (Mietskasernen) accessed via dark courtyards with poor ventilation. Berlin's large block plan can be interpreted as an attempt to shift the basics of human settlement need from government to private developers, with a minimal amount of public oversight. The "market" (developers) was supposed to fill in the blocks with side streets and public spaces—but this didn't happen. Berlin's Mietskasernen can thus be evaluated on the basis of what it excluded—local streets and open spaces on the interior of large superblocks, life-sustaining elements that public planning should have insisted on.

Even where the objective of the superblock was to increase access to green space, reduction of road-building cost was still a strong motive (as it is for features like quadrangles and courtyards). The problem was that, freed from the constraint of needing to build to the street, enveloping green space could be overblown. In Hampstead Garden Suburb, the vast common green was City Beautiful–like, too

Figure 28.2 Jackson Heights, Queens, New York, USA. *Apartment buildings set in gridded green space, an evolutionary step toward the superblock.*

big for a small suburb and prone to be "deadspace." Peter Hall said it looked like a space that was "waiting for an Imperial Durbar" to take place.[3] Clearly the scale was meant to impress rather than to provide functionality or civic utility.

In the United States, an interesting evolutionary step toward the superblock was the case of apartment buildings set in gridded green space. Jackson Heights in Queens, New York, is rooted in New York's existing grid but consciously distinctive in its quest to be more suburban—green—than urban (Figure 28.2). In a 1919 article "What Is Home without a Golf Course?" a reporter extolled the virtues of a "community settlement" that was not for the "poor working classes" (as apartment groupings were then labeled), but was solidly for "the great middle class" (Figure 28.3).[4] The design was novel at the time—a community composed of six-story apartment buildings set in a grid with plenty of green. From there, the next step toward modernist superblock form was to eliminate all but the outermost streets and embrace the freedom to locate buildings randomly within the created park.

Radburn, New Jersey, built in 1929, is the quintessential superblock community (Figure 28.4). According to Dal Co, Radburn was modeled after Central Park, since it was there that the separation of traffic was introduced into the American consciousness. It also shows the influence of both the neighborhood unit and the garden city: large, superblock-based neighborhoods were supposed to form a "complete garden city" for 25,000 inhabitants (lacking industry or other major source of employment, it was a goal that was never achieved). Like the neighborhood unit, Radburn's neighborhoods had a school and playground at the center, but with green spaces rather than streets as boundaries. Open green spaces in the center of the development functioned as sheltered space and were not really meant to be public. The result was the "Radburn Idea"—superblocks used for complete

Figure 28.3 *A page from the* New York Tribune *extolling the virtues of Jackson Heights in New York City. What Is Home without a Golf Course?* By Elene Foster, September 28, 1919, Page 3, Image 79. Public domain, via Wikimedia Commons, https://comm ons.wikimedia.org/wiki/File:What_Is_Home_Without_a_Golf_Course%3F_ %E2%80%94_illustrations_(chroniclingamerica).png.

Figure 28.4 Radburn, New Jersey, USA. *Street hierarchy and superblocks shield people from cars; front doors face green space rather than the sidewalk, and the backbone of the community is a park.*

Figure 28.5 Baldwin Hills, Los Angeles, California, USA. *Like living at summer camp.*

separation of pedestrian and car, where the "community heart and backbone" is a park. In the decades that followed, neighborhoods conceived as grouped housing around a central open space were imagined in every which way. Golf courses as the central green were a popular option. Baldwin Hills Village in Los Angeles, now called the "Village Green," was a superblock champion, one website boasting, "there is so much greenery and open space it feels like living at summer camp!" (Figure 28.5).[5]

In some ways, the superblock is really nothing more than one version of a very large block. But the obvious liability of any large block is that it cuts off access. Even if traversed with pedestrian pathways as at Radburn, the paths are not lined with activities, and if there is no meaningful destination at either end, and no variation in the scenes one can experience along the way, the pathways can become somewhat meaningless.[6]

On the positive side, the superblock does allow more options for building arrangement. And if buildings do not need to be street-facing they can be oriented to maximize sun access. Where this is accomplished, the superblock might even be interpreted as a promoter of spatial equity. In the case of the Soviet mikrorayon, high-rise slabs provided sun exposure on two sides for every unit, thanks to superblock freedom. In addition, buildings could be arranged to provide internal collective space—a protected communal area that isn't relegated to the street where it competes with traffic and commerce.

Jane Jacobs, for one, denounced these surrounded interior greens, which she called "sheltered 'togetherness' worlds." She argued that they are exclusively matriarchal and really only of use to very small children—which means they are yet another form of specialization and separation. With buildings turning their back on the street, superblocks are emblematic of the travesty that private cars have been given the authority to dictate the urban pattern. Social connection is also a challenge, as exchange is more conducive to active streets than passive green space. As one resident of Radburn admitted, "life is more oriented towards that peripheral access road than towards the common green," which "abruptly evaporate(s)" beyond each resident's private backyard.[7]

29

Plazas and Squares

Plazas and squares are two main types of civic space: the infrastructure of civil society. There are other types of spaces to consider, such as the campo, piazza, green, or grand place, and any kind of space in a city can be "civilized"—even the wastelands left over from the industrial era, such as highway underpasses, can be repurposed. But this chapter focuses exclusively on plazas and squares, the open spaces of cities and towns that aren't sidewalks, parks, or someone's front lawn. Technical distinctions between plazas and squares tend to be more about design and use rather than meaning and interpretation (plazas are paved, squares don't have to be), but they are used here interchangeably.[1]

Plazas and squares have been assigned a wide array of social interpretation. They are the heart of the community, or they are in service to empire-building. They are for collective life, or they are for social segregation. They are an essential physical manifestation of civic culture, or they were created—as one historian remarked about squares in colonial plans—to create "hierarchies of space and power." Savannah's squares were established as places of refuge for settlers living outside of town, in case of attack. Thus, the positioning of squares was an attempt to calm the fears of would-be settlers. The square in central Belfast seems to be devoted to nothing more than dignifying City Hall (Figure 29.1).[2]

It is commonly understood that the provision of civic space is a reciprocal process: a sense of community helps ensure that adequate civic space is built, and civic space generates a sense of community. Raymond Unwin, in his 1909 *Town Planning in Practice*, was a believer: "adequate expression of corporate life in the outward forms of the town will both stimulate and give fresh scope to the co-operative spirit from which it sprung." Historically, and more practically, civic spaces were thought of as providing the city with "lungs" so people could breathe ("for the benefit of people dwelling at the centre").[3] The more compact and dense the urbanism, the more precious any open space was.

Civic spaces are supposed to be the places of spontaneous and face-to-face social interaction: "meetings, conversations, encounters and flirtations," not to mention sporting events as well as government, religious, and commercial functions. The activities taking place, even if "habitual," are mostly "unformalized." But there are cultural limits to this social exchange. The traditional Islamic city was socially introverted, such that collective life involving the world outside of the family was restricted to the open space adjacent to a mosque—not in a public plaza or square. In Western democracies, civic spaces are supposed to be open for all to

What Cities Say. Emily Talen, Oxford University Press. © Oxford University Press 2024. DOI: 10.1093/oso/9780197647769.003.0030

Figure 29.1 Belfast City Hall, Belfast, Northern Ireland, UK. *A square devoted solely to dignifying city hall.*

converge in, although the reality is that subvert and overt "cues" dictate who actually "belongs."[4]

In medieval cities, civic space functioned as the physical representation of common life, which was especially important in times when urban dwellers lacked political power. Socially, medieval civic space was more complicated than in antiquity, since a number of entities needed accommodation: the wealthy, merchants, clergy, administrators, royalty. There was civil authority and there was religious authority, and there was civic space that, as a setting for common life, could be of different character from either of those. Such differentiation did not exist in antiquity.

Squares and plazas used to serve practical purposes. When there was no "mass communication" via newspapers, telephones, and the internet, the town square was the locus of communication about one's fellow citizens. And when there was no municipal water, the town square provided a public fountain, which was also a social gathering point. In the Renaissance, there was great concern for the urban context of churches, and much attention was focused on the visual space around a cathedral and how it could be used to enhance the building's size and stature. These civic spaces had a practical value as staging areas, whereby crowds could gather and organize for church ceremonies that took place outside.[5]

The square was a setting for all sorts of rituals that are no longer part of civic society, including public beatings and hangings. If plazas and squares seem quiet to modern eyes, it's because some of their basic social purpose has ceased to be

Figure 29.2 Seagram Building Plaza, New York City, New York, USA. *An open, urban plaza set in front of a corporate building often lacks civic purpose and can become dead space.*

relevant. Now, civic space plays a leading role in consumption—of recreational activities, or food carts, or public art. The United States is especially geared to this. The squares inserted in New York City's 1811 grid, which were considered woefully deficient, were in service to consumerism. And, of course, many of these civic spaces are now privately owned, outwardly open to the public but more for the purpose of adorning an adjoining corporate building than for providing a place of civic identity and democratic life (Figure 29.2). New York's mid-20th-century plazas, which emerged out of a zoning rule requiring them, were later ridiculed as dead spaces.

In general, open space in the city is hard to hold on to, once the desire to congregate and pressure to densify sets in. William Penn's plan for Philadelphia was composed of large blocks with plenty of open space, but over the centuries the blocks were filled in. A similar encroachment happened to Savannah's reserved open blocks. The market value of such land is simply too much of an allure, and political leaders are unable to reserve the land for public plazas and squares. Encroachment is a sign that the private realm has gained enough power and clout to overtake civic purpose.

Plazas and squares are often great examples of enclosure and the public outdoor room—outdoor space that is "formally disposed" and defined by building frontages. Some constraint is necessary. London's Wellington Arch was mocked for its undignified placement in a square surrounded by traffic and "cut up into irregular leg of mutton shapes" (a treatment that, one critic claimed, would not have been tolerated in Paris) (Figure 29.3). Even Camillo Sitte, the great champion of medieval irregularity, agreed that where plazas were too irregular, they were tortuous. A plaza's irregularity did not always translate to an art form, in other words. Blumenfeld was

Figure 29.3 Wellington Arch, London, UK. *The monument was ridiculed for its undignified placement in a square surrounded by traffic.*

Figure 29.4 Place de la Nation, Paris, France. *A plaza that is too large weakens the spatial experience, becoming more like a field than a plaza.*

more exact: a plaza has a "definite upper limit" of 450 square feet. Where it is much larger, such as the Place de la Nation in Paris (Figure 29.4) or the Civic Center in San Francisco, the spatial experience becomes "weak" and the plaza functions more like a field than a plaza.[6]

This exact dimensioning is less relevant where squares emerged more organically. The "artisan" example of the square can be seen in places around Barcelona (e.g., Garcia, Sant Andreu, and Poble Sec), which were agricultural estates that

Figure 29.5 Place des Vosges, Paris, France. *The perfectly equal-sided square focuses attention on the space rather than any particular architectural feature surrounding it.*

were urbanized by inserting a square, usually with a fountain and a market. Streets were eventually connected to the square, producing a grid to "ensure flows."[7] Or a square may have been incidental at first, a mere opening up of space in the city's site plan.

There are "squares" that don't function like squares at all, such as "Times Square." They are viewed as "amorphous" and not particularly valuable as an urban spatial experience. The amorphous square might be contrasted with the perfectly equal-sided Place des Vosges in Paris, where the equanimity focuses attention on the space rather than any particular architectural feature surrounding it (Figure 29.5). There is no "directional axis toward a culminating monument"—just perfect enclosure.[8]

Using the more formal definition of a square, there are two main types, the public square and the residential square. Renaissance Italy was a significant generator of the former, while France and especially England were generators of the latter. In Renaissance urban design, formal squares were inserted as islands of order in seas of medieval disarray, such as the Place Vendôme in Paris (Figure 29.6). The Renaissance plan for Pienza is said to be one of the earliest examples of Renaissance urban design—a square placed in the middle of a village (Figure 29.7). But its top-down conception (commissioned by Pope Pius II, as it was his birthplace) meant it was, according to Braunfels, destined for failure, because the square "never took on a life of its own."[9] A plaza that appears vastly over-sized was most likely scaled for military purposes, originally. The plaza in front of the tsar's Winter Palace in St. Petersburg is vast for exactly this reason. Paul Zucker criticized this kind of scale for public squares; because of their size, they were simply voids, not settings for civic life.

The intermittent placement of city squares was a way of organizing urban growth. Such systems varied in their centrality: the centrality of squares in Avola, Italy

Figure 29.6 Place Vendôme, Paris, France. *An island of order in a sea of medieval disarray.*

Figure 29.7 Pienza, Italy. *An example of Renaissance urban design that was criticized as top-down and lacking a life of its own.*

(Figure 29.8), can be contrasted with the placement of squares in Savannah and Philadelphia, which sought an even distribution. The American system of wards and squares tended to result in a more repetitive, perhaps egalitarian pattern, as opposed to an overall central focus. In New Orleans and Savannah, urban squares appear at regular intervals and serve to mark residential neighborhoods.

In the "habitually non-centric orthogonal array" that is the grid, squares were used as "points of emphasis." In Washington, DC's grid, these points of emphasis were fifteen squares symbolizing the fifteen states of the newly formed union. Washington's set of squares and monuments are thought to be less a unified and

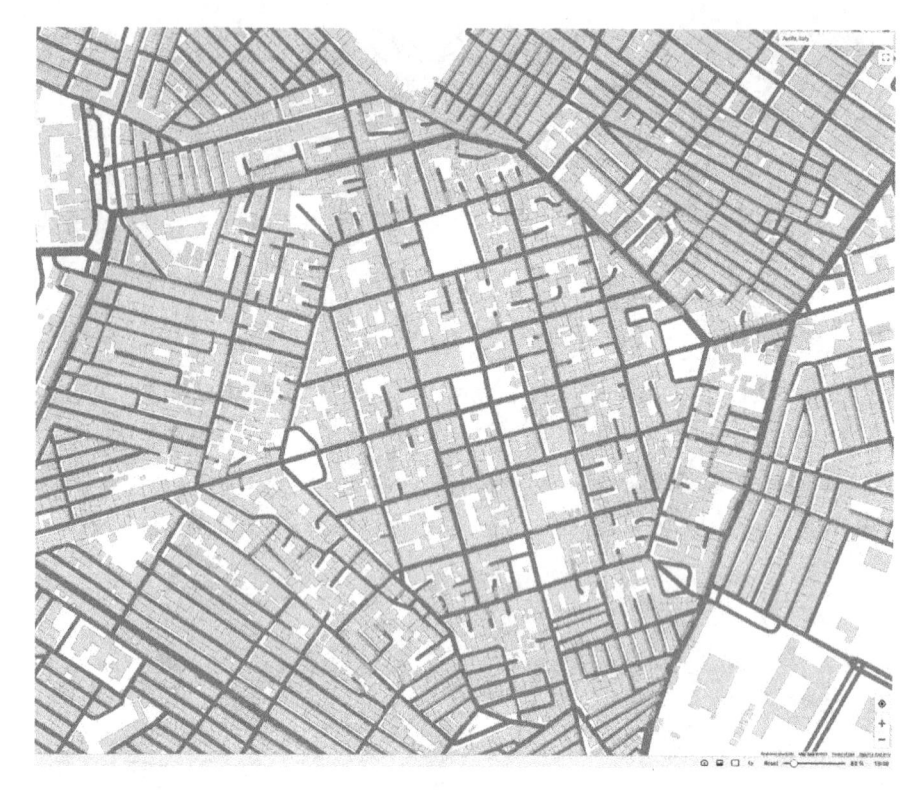

Figure 29.8 Avola, Italy. *The intermittent placement of city squares was a way of organizing urban growth.*

integrated whole and more like a set of detached monuments that, although positioned at the end of axes, do not seem to cohere.[10]

Small squares have the advantage that fewer functions around them are needed to activate them. And they can be created with minimal effort, for example by widening part of a street and situating buildings around to create spatial definition. In contrast, large open plazas in the city can seem bleak and wind-swept, requiring much more investment in activities to make them seem active. This is why Mumford argued that there was an intrinsic benefit to the burden of having to contend with crowded places and irregular topography: a plaza "became pompous and empty when the planner had limitless resources and no natural or human obstacles to overcome." Alexander et al. argued the importance of small civic spaces as an empirical matter: 70 feet across is the maximum at which it is possible to "make out the faces and half-hear the talk" of the people in a space. If kept below this dimension, people will feel at least "half-consciously tied together."[11]

What or who adjoins, and therefore dominates, an urban square is an important part of interpretation. At certain times in history—the Greek agora or the Roman forum—the central square had multiple functions, and civic life predominated. Medieval squares broke functions apart such that there would be a cathedral square outside of a central market square, and the former was subordinate to the latter.

Figure 29.9 Ieper, Belgium. *The cathedral, set in its own space down a narrow street, entices and surprises the visitor, who is compelled to look upward.*

The separated plazas around the market and the cathedral in Ieper, Belgium, is one example (Figure 29.9). There might have been pronounced and purposeful separation, with the marketplace forming a central square, while the cathedral, set in its space down a narrow street, would entice and surprise the visitor. The advantage was that the visitor would be "forced to look upward at the towering church with its torrent of sculptured figures." Some of the great public squares in Italy, such as the Piazza di San Marco in Venice, actually started as marketplaces around the approach to a church.[12]

Squares provide physical evidence of the importance of whatever adjoins, which is why Renaissance monarchs demanded a palace square. After the fall of monarchies and the rise of state power in the 19th century, vast squares were created in front of parliamentary and institutional buildings, which were settings for displays of military power. But the approach leading to and surrounding a plaza or square could be very different. There is an interesting contrast to be made between London's vs. Paris's most important monuments to military victories and heroism—London's Trafalgar Square (Figure 29.10) vs. Paris's Arc de Triomphe (Figure 29.11). Paris's monument has twelve avenues radiating from it, while London's has no surrounding axes. Braunfels interpreted London's lack of ceremonial approach to Trafalgar Square as "a symbol of national political self-confidence."[13]

Figure 29.10   Trafalgar Square, London, UK. *With no surrounding axes aimed directly at it, the monument to military heroism is understated and perhaps a symbol of political self-confidence.*

Figure 29.11   Arc de Triomphe, Paris, France. Paris's monument to military might has twelve avenues radiating from it, a sharp contrast to London's Trafalgar Square.

An important source on the topic of squares is Paul Zucker's *Town and Square: From the Agora to the Village Green*, where Zucker argued that the "physical and psychological function" of a square does not depend on the square's scale or size, it depends on whether the square's space as a "frame for human activities" is successful. This depends, in turn, on what surrounds it. Zucker argued that if a square is oriented around a central axis, then it is really a street; movement and vista dominate, not civic life. But if not aligned with an axis, the square can function like an outdoor room. In their book *Fundamentals of Urban Design*, Hedman and Jaszewski articulated why this matters. In an enclosed plaza or square, one has a feeling of being on "a stage" such that "every gesture suddenly becomes important." The surrounding buildings create the space, but they are "ancillary to a space that has become a separate entity." What the plaza creates is "a positive sensory experience that enhances the perception of self by giving each movement special significance." This builds sense of community, since those sharing the space are brought into a "perception of community" through a "heightened awareness of their physical relationship to others." Where there is no such enclosure, where space is vast, people are reduced to marginal entities "whose fragile position in the universe is laid bare."[14]

To complete the conception of a plaza or square's "firmness," it is necessary to limit the number of connecting streets. Having streets enter at the corners of a square (known as a turbine square), and preventing them from joining at each end, is a way of limiting through-traffic. On the other hand, limiting the entry points around a square can make the square seem more exclusive. The enclosure around the Place des Vosges suggests a special kind of inclusion for the residences lining the square, but the enclosure excludes everyone else. Inclusiveness might have happened if the square included more access points, such as at the 17th-century Place des Victoires in Paris (Figure 29.12). There, the surrounding neighborhood seems more integrated.

And yet the Place des Vosges did produce one kind of "integrating idea"—the aristocrats aligning their houses around the square formed a "background" for the monarchy. At least the noble families were acting as a collective to create an enclosed space, rather than establishing their own separated palaces. The idea became popular in England, but there are also American examples, such as Louisburg Square in Boston.[15]

London produced famous residential squares, such as Covent Garden, Grosvenor Square, and Bedford Square (Figure 29.13). They were resident-only—communal but not public—and yet they had an outsized ability to affect neighboring areas and functioned like mini-towns. Barnett labeled these squares a "bourgeois counterpoise" to royal power that tended to be focused on elements like the axis and the vista. They were stately, the equivalent of a palace courtyard. Rasmussen likened them to the interior garden of a convent (which, in fact, Covent Garden had originally been). The basic arrangement was predicated on the "form of the rural estate,"

Figure 29.12 Place des Victoires, Paris, France. *The square has multiple access points, which makes the surrounding neighborhood seem more integrated.*

Figure 29.13 Bedford Square, London, UK. *The residential square was the "bourgeois counterpoise" to royal power, the equivalent of a palace courtyard; identical buildings promoted social sameness.*

placing a centerpiece (square with garden) around which aristocratic townhouses developed. Above all, the residential square was a social segregator—houses fronting the square were all of the same social status. Identical building enabled social sameness, not, as in other instances, a uniformity intended to mask underlying social differences.[16]

30

Centers

What forms a city's center, its nucleus or core, says a lot about what is valued and who holds power. Its composition has changed dramatically over the centuries. In ancient cities, an elevated sacred precinct (the acropolis) might be joined to other religious buildings to form the city's "cultural nucleus," a physical expression of "permanence, continuity, accumulation." The center of Beijing, the temple city, was a product of ritual: rules that created a place for the emperor at the center, who was protected in the extreme (Figure 30.1). In Lingang New City, China, the center of the city is a lake. The buildings around it articulate a natural metaphor: concentric ripples of a pond expanding outward. Greenbelts inserted between each band of building are an attempt to merge city and nature (Figure 30.2).[1]

Centrality gradually usurped elevation as the primary means of expressing dominance. Previously, the Acropolis in Athens, which is not centralized, asserted importance by its location on a commanding hilltop. As the ancient world colonized, important buildings were "brought down" and integrated with the town. The urban fabric thus began to establish a closer dialogue between temple and town, between the sacred and the profane.[2]

There was also the agora ("no mere public place"), whose importance was revealed by its placement as close to the center of the town as possible, or near the port if it was a harbor town. It was sized according to the population served ("neither too small nor too large"), implying a static quality, as if the population count would never change. Centralized placement, and the fact that streets ended at the agora rather than crossing it, was indicative of how the Greeks put communal life above private home life. It was this social function that meant the agora's importance gained "at the expense of the acropolis," and eventually it became the most important part of the city.[3]

Later throughout Europe, it was the cathedral that was at the center, especially in small towns. These "skyscrapers of God" were admired by no less a modernist than Le Corbusier, who called the small cathedral town "an act of optimism, a gesture of courage, a sign of pride, a proof of mastery!"[4] The cathedrals were meant to be seen from miles outside of town, an expression of dominance, or, as Lefebvre interpreted Europe's great cathedrals, a "political act." The imposing dome of Santa Maria del Fiore in Florence, Italy, the only part of town seen distinctly from a great distance, accomplishes this supremacy, providing identity and gravitational pull at the same time (Figure 30.3). The rules for cathedral placement in the *Laws of the Indies* had the same objective but used placement and content alongside size and height to

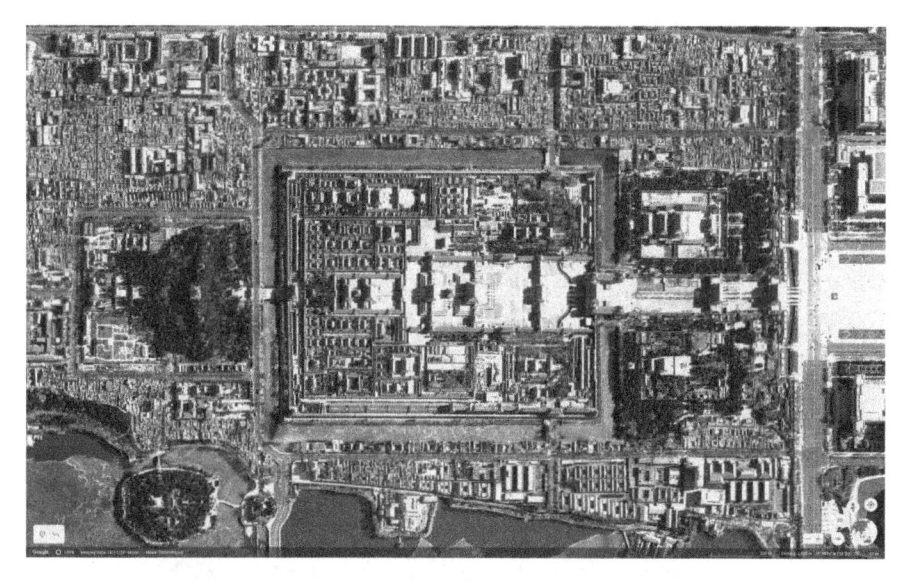

Figure 30.1 Imperial City, Beijing, China. *The emperor's protected center was a product of the ritual of progressive access.*

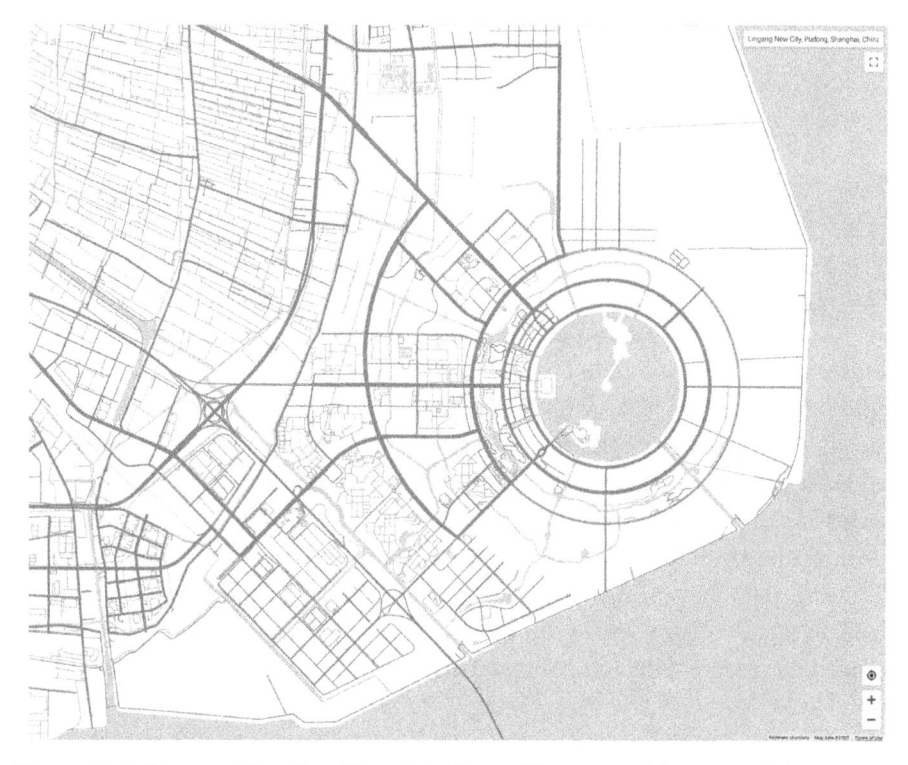

Figure 30.2 Lingang New City, Shanghai, China. *The center of the city is a lake, a metaphor for the merger of city and nature.*

Figure 30.3 Santa Maria del Fiore, Florence, Italy. *The imposing dome, which can be seen from a great distance, provides identity and gravitational pull.* Credit: PROPOLI87, CC BY-SA 4.0 <https://creativecommons.org/licenses/by-sa/4.0>, via Wikimedia Commons.

express dominance: "the church should not stand on the perimeter of the square, but at such a distance as to appear free, separate from other buildings . . . in this way it will appear more handsome and more imposing."[5]

The central plaza was especially important under the *Laws of the Indies*. Although the *Laws* dictated street pattern and the location of important buildings, the central plaza, Kostof argued, was "the key to the entire settlement." The civic prominence of the central plaza was evident in the requirement that the most important buildings had to front the plaza, with more noxious uses relegated to the edge of the city. The size of the plaza was based on what was considered best for festivals with horses involved: the length one and a half times the width (600 feet by 400 feet was considered a well-proportioned medium-sized plaza). The four streets extending from each corner of the plaza were to be arcaded for market stalls and pointed toward the cardinal directions to minimize wind.[6]

Plazas were often unambiguously centered, but city centers could also grow out of other considerations. For example, a town center might be adjacent to water rather than geographically central, for reasons having to do with trade. New Orleans' Jackson Square is an example (Figure 30.4). This practical application can be contrasted with Indianapolis' center, the Soldiers' and Sailors' Monument, which

Figure 30.4 Jackson Square, New Orleans, Louisiana, USA. *A town center might be adjacent to water rather than geographically central, for reasons having to do with trade.*

Figure 30.5 Soldiers' and Sailors' Monument, Indianapolis, Indiana, USA. *A tall monument marks the city center, but the space can feel static.*

stands as an exclamation point marking a spot (Figure 30.5). Such centers tend to be passive and static rather than places of active participation in public and social life. The symbolic importance of a center is emphasized by forcing roads to lead to it. A baroque city might have streets driving "headlong" into its center, symbolizing the centralization of power. The clearly demarked center of the Renaissance city

Figure 30.6 Vitry-le-François, France. *The bastioned walls are still visible, but the center, with four avenues leading to it, is the most important part of town.*

Vitry-le-François, with four surrounding avenues leading to it, provides an unequivocal sense that the center is the most important part of town (Figure 30.6). Garden cities and suburbs (e.g., Mariemont, Ohio), built in the early part of the 20th century, often use the same device—diagonal roads leading to a central place, which also offers a relief from the surrounding grid. Such a physical declaration of centrality can be contrasted with the weak center of Letchworth Garden City, which Peter Hall described as "a terrible mess." The streets leading to it seem to go nowhere.[7]

The strategy of pointing roads to the center as a way of declaring importance contrasts with the approach of the medieval city. There, the center was created by the "opposing forces" of protection and attraction—a place of civic confluence that was at the same time protected by a surrounding labyrinth of irregular streets. Only a few streets came together in the center of town. This did not diminish the symbolic importance attached to the central square, which was the key to the whole social structure of the town. It maintained centrality by ensuring that

Figure 30.7 Veurne, Belgium. *Despite being a medieval merchant town, public buildings were arranged around a stately central square, which anchored and centralized social life.*

the surrounding structures fronting the square were imposing. One example is Veurne, Belgium, where, despite exemplifying "the medieval conception of a business town," all manner of public buildings were arranged around a stately central square, which anchored and centralized social life (Figure 30.7). The center was the place where a sense of community, and the whole identity of the town, was physically rendered.[8]

Yet the city center was not uniformly a place for boisterous civic life. In the medieval town, open space at the center could also be reserved for a monastery, which provided the crowded town with a "spirit of enfolding and protection." It was an opportunity for "isolation and contemplation" in the heart of the city. To Mumford, these "forms of escape" were what made the city more than a "camp," in contrast to modern cities, which he critiqued as lacking places for quiet solitude.[9] Later, garden cities sought contemplative centrality by putting green space at the core—although this generated ambiguity about ownership, control, and identity.

The placement of a square at the city center has been common for centuries: Spanish colonial town planning required them, William Penn established them for Philadelphia, James Oglethorpe for Savannah, and hundreds of centralized courthouse squares were established for towns throughout the United States. Robert Veselka analyzed the latter case in Texas, where the square, with its "symbols and rituals," had strong symbolic importance. There was no ambiguity that it was meant to be a physical expression of community life and "shared values"—but it was also meant to be authoritative, with mixed success. In the American colonial period, local governments needed to be established and, absent a town, counties simply built courthouses and hoped that a town would eventually form around them. The Gloucester Courthouse was successful in stimulating this adjacent urban context (Figure 30.8), but King William County was not (Figure 30.9). The latter, an

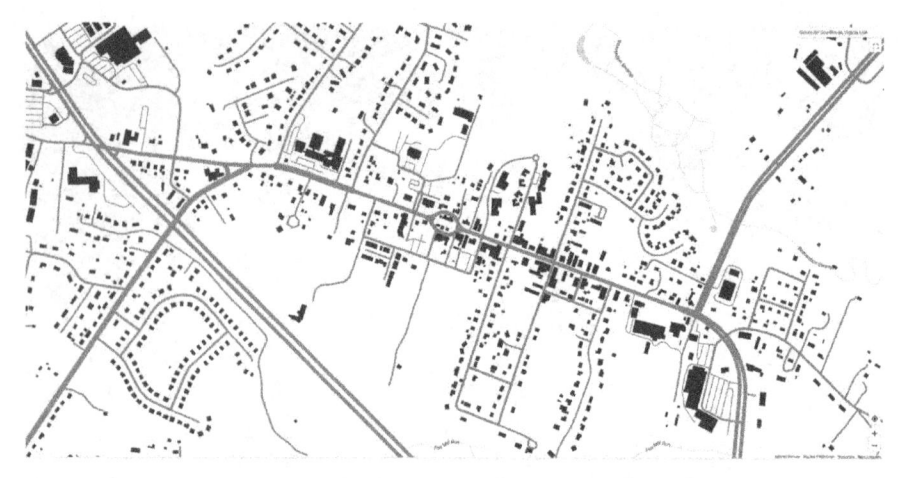

Figure 30.8 Gloucester Courthouse, Virginia, USA. *Absent a town, county governments built courthouses and hoped that a town would form around them. The Gloucester Courthouse, within the center circle, was somewhat successful.*

Figure 30.9 King William County Courthouse, Virginia, USA. *Unlike Gloucester, a surrounding town never materialized, and the courthouse stands in the middle of the county as a solitary, unanchored symbol of government.*

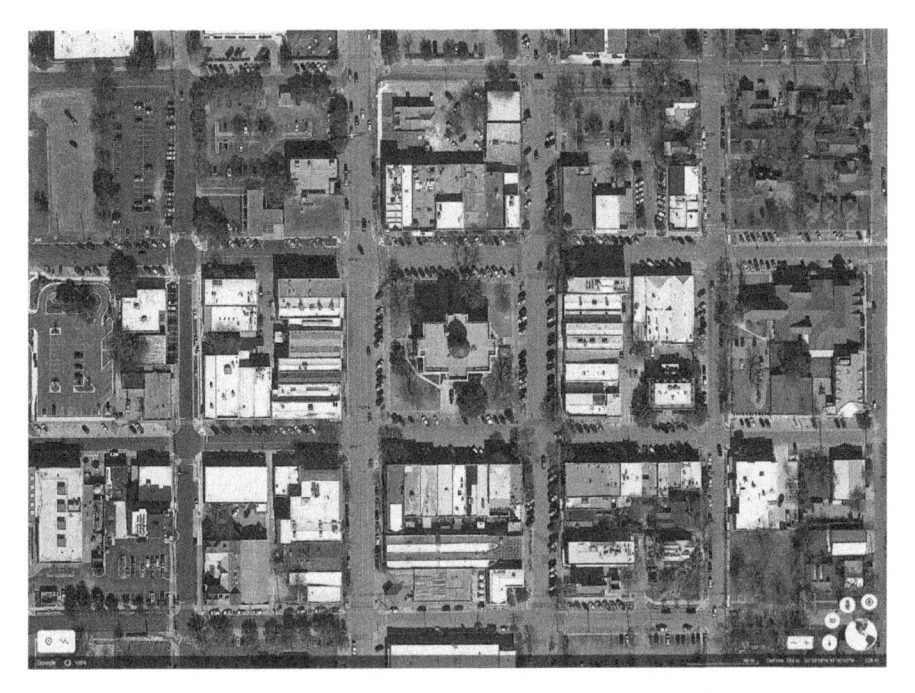

Figure 30.10 Williamson County Courthouse, Texas, USA. *A predominant courthouse square, where the streets converge on the site and the business district surrounds and frames it.*

18th-century courthouse, stands in the middle of the county—a solitary, unanchored symbol of government.[10]

Courthouses were especially important in the American frontier because they were the place of legal authority, and therefore civic legitimacy. Veselka worked out the subtle differentiations in courthouse square design and what they meant. Courthouse squares are "predominant" if they have a central focus, occupying "an honored space for civil authority" in which they "dominate their townscapes." "Codominant" squares share their civic role with another site, such as a city hall. "Subordinate" squares lack focus, and their role in the life of community is ambiguous, owing to their removed locations. An example of a predominant courthouse square is Williamson County, Texas (Figure 30.10). The courthouse square has streets converging on the site, and the town's central business district surrounds and frames the square, reflecting "numerous connections and affective ties" with the community. In contrast, the subordinate square at Mertzon sits on a hilltop, which is the only feature it dominates (Figure 30.11). It is physically, symbolically, and practically removed from community life. One wonders if the decline of the courthouse square as the defining center of a town symbolizes a loss of faith in commonality and shared values.[11]

Perhaps collective identity, reflected in a center, would be more relevant at the smaller scale of a neighborhood as opposed to a whole city or town. In a smaller setting, the center might be more realistically interpreted as a physical expression

Figure 30.11 Mertzon, Texas, USA. *The subordinate square sits on a hilltop (in circle at center), which is the only feature it dominates.*

of social connectedness. At least symbolically, where all paths in the neighborhood lead to the center, the outward goal could more realistically be to strengthen the "bonds of community." The neighborhood center provides a visible, literal focal point, and perhaps a permanent symbol of the common bond that people living in the same neighborhood share. This is why centers are believed to be more important than boundaries in neighborhood definition.[12]

In sharp contrast to a neighborhood center, or to the historical urban experience in general, the nucleus of the modern city has evolved into a cluster of downtown skyscrapers that overpower any centralized experience in the form of a cathedral, plaza, or square. Starting in the late 19th century, commercialism "aggressively disrupted" what had been the established hierarchy for centuries, in which civic and religious buildings dominated the center (and the skyline). The transformation began in the late 19th century, starting as a single cluster of tall buildings, but evolving into several clusters, for example in Milan, Italy (Figure 30.12). The multi-center skyscraper city is a monument to commercialism, to the power of money, and to centralization itself. Gutkind thought that it created a class of "slaves" in the surrounding residential zones, who became governed by a "despotic force" (money)— "the old game of ruler and ruled, but with other symbols."[13] But is the downtown the centralization of power for the few, or a consolidated source that emanates outward and distributes power to the surrounding domains?

Figure 30.12 Milan, Italy. *The multi-center skyscraper city is a monument to commercialism.* Credit: Daniel Case, CC BY-SA 3.0 <https://creativecommons.org/licenses/by-sa/3.0>, via Wikimedia Commons.

The existence of the modern intensive core, which in the span of history is a recent phenomenon at least in terms of the height differentials involved, signals an intense competition for centrality. In raw economic terms, it is the result of land value gradation—Alonso's bid-rent theory. Centralized access is the key to corporate profits, reflected in a steep gradient of land values moving outward from the center. Blumenfeld thought that the "fantastic skyrocketing of land values" that created the crowded agglomeration at the center starting in the 19th century was an aberration and essentially the result of a "time lag" between interurban and intraurban traffic that had since been overcome. The end of the time lag translated to more dispersion, although the skyscraper core remained strong.[14]

We can also read the skyscraper downtown as living proof of the success of private over collective interests, the ability of corporations to completely overpower the city core. This need to be "close to the action" creates vertical monumentality, with powerful corporate owners vying for inclusion in a relatively constrained area. Central Business Districts—the "CBD"—are thus a feature of business life, not public life. The result is often a fragmented kind of urbanism, a free-for-all expression of capitalist interests that is unlikely to offer something representative of the city as a collective, social enterprise. There's a lack of stability, too—the skyscraper core, like capitalism, needs to constantly reinvent itself and build the world anew.[15]

CBDs, which constitute the modern urban center, might seem overpowering and too big to fail, but they can be vulnerable. The COVID-19 pandemic created an implosion of office and retail demand in the urban core, demonstrating the core's lack of resilience and a reminder that the CBD's dominance can be challenged. Cultural shifts in preference can also undermine a once-dominant core. In Hong Kong, a wealthy class previously obsessed with the "fetish of centrality" is now increasingly interested in the "cult of isolation" at the periphery (Figure 30.13). Their gated and walled communities are not so much about keeping others out as they are about creating a spatial distinction that elevates the importance of life inside, rather than outside the home.[16]

This is not to say that modern skyscraper downtowns are the only instances where money and private interests dominated the center. From the Greek agora to the medieval town square, centers were marketplaces. In the medieval bastides, the access points to the central marketplace were restricted to just four entrances, at which fees could be collected—making the center, although public and ceremoniously marked, primarily a revenue source. Over the centuries, this function has been constant. Whether a downtown skyscraper core or a medieval central marketplace, what the center demonstrates is the success of consolidated wealth: corporations or merchants vying for centralized locations as validation of their importance and outsized role in the life of the city.

There are those who don't think much of the city center to begin with. One expression of this is the critique that centralized institutions in the heart of a city is a significant barrier to human progress, because consolidation limits access. The antidote, the imperative, is decentralization.[17] Taken to extremes, as in the case of American sprawl, one's private home is the center of one's "city" life, in which case there really is no need to prioritize a physical urban center.

Figure 30.13 Hong Kong, China. *A wealthy class previously obsessed with the "fetish of centrality" is now increasingly interested in the "cult of isolation" at the periphery.*

Figure 30.14 Librino, Sicily, Italy. *Meandering open space, a rejection of centrality, and a vegetative framework were supposed to embody organic growth, but green spaces were left unimproved.*

There is an interesting case of outright rejection of centrality that was tried for the new town of Librino in Sicily (Figure 30.14). Built in the 1970s, it used meandering open space to connect its buildings and purposefully exclude a center. The idea was that a natural vegetative framework was more aligned with the design philosophy of "metabolism"—a city of flexible, expandable structures that somehow embodied the processes of organic growth. Unfortunately, such ideologically motivated schemes fail if the money required to support them runs out, which it almost always does. Librino today is a poor area with a poor reputation, where people improvise their social space in streets or unimproved green space.

31

Government

Government buildings like courthouses might constitute a city center, but the location and centrality of government functions is a broader topic. Where government is positioned is a political message. In Putrajaya, the administrative capital of Malaysia, the location of the executive branch is not only superior to that of the legislature, but it turns its back on it (Figure 31.1). Executive functions are removed from "the gaze" of the legislature, considered a "profoundly political action."[1]

Sometimes government structure is manifested explicitly. In Suzhou, China, the central focus of the city was a walled and moated government complex, around which there was a relaxed grid (Figure 31.2). Kostof admired the plan because it was not as rigid as other capital cities, and instead offered "a supple rhythmic complexity free of dogmatic symmetry" complete with zigzags and looping streets. Although the plan was "clearly premeditated" and "executed according to precise calculations," the straight streets vary in their length; the blocks, although rectangular, are not uniform. Kostof interpreted this as evidence of the "loosening up" of the usually more rigid administrative Chinese city before the 10th century. It might even reflect a more relaxed form of control over citizens.[2]

In more recent times, there are, in general, two types of capital cities, classic and modernist. The classic model has nodes that distribute functions along connected axes. Washington, DC, St. Petersburg, and Canberra are of this type. The modernist mode—Brasília, Islamabad, Chandigarh—relies on a hierarchical road system, and with a corresponding low density, concentrates government functions in a single complex.[3] Dominance is indicated wherever roads converge. Symbolism is reflected in the degree of centrality and in the connections and hierarchies between important buildings and places.

Above all, where a national capital city is explicitly founded as such, it is an opportunity to render a nation's system of government in material form. Washington, DC, is partly this, but it doesn't go all the way. It has been critiqued for missing the opportunity to truly reflect the American system of government. Why, for example, isn't the Supreme Court located more prominently, perhaps where the Lincoln or Jefferson Memorials are located, instead of being embedded in a cluster of buildings?[4] The Brazilian capital, Brasília, was more successful in this regard, reflecting political structure explicitly. The dominant central axis organizes political power and reinforces the hierarchy of government bureaucracy.

With capital cities, "cultural codes" can be forced on a populace in top-down fashion. The resulting structure can seem artificial and not reflective of the

What Cities Say. Emily Talen, Oxford University Press. © Oxford University Press 2024. DOI: 10.1093/oso/9780197647769.003.0032

Figure 31.1 Putrajaya, Malaysia. *Government sites are positioned to give a political message: the location of the executive branch (foreground) is superior to—and turns its back on—the legislature (background).*

embedded values that would likely emerge if city-building proceeded incrementally. The "vernacular city" struggles to survive. A difficult balance is required since a capital city needs to represent an entire country, which is often quite diverse, but also exhibit a "metaphor of unity" that might be described as "contrived." Paradoxically, the capital city has to express openness and accessibility in the face of hierarchy, power relationships, and bureaucracy. The "capital T" form is thought to be good at this, expressing both openness and hierarchy, for example in Ottawa, where all government buildings are situated in relation to whatever building is designated as the "chief artifact" (Figure 31.3).[5]

Ideal cities that were actually built, and that were not primarily intended as a commercial venture, are rare, but they express political values in built form. Notable examples are from the Renaissance—Livorno, Sabbioneta, and Palmanova. As Argan argued, "the ideal city was, in fact, an artistic and political invention of its time, founded on the principle that the perfect architectural and urban form of the city corresponded to the perfection of its political and social arrangements." They were cities that reflected "the plans of theoreticians," based either on ideals about utopian government or on ideals about the military.[6]

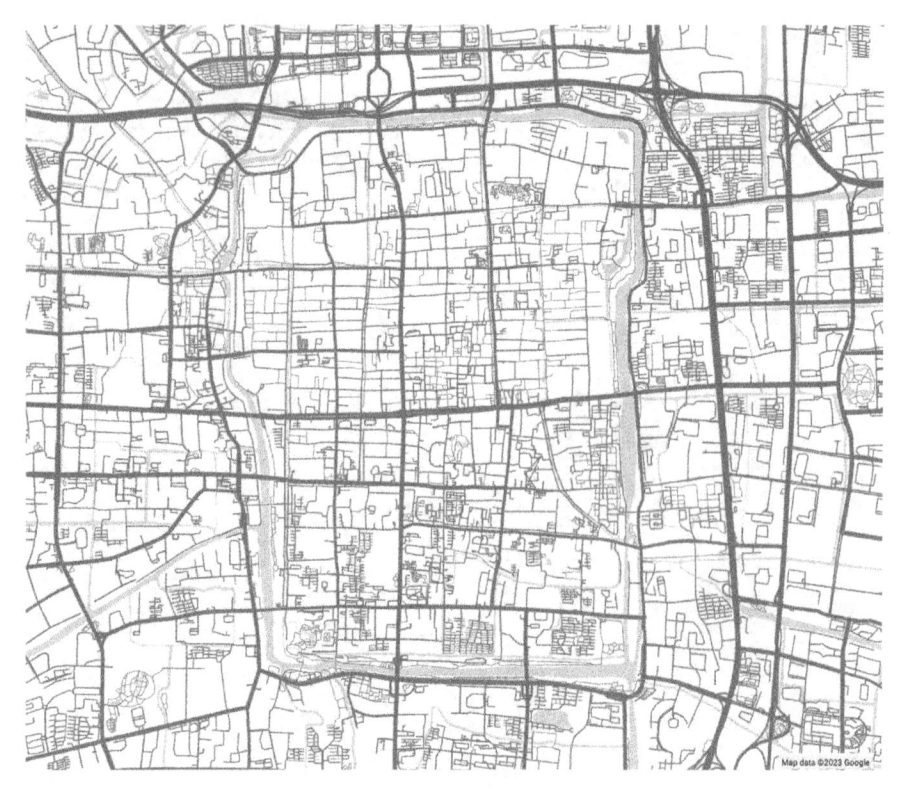

Figure 31.2 Suzhou, Jiangsu, China. *A relaxed, although precisely calculated grid possibly reflected a more relaxed form of control over citizens.*

Figure 31.3 Ottawa, Canada. *A capital city might seek to express openness in the face of hierarchy. The "capital T" form is thought to express both.*

Renaissance city planning ideals eventually translated to capital cities throughout Europe. The construction of settings for state authority represented a complete transformation of the medieval city. Cities began to express political power in new ways, orienting themselves to a new urban elite that was not spread among a merchant class but was dominated by perhaps a single family or despot with complete control and power. This was very different from the old urban middle class that had united merchants and craftsmen in medieval towns. It follows, then, that the city plans of the 15th and 16th centuries saw the birth of cities conceived in ideal form, supported by a city planning science that separated the liberal arts from the mechanical arts, and that was put in service to governments and their political aims.[7]

32

Towers in a Park

While baroque plans asserted power horizontally, 20th-century monumentalism was vertical, although the practice of using tall buildings as expressions of power and of "a great, visible ego" has a long history. The quest to "articulate oneself politically by means of large buildings" was, according to Braunfels, something the Italians during the Renaissance were especially adept at. Italians asserted that this was an example that their politics had "pride of place."[1]

By the late 19th century, the skyscraper had ushered in a new level of vertical monumentalism. The power revealed by a skyline was exclusively corporate and commercial. For a time in the early 20th century, City Beautiful proponents thought that their expansive baroque plans could compete with the vertical commercial city. Perhaps the integration of horizontal monumentality, they reasoned, could help resolve the incongruity between the commercial and the civic city. But the effort failed. Tall buildings signified freedom, liberty, gumption—they were understood as "monuments to entrepreneurial daring." Le Corbusier was convinced that the skyscraper created the utmost in individual liberty because, guided by the laws of geometry and technological perfection, it freed people from "ignorance and conflict."[2]

Tall buildings set in parks were that much more visible as monuments to rationality and the "rule of reason." But Jacobs saw towers set in open space differently: as a celebration of "the potency of statistics and the triumph of the mathematical average." It was another example of segmenting, sorting, and viewing the city as a problem of disorganized complexity. For Mumford, the tower symbolized machine living, the monotony and regimentation of human life by invisible corporate forces. It signaled the rule of bureaucracy, "an illusory image of freedom at the very moment all the screws of organization are being tightened."[3]

It is hard to read towers set in parks as manifestations of individual liberty, since they separate people from the ground and therefore their surroundings—a separation that extends, potentially, to their sense of place, their sense of belonging, and their sense that their individual actions matter. Social and civic life tends to become an afterthought, or forced. This is why urban districts composed of high-rise living are regularly interpreted as places where people are alienated from each other and from the outside world. Given the distance between home and the outside, accessed only via elevators, there is no natural or easy social mingling: one must have a dedicated reason to venture out and socialize, and the extra effort needed means that people tend to stay sheltered inside. Being cut off from the

What Cities Say. Emily Talen, Oxford University Press. © Oxford University Press 2024. DOI: 10.1093/oso/9780197647769.003.0033

Figure 32.1 Prairie Shores, Chicago, Illinois, USA. *Isolated buildings, lined up like dominoes.*

Figure 32.2 Parkchester, The Bronx, New York, USA. *An early rendition of "towers in a park," built in the 1940s, before Stuyvesant Town.*

ground is, in other words, alienating and impersonal. This is why Christopher Alexander advocated a four-story limit for apartments, for "connection to the ground and to neighbors."[4]

But if set in parks, skyscrapers can be thought of as a reconciliation between density and green space: the ground has been "freed" for greenery. There is certainly a bold symbolism expressed in a skyscraper set in green space. One is seclusion—or isolation. Each building is an island or, if lined up in succession like Chicago's Prairie Shores, a domino (Figure 32.1). Parkchester in New York was an early cluster of towers in a park, built in the 1940s (Figure 32.2), followed by Stuyvesant Town. High-rises set in parks were not garden city decentralization, but there was a certain relationship between the two concepts, as both involved trying to get nearer to green space.

Which is preferable, parks in cities, or cities in parks? There are different ideas about how "open" the city should be—dense and compact with intermittent open spaces, or open green landscape with buildings set within. If the latter, one has to worry about how such buildings engage the street, although, according to Le Corbusier, skyscrapers are simply vertical "streets in the air."[5]

There was a good rationale for towers in parks, some argued. The 20th-century habit of setting towers in green space was a response to congested urbanism that needed opening up. For Le Corbusier, the ideal was not just a tower in a park: aspirationally, he wrote, "the whole city is a park," a sentiment not unlike what proponents of garden cities and suburbs believed. Founders of Ocean Grove, New Jersey thought of the whole development as offering "Edenic nature" and thus reasoned there was no need to designate parks (later, parks were developed in leftover land near railroad tracks or small unusable parcels). Ecoville, an edge city of Curitiba in Brazil, manifests the Corbusian vision, but since the towers are set in private parks, the result is a vertical gated community, a "controlled and exclusionist" approach to collective life. There is no way to aggregate park space, no way in which a community-oriehted sense of space might be formed (Figure 32.3).[6]

In more technologically constrained eras, the city was opened up by inserting boulevards and urban parks. This provided benefits to other sectors of urban life, such as helping to move traffic or provide settings for commerce. But towers in parks seem only distantly related to what transpired in cities like Paris where the quest to bring green space into the city inspired widened boulevards. Towers set in parks are a whole other category: landscape becomes the structural basis of urbanism, eclipsing the usual elements of streets and blocks.

Figure 32.3 Ecoville, near Curitiba, Brazil. *Towers set in private parks: there is no way to aggregate park space to create a community-oriented sense of space.*

The difference between the towers in a park approach to greening and the City Beautiful movement is significant if viewed in terms of the rules of traditional urban form, where streets create blocks and buildings line streets. City Beautiful planners would have worried that their open spaces not become lifeless, since their primary concern was the civic realm. But the modernist isolation of buildings resulted, as Oscar Newman and others pointed out, in a disregard for the functional use of the spaces surrounding buildings.[7] Modernist planners did not seem to appreciate the crucial difference between visual open space and habitable open space, and thus they became like sculptors working in an unencumbered sculpture garden. They believed there was no misalignment, since buildings did not have to be subordinated to the urban fabric as a whole. Freestanding and competing towers could just vie for attention. This suited the commercial American city well. If there was enough capital, the individual building could be aggrandized even if it lacked civic, cultural, or religious significance.

But there was a problem—the park wasn't always a given, and, absent the park, the tower became something much less likable. Because of the failure to appreciate the importance of context and the need to create connectedness between buildings, buildings became ensconced in vast expanses of asphalt, useless plazas, and other forms of what Trancik labeled "lost space." Cultural centers of major US cities often exhibited the basic form of isolated buildings set in open space, part of a "master planned" project. And because they were "projects," they were, by definition, separated from the city. They were single-purpose and alienating, a product of open space that seemed unrestrained and purposeless. And they could hardly exhort much civic prominence if surrounded by acres of parking; their civic role became "muffled."[8]

The isolated building spawned all manner of non-standardized arrangements and patterns, creating a chaotic urban fabric that has now become a defining characteristic of sprawl. The American urban pattern plunges abruptly from edge city high rise to single-use residential development, creating a non-hierarchical city devoid of any clear pattern of spatial differentiation. The strangely named "Greenwood Village," an edge city outside of Denver, fits the description (Figure 32.4).

Jane Jacobs ridiculed this form of city-building, and for a time the model seemed universally disliked for all the reasons she identified: loss of eyes on the street and no sense of enclosure, for example. But after the turn of the 20th century, a new movement emerged that attempted to reactivate the towers in the park model. The movement known as "landscape urbanism" sought to employ nature's "indeterminacy and flux" to allow freely designed buildings as freestanding objects within a landscape, both buffering and unifying their individualism. Set in landscape, as in Shenzhen, unconstrained form-making was again possible (Figure 32.5). Rather than an urban fabric based on the spatial definition set by buildings, landscape would provide a new kind of "structuring medium." "The look and shape of the city" was to be a matter of "open space within which buildings are set."[9]

Figure 32.4 Greenwood Village, Denver, Colorado, USA. *A "village" in name only, the collection of towers in parking lots lacks spatial differentiation.*

Figure 32.5 Wuzhou Guest House, Futian District, Shenzhen, China. *Modern "towers in a park" exemplify the ideals of landscape urbanism.*

City-building in Northeast Asia has embraced the tower in a park model full-steam. Global city developments like Lingang New City in China are mammoth-sized and sold to the public on the basis of being technologically and ecologically advanced. With green inserted everywhere, the attempt is to synthesize "the calm of the countryside" with "transnational bustle." And they are built fast. Speculative sky-scraper clusters exude "instant city making" that is "built to thrill" to reflect national pride and economic power—and to keep up with the West. Global corporations make money, and the city is rewarded with an impressive skyline. The speed squashes any hope of public input, and the scale is "megalomaniacal," but what the state sees is a reasonable response to an "emergency of national survival." Cities are in service to national interests, and macroeconomics has clearly overshadowed the needs of daily life. Rhetoric about local shopping and self-contained communities is still invoked, but the global outlook and dependency create an inescapable irony.[10]

33

Buildings and Settings

The siting of buildings has been touched on in several chapters already, but this chapter hones in on the context of, and linkages between, culturally significant buildings. How do we interpret the location of important buildings? Do civic buildings stand like individual monuments, or are they meant to be connected, or to form an ensemble? What can be interpreted from the connections between sites?

Sometimes buildings block a connection. Perhaps the blockage served some purpose, or the connection was not deemed especially important. Case in point: in Washington, DC, the Treasury Building blocks the view between the Capitol and the White House, indicating that the connection between these two major branches of government was not considered important, even symbolically.

Vitruvius's first-century treatise had dictated the location of temples and all other public spaces based on considerations like "the very highest point commanding a view" for the temples of gods, "under whose particular protection the state is thought to rest." Freestanding buildings and monuments would be reserved for places that deserved the highest respect. Centuries later, medieval churches commanded similar deference. They were often monumental, but even smaller churches were sited to symbolize their central role in the life of the town. Mumford lamented the focus on the church, however, because he thought it meant that "the polis" had "now shrunk to a church."[1]

As buildings increased in scale because of technological advances, they could dominate without being on higher ground. The acropolis was large, but it was its towering height that gave it gravitas. Later, if buildings were large enough, they could inspire awe even though they were on the same topographic level. Without this dominant scale, orientation and legibility could be lost. Barnett argued that the modest buildings at the center of Hempstead Garden Suburb lacked legibility for this reason. An original proposal for two large central churches was rejected, and the smaller size of the buildings meant that they could not be seen from many parts of the development. But the developers had argued that Hempstead was a suburb and was not meant to be a medieval village dominated by a church.[2]

Unlike baroque town planning with its precise notions of order and symmetry, the medieval church and adjoining square were not centered in a literal way. The only precision in terms of site design was that the nave of the church ran east to west and the altar pointed east, no matter the surrounding block context. This could make the church seem out of sync with its surroundings. For example, in Freiburg im Breisgau's cathedral square, the church was supposed to remain isolated, but

What Cities Say. Emily Talen, Oxford University Press. © Oxford University Press 2024. DOI: 10.1093/oso/9780197647769.003.0034

Figure 33.1 Freiburg im Breisgau, Germany. *The church was supposed to remain isolated, but development occurred around it, making it seem out of sync with its surroundings.*

development occurred around it. The result is that the spaces surrounding it seem to have no particular meaning or use (Figure 33.1).[3]

The linking together of important sites could create a certain unity. Argan wrote that the "historical-artistic basis" of the Renaissance city, exemplified by Rome, was that the form of the city was based on its monuments, such that "the monument assumed a dominant role in the context of the city; it became the focal point of Rome's urban perspective." With the linking of buildings, as monuments, it became possible during the Renaissance to think of the city as a totality and a collective form. This played out in the Pope's hometown and summer retreat, Castel Gandolfo, where a country village was transformed by arranging patrician palaces in relation to the cathedral. This created an architectural unity: an urban whole by way of linked buildings (Figure 33.2).[4]

Another kind of setting is created when radiating avenues terminate (or originate) at a particular point. According to Kostof, an early version of this idea derived from hunting grounds, where paths were cut through the forest and a central gathering spot was created (essential for cornering the stag). Later, round points manifested urban design theory about infinite space, with their avenues extending in all directions into a boundless horizon, space perpetually stretching outward. The round point with radiating avenues also had a military application, as at Palmanova, where centrally positioned troops could defend in all directions. Reps thought that the design was aesthetically pleasing as well, and thus "the desires of architects and military engineers coincided and blended."[5]

It is hard to think of a more explicit site design for expressing centrality and power than a radial pattern with all streets pointing to a particular location. But what streets might be pointing to varies significantly. Baghdad's radial-concentric

Figure 33.2 Castel Gandolfo, Italy. *Patrician palaces were arranged in relation to the cathedral, creating an urban whole.*

design was a political diagram, with a palace at the center. Pope Sixtus V used radiating avenues to focus attention on religious sites. In Hamina, Finland (founded 1723), all roads point to the Town Hall. The center of the radial plan of Karlsruhe, Germany, is a palace, so all roads lead to the prince.

But is it better, from the sovereign's perspective, to situate important buildings at the termination point of a main road such that they can be viewed from a distance, or should important buildings have their own enclosed precincts with deferential buildings surrounding and contextualizing them? The divergence in meaning is quite evident: axis and terminated vista are the language of power; enclosure is the language of collective life. Missing the distinction, American cities sometimes tried to simulate a terminated vista by awkwardly rotating a building on its axis, hoping to elevate the importance of a building otherwise obscured by its placement on a block with no particular distinction. More commonly, siting considerations were secondary. There seems to have been no great concern that large and important

Figure 33.3 Place de l'Opéra, Paris, France. *The ultimate case of "disencumbering": open on all sides, but also jammed in a hole and buried in a quarry.*

buildings, even in the largest US cities, could be viewed all at once from top to bottom. Obviously if this required clearing around a building, a practice known as "disencumbering," there was a significant cost to that.

The disencumbering of the Place de l'Opéra in Paris prompted vehement critique in the 19th century (Figure 33.3). The architect, Charles Garnier, was not happy with the treatment of his building in the least: "The Opéra [is] jammed into a hole, pushed back, and buried in a quarry!" He meant that there were too many openings in the plaza that the Opéra sat on; corners of plazas needed "firmness." To Sitte, a disencumbered building was "like a cake on a serving platter" and therefore artificial. Joseph Stübben, on the other hand, praised Paris's Opéra site as an example of a civic building capable of standing in "artistic relation" to the streets and allowing traffic to flow around it. He wrote that City Hall in Philadelphia (Figure 33.4) and Elisabeth Church in Vienna, with no such circulatory design, were "keenly felt hindrances" to traffic flow and examples of what not to do.[6]

Ultimately, disencumbering treats a building like a work of art. The cost is justified because "the millennial monuments" of history need to "loom gigantic in their necessary solitude." Unfortunately, what needed to be cleared from these works of art was often humble, but not necessarily unloved urban fabric capable of supporting everyday life. Entire neighborhoods were simply wiped away. A version of this was common under "urban renewal" in the mid-20th century, which essentially involved wholesale destruction of neighborhoods to produce unencumbered building sites, although the cleared sites were usually not for the purpose of disencumbering works of art.[7]

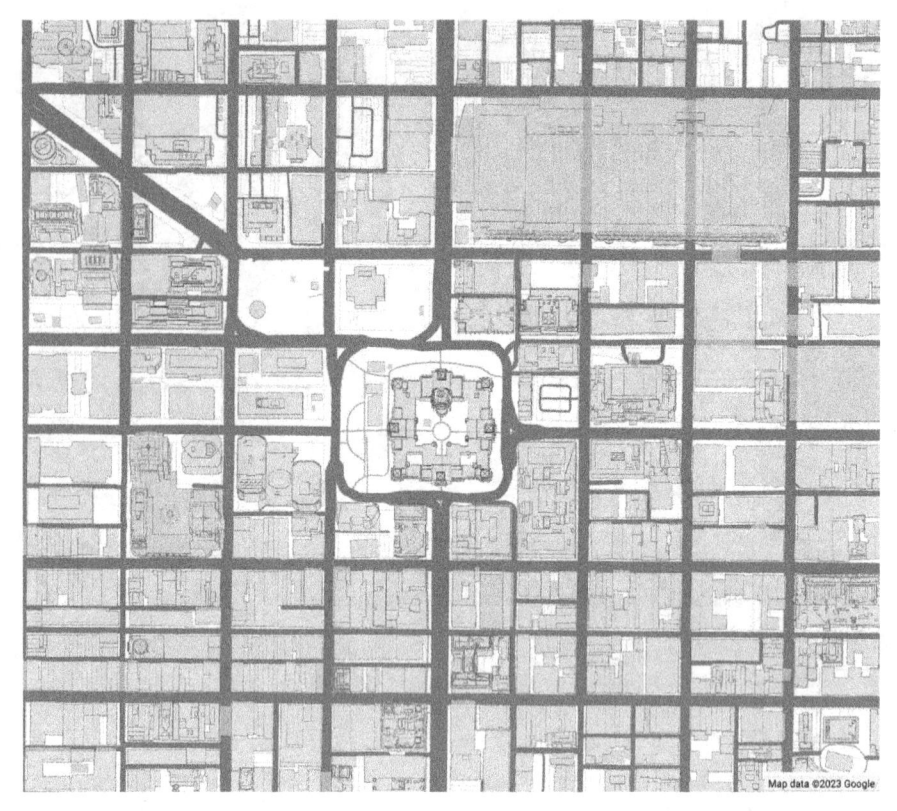

Figure 33.4 Philadelphia, Pennsylvania, USA. *Some early 20th-century planners lamented the hindrance to traffic flow posed by the placement of Philadelphia's City Hall.*

According to some critics, many modernist, object-buildings don't do well on unencumbered sites, and can only really be valued if they are embedded into, and embraced by, an exemplary surrounding urban fabric. In other words, they have a hard time standing on their own. Andrés Duany argued that this is why the star architects of the late 20th century "demanded" inclusion in the historic areas of London, Milan, St. Petersburg, Washington, and Paris, refusing available sites in modernist enclaves such as Crystal City, La Défense, and the Docklands because their buildings succeeded only when they parasitized traditional urban fabric. When placed among other object-buildings, they coalesced into a strada comica, as Rem Koolhaas eventually demonstrated with his Starchitect Collage.[8]

The position of the residence of a ruling authority, which is almost always monumental, is revealing. One can contrast palaces surrounded by walls and moats with the residences of monarchs and leaders with a much less dominant footprint. A castle can tower over a town (Heidelberg), or nestle within it (Urbino). Both the White House in Washington, DC, and the castle, Prinsenhof Delft, of William of Orange (the 16th-century "father" of the Netherlands), are large, but they do not dominate the city or command the center (Figure 33.5). Following

Figure 33.5 Prinsenhof, Delft, the Netherlands. *The castle of William of Orange is large but does not dominate the city or command the center.*

Figure 33.6 Zwinger, Dresden, Germany. *18th-century palace grounds were a theatrical stage set for the display of power and wealth.*

Machiavelli's logic about walls, a more physically embedded authority is an authority that is confident and secure.

At times the ruling class wanted to create a theatrical stage set for the display of their power and wealth. The buildings of Dresden's Zwinger, an early 18th-century palace grounds complex (meant to adjoin a palace that was never actually built)

Figure 33.7 Bessemer Park, Chicago, USA. *The civic importance of the fieldhouse is emphasized by its central placement, flanked by smaller buildings (although the stateliness of the setting was later disrupted by the construction of I-90).*

have been likened to a ballet: a pair formed from the oval pavilions, a quartet created by four salon buildings, a solo dancer as the ceremonial gate, and the orangery forming the chorus (Figure 33.6). Braunfels wrote that it is "the stage setting for a fantasy and the fantasy itself."[9]

But building placement can have meaning in the commonest of settings. Chicago developed a system of small parks in the early 20th century and building placement within these parks was meant to instill civic pride. The civic importance of the main building or fieldhouse, for example at Bessemer Park, was emphasized by its central placement at the end of an axis, flanked by smaller buildings—a kind of mini-version of the symbolically hierarchical placement of the US Capitol Building at the end of the Washington Mall in DC.[10] A major interstate (I-90) later disrupted the stately setting (Figure 33.7).

34

Enclosure

Enclosure is the principle of giving space dimension by using aligned building frontage (or some other element, like trees) as walls to create an outdoor room. This is important because the room created is public and thus can function as a setting for social and civic life.

Outdoor rooms come in lots of sizes, but sense of enclosure is thought to be lost if the ratio of street width to building height exceeds 1:3 (although some urbanists set the maximum ratio at 1:1). Noting the empirical regularities of the medieval plaza, Sitte prescribed the proper relationship: the width of a plaza was to be at least equal the height of the main building fronting it; the length of the plaza was not to exceed three times its width (this ideal proportion was also suggested by Alberti). Renaissance and Baroque plazas employed greater distances—an observer needed to stand back twice the height of a building in order to see the whole facade; a group of facades might require standing back three heights' worth.[1]

Spatial dimensioning was a conscious act in the Renaissance and Baroque periods, and the result was much vaster in scale than the medieval city, whose narrow streets and tight spaces provided more intimate settings for social life. Squares seemed literately carved into the medieval urban fabric, creating an extraordinary contrast and a bold statement that space was going to be treated differently than in medieval times. But if the proportions were off, enclosure was lost. In Paris's Place de la Concorde, for example, "space is almost completely released." The only group of buildings actually facing the square are across the river Seine. Considered much more successful is the Baroque era Piazza Navona in Rome, which is a spatial reproduction of Domitian's stadium (Figure 34.1). In the 16th century, Michelangelo designed the Piazza del Campidoglio (Capitoline Square) not as a void but as a "solid plastic space." An early Renaissance example, Florence's Piazza Annunziata, is said to exemplify the idea of "limited space at rest" and stands in stark contrast to later eras that were more interested in unlimited space (Figure 34.2).[2]

There is usually no sense of enclosure in suburban contexts. In the green and leafy picturesque settings of suburbs, three-dimensional space is irrelevant. This is why a common critique of the suburb is that it fails to use the street as a spatial element, whereby an outdoor room—a civic realm—can be created. Buildings are placed *within* space; they do not *create* space. Buildings are set in open land, and although people within the buildings gain immediate access to openness, the ability to define space and create enclosure is lost. Continuity in suburbia is by

What Cities Say. Emily Talen, Oxford University Press. © Oxford University Press 2024. DOI: 10.1093/oso/9780197647769.003.0035

Figure 34.1 Piazza Navona, Rome, Italy. *A Baroque reproduction of Domitian's stadium: spatial definition at its finest.*

Figure 34.2 Piazza Annunziata, Florence, Italy. *Space in solid form, said to be "at rest."*

way of linkages between open spaces, a "continuity of voids," as Choay wrote.[3] Value is based on the amount of light, air, and green space available, not on the creation of a public room. Houses are in their own private domains, and although they might present the illusion of collective ownership of the "park" they occupy, the park is not a setting that stimulates collective action. In the suburban context, green spaces are not so much contributions to public life as they are extensions of private life.

There are suburban exceptions. One early suburb, Bedford Park, was thought to provide a compromise—single-family houses that, through a common

Figure 34.3 Battery Park City, New York City, New York, USA. *A rejection of the "tower in a park" model, and a step toward enclosed space, lowered building heights, and aligned frontages.*

architecture and close relationship to each other and to the street, were in fact capable of containing the space in front of them. An "assembly of facades" can thus create a setting for the social life of suburbs, which, the theory goes, increases social connection because people are encouraged to linger in such spaces.[4]

Mid-century modernism with its towers set in parks was the opposite of enclosure. But there was a counter-response, toward the end of the 20th century, that sought a return to enclosure through lowered building heights and aligned frontages. This was reconstituted at a variety of urban intensities. At the urban core, there was Battery Park City (Figure 34.3). Further out, in more suburban locations, various New Urbanist developments, such as Prospect New Town, took up the "suburban wing of the enclosure movement" (Figure 34.4).[5]

The return of enclosure was in part a recognition of its economic advantage: enclosure makes use of every inch of frontage, which is valuable real estate. But it also shows respect for the public realm. If the frontage line is relatively straight, with no projecting buildings, it shows deference to the street and sidewalk and an acknowledgment of the street's role in the city's social life. Disciplined frontages work collectively, even when individually and privately owned. If, on the other hand, the frontage line is irregular, with buildings set back at a variety of distances, it makes the public space in front seem more ambiguous and less cared for.

A covered arcade (a series of arches) or a colonnade (a series of columns) can create an intimate form of enclosure for the pedestrian. In antiquity, these enclosure devices transformed streets into social spaces. A writer from 360 CE bragged about the colonnaded city of Antioch and how "bad weather," unlike in other towns, was unable to "interrupt our continuous intercourse." The English called these covered sidewalks "piazzas" because they were brought from Italy in the 17th century. Elbert Peets thought they were an oppressive invention. While they might have been "the

Figure 34.4 Prospect New Town, Longmont, Colorado, USA. *A New Urbanist new town takes up the "suburban wing" of the enclosure movement.*

height of civility" in the "pre-umbrella day," they blocked the sun from building interiors and were "an additional instrument of darkness."[6]

Enclosure does not require straightness, only alignment at the right scale. There are plenty of examples of enclosure on curved streets with aligned frontages (e.g., Bath, England). But where curvilinearity is associated with widely separated houses, such as in the curving street patterns of modern suburbs, even aligned frontages fail to create an outdoor room or the sense that private houses are working collectively to create a shared space.

With no buildings lining the street, there are no eyes on the street. And so, for Jane Jacobs, lack of enclosure meant a lack of safety because it meant that no one was watching the street. Mumford scolded Jacobs for prioritizing enclosure, and the street life and safety she thought it enabled, because, he argued, there was too much emphasis on its role in crime prevention. What, Mumford asked, should we make of the fact that 18th-century London met "all of Mrs. Jacobs' planning prescriptions," but it was a "nest of violence and delinquency"?[7]

35

Boundaries

Boundaries come in many forms, including walls, gates, greenbelts, highways, open land, and buildings. Many are innocuous, like the low stone walls of Ireland that demark property lines and keep the sheep enclosed. But where boundaries are meant to exclude and segregate, social control and superiority seem to be the objective. Protection and exclusion, in other words, go hand in hand.

Walls are the easiest to read, signaling some combination of protection, enclaving, or separation. Premodern walled cities were built for protection, but separation was a motivation too: there was to be separation of the sacred (wilderness) from the profane (human-built cities)—or, barbaric life outside the wall from the civilized dweller within. In contemporary culture, walled villages might still be about protection, not from marauding barbarians, but from people unlike those within. As Mumford put it, walls created an island effect that instilled "a fatal sense of insularity," where "unity and security reversed their polarity and passed over into anxiety, fear, hostility, and aggression."[1]

A more forgiving interpretation is that boundaries, even in walled form, help concentrate and contain the resources a city or neighborhood needs, ensuring that resources don't spill out. Boundedness is also an assertion that there is a natural limit to the size a human settlement is supposed to be. This is the Aristotelian concept of the city: boundaries are a rational form of control against city-destroying forces. In China, walls were considered sacred, like a cathedral, and cities were built from the periphery inward.[2]

There are many examples of cities that were once completely walled, although the original walls have usually been reduced to remnants. Where walls surrounded small settlements, such as Castelfranco outside of Venice, they gave the impression that life inside was fixed and definite (Figure 35.1). The Bastides throughout France were walled, as were villages in precolonial China. If the walls have survived, such places are now tourist attractions, perhaps because of the sheer novelty of containment. The walled city of Dubrovnik, with its 14th-century walls still intact, is one example, especially since it was used for the filming of *Game of Thrones* (Figure 35.2).

The medieval town was like a fortress, but its walls had significance beyond protection. According to Rykwert, they represented the uniting of heaven and earth, and breaching the wall meant you were severing that union. Walls thus represented both security and unity. As Rykwert wrote, "the wall was valued as a symbol as much as the spires of the churches." The town gates were also symbolic, marking the boundary between two realms, the rural and the urban. Medieval gates also had the

What Cities Say. Emily Talen, Oxford University Press. © Oxford University Press 2024. DOI: 10.1093/oso/9780197647769.003.0036

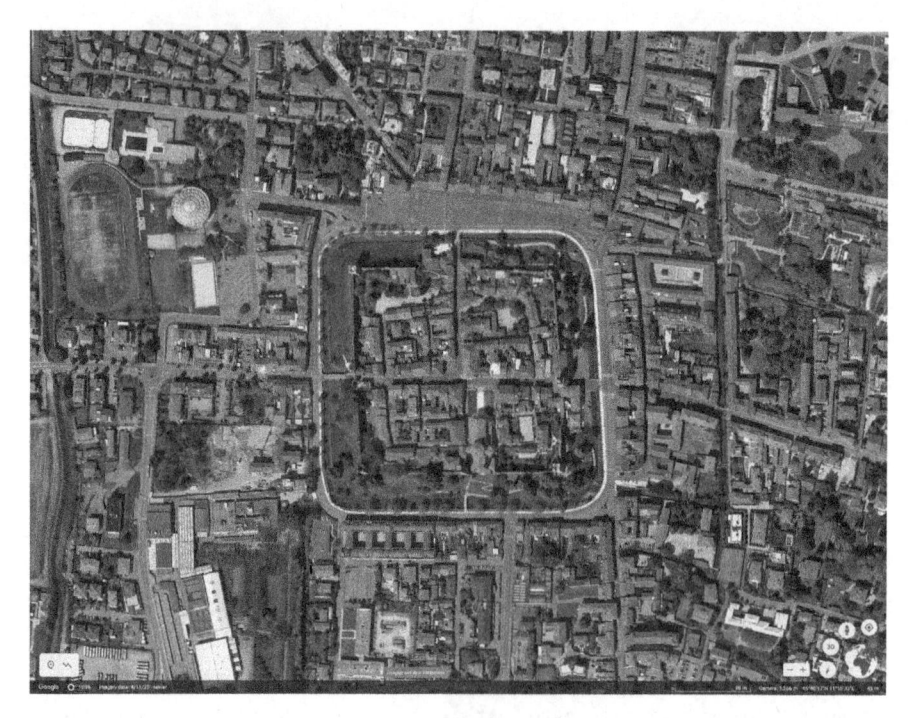

Figure 35.1 Castelfranco, Italy. *Walls gave the impression that life inside was fixed and definite.*

Figure 35.2 Dubrovnik, Croatia. *With its 14th-century walls still intact, the* Game of Thrones *city is being overrun with tourists.* Credit: Chensiyuan, CC BY-SA 4.0 <https://creativecommons.org/licenses/by-sa/4.0>, via Wikimedia Commons.

effect of creating economic districts around them, as the movement of goods and vendors tended to set up there. This had the added benefit of reducing congestion in the marketplace at the town center.

Boundaries always come with some means of entrance. Christopher Alexander liked the feeling of transition that "solid" gateways inspired and endorsed the practice of marking every boundary to help people understand the importance of transitions. If gates (in various forms) offer "slow, progressive access," such as the series of layered compounds one had to go through to reach Beijing's Inner City, then gated-ness becomes more of an experience—and more profound. As cities are no longer moated and gated, any civic space within the city can serve as a point of entry. A city railroad station or airport terminal might serve the entrance function.[3]

Like the medieval town, Renaissance cities were initially walled, for defensive purposes. By 1600, bastioned curtains were the walls of choice. These walls would be applied to both old and new cities, where they were encased in "an elaborate, often star-shaped, ring of pointed low-spreading bastions with an enormous physical reach." Kostof describes the layout as "a sunburst for warfare." Philippeville, Belgium (Figure 35.3), and Vitry-le-François, France ("Centers" chapter, Figure 30.6) are two examples where we can still see the imprint of these bastioned walls. Cities might be star-shaped or polygonal in terms of their overall shape, with thick sloping walls, but the interior of the city was gridded. Urban form was, as Argan writes, "purely instrumental"—dictated by defensive function. Star shapes and other geometric elements were abstractions with no social purpose other than defense.[4]

The phenomenon of these walled cities, ubiquitous in Europe by 1600, is interesting because of the new relationship between city and hinterland it expressed. It was, as Argan wrote, "A new interpretation of the relationship between the city in its enclosed form of volumetric unity and the surrounding territory." Earlier, in the 14th century, the countryside surrounding a town was considered "the natural

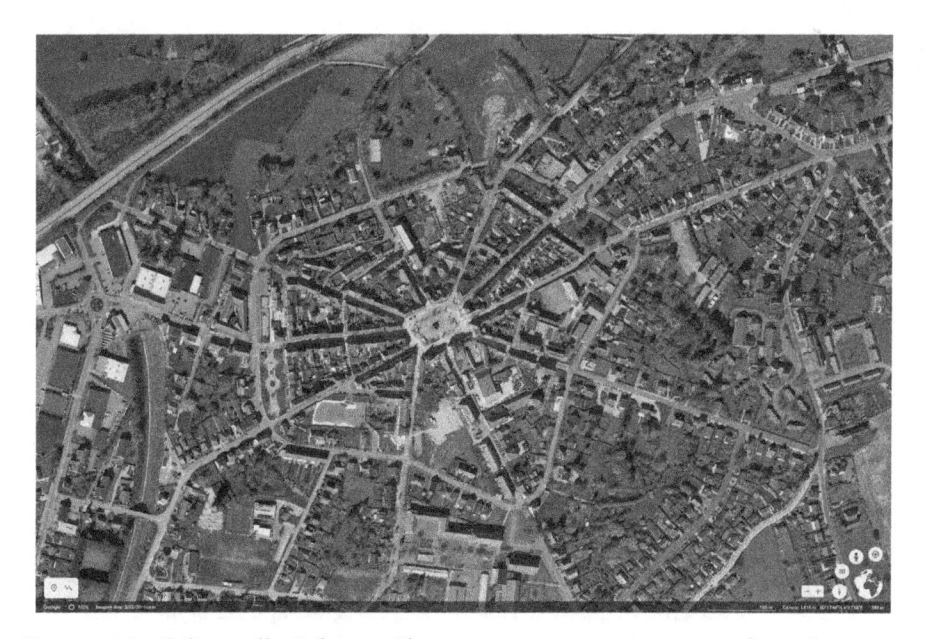

Figure 35.3 Philippeville, Belgium. *The permanent geometric imprint of war; the bastioned walls are now a ring road.*

complement of the city's economy and social life." But as walls became thicker and more complex, the city began to resemble "an armored coffer full of precious objects."[5] Elaborately engineered battlements created more physical distance between town dweller and the open land beyond, disrupting the close relationship between town and countryside that had long existed—and that had made compact living with scant internal open green space seem less problematic.

European ring roads, which emerged in the baroque period, entered the landscape after encircling city walls came down. They were often used as social separators. Vienna's Ringstrasse created a "Baroque sequence of spaces" out of its demolished fortification wall to create a ring that, ostensibly, was meant to connect its inner and outer parts (Figure 35.4). But the Ringstrasse created a barrier zone between the city center of the elite and the working-class suburbs beyond. Not only did this create significant traffic problems, but it separated classes. The "military insulation belt" had become a "sociological isolation belt." However, the massive undertaking has also been described as a "total work of art" not unlike a Brahms symphony, "a testimony to the self-confidence of the Danubian monarchy." Buildings were separated in the Ringstrasse's adjoining parks so that people could wander around them, look at them from a distance, and marvel at the greatness of Viennese culture.[6]

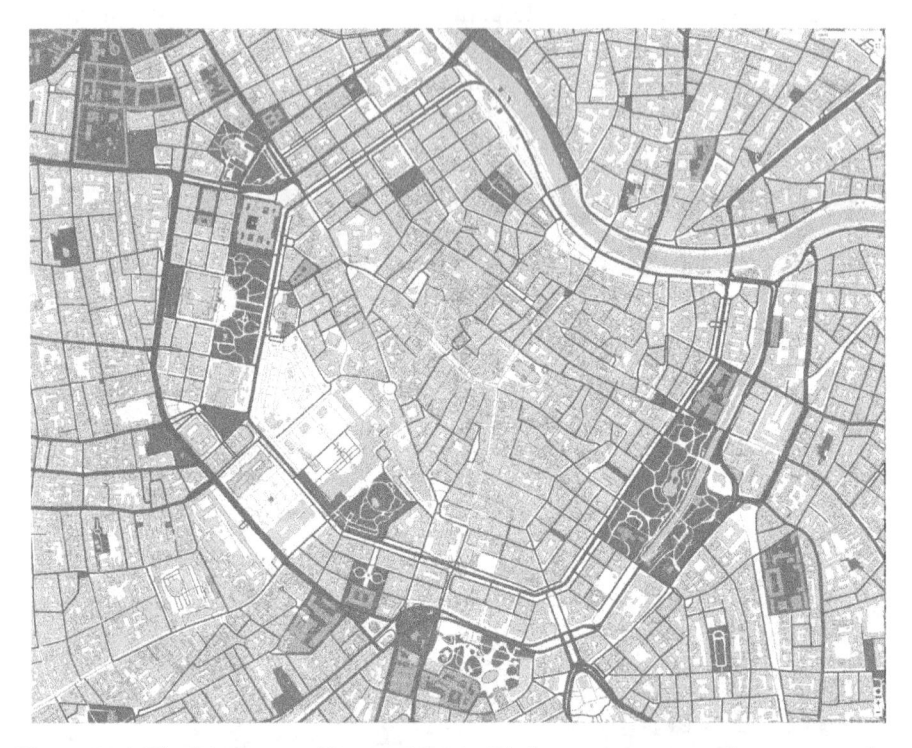

Figure 35.4 The Ringstrasse, Vienna, Austria. *The baroque sequence of spaces created a barrier zone, but people could marvel at the greatness of Viennese culture.*

Figure 35.5 Römerstadt, Germany. *Nature was integrated by putting a greenbelt between housing and industry; the green functioned as a "reservoir of recovery."*

These greenbelts are horizontal boundaries with ancient roots. Although initially they were used to keep the open countryside close to city centers, in later times, they provided recreational space. Jane Jacobs thought that the point of a greenbelt was simply to stop a town from ever becoming a city. But there was an ameliorative purpose, too. Socialist cities used greenbelts as boundaries that would delimit city from countryside, aiming to keep each realm pure, which aligned with socialist ideology. In Römerstadt, a German garden city built during the Weimar Republic, the greenbelt was "no bourgeois pleasure ground" but an insulating green that would function as a "reservoir of recovery." With "earth beneath their feet" people would be "confident and self-reliant" (Figure 35.5).[7]

While greenbelts are often conceived as recreational boundaries, highways and arterials, especially those slicing through cities, have no such claim. Highways are about mobility, but they are also great dividers, not unlike the moats around medieval cities. But unlike the protective moat, the highway is unlikely to benefit adjoining residents, who are forced to live with noise and emissions. Arterials are boundaries composed of wide roads meant only for traffic, creating a kind of insularity and internal focus for the areas they surround. The roads themselves are unlikely to have much value as habitable places. This was the explicit intention in the plan of Chandigarh, India, where traffic around large blocks was supposed to stimulate internal coherence and unity, but also separation and exclusion (Figure 35.6).

A surrounding green space, even if not a complete belt, has been used to demarcate and separate a suburb. Chatham Village in Pittsburgh is surrounded by green space and hills on three sides, presenting "only one inhabited face to the neighborhood, and its expression is distinctly aloof." Houses "literally turn their backs" on the surrounding area. Connections to adjacent roads, which could

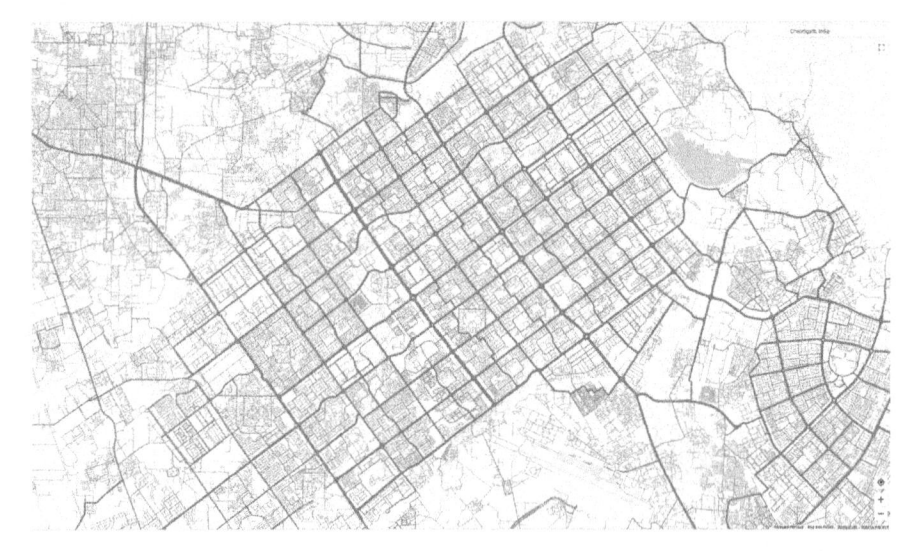

Figure 35.6 Chandigarh, India. *Wide arterials around large blocks were supposed to stimulate internal coherence and unity, as well as separation and exclusion.*

Figure 35.7 Chatham Village, Pittsburgh, Pennsylvania, USA. *Surrounded by green space and hills on three sides, houses "literally turn their backs" on the surrounding area.*

easily be accomplished by simply connecting to the surrounding grid, are avoided, which makes clear that the Village prefers to limit connection to the outside world (Figure 35.7).[8]

Suburban separation is often even more explicit. Walled and gated suburbs are not uncommon and attempt to keep the enclosed development unified. The symbolism is not discreet: here is the middle-class version of the walled castle compound, in which case it is not so much social escapism as social dominance.

Figure 35.8 Alphaville (right), outside of Curitiba, Brazil. *Suburban separation by way of an extreme contrast in form.*

Figure 35.9 Seoul, Korea. *In high-rise districts, exclusion is reinforced not by walls but by private amenities and large-scale commercial buildings.* Credit: Republic of Korea, CC BY-SA 2.0 <https://creativecommons.org/licenses/by-sa/2.0>, via Wikimedia Commons.

Alphaville, a planned suburb in Curitiba, expresses separation by way of being gated, surrounded by green, and presented as an extreme contrast in form.[9]

Fishman identified a central irony to the gated suburb: that instead of shutting people out, the residents have instead shut themselves in. The result is a narrowing of perception and of the capacity to care about, let alone intervene in, the world

Figure 35.10 No Man's Land, Berlin, Germany. *A "No Man's Land" now occupies the "Death Strip" that was between the two walls that comprised the Berlin Wall. The area stands as a metaphor for Germany's complex history: simultaneously a green space and a scar.*

beyond the gates. Taken a step further, there might be walls around each individual house and yard, for example in the 1970s-era suburbs around Phoenix, in which case walled separation cannot really be attributed to a quest for collective unity.[10]

It is not only suburbs that seek boundedness. Grady Clay noted that industrial complexes can mimic medieval castles, complete with turrets and patrolled outlook posts, surrounded by open fields, and with fences in place of moats. Or there is the office complex, consisting of a tower on a pedestal base—"easy to defend, accessible through one entrance, negotiable through one lobby . . . turning cold shoulders" to all surrounding neighborhoods. Clay called these examples of "turf," resembling walled fortresses. In high-rise districts, such as the apartment complexes of Seoul, Korea, exclusion is reinforced not by walls but by surrounding high-rise clusters with private amenities and large-scale commercial buildings (Figure 35.9).[11]

The most dramatic, and violent, walled experience in modern times was the Berlin Wall, which was actually two walls. A "No Man's Land" now occupies the "Death Strip" that was between the walls. The area stands as a "stunning metaphor" for Germany's complex history: "a green space, an urban wilderness, a scar, a 'zipper' and a souvenir" (Figure 35.10).[12]

Conclusion

This book has grappled with questions about motivation and meaning: what inspired an urban pattern or form initially, and what meaning does it hold for us now? Cities as physical places say a lot about a society and a culture in terms of what is valued and where power resides. One can "read" the city and its parts as expressions of cultural preferences, aesthetic taste, and political and economic influence. Understanding what patterns and forms have meant, what they mean now, and what they might mean when implemented in the future—that has been the essential aim of this book.

As a way of summarizing, I conclude with a set of evaluative questions the reader might pose when looking at their own city, town, neighborhood, or place within. I hope the list will benefit anyone trying to understand what cities say.

Order

- How ordered is the city? Does the pattern seem overly diagrammatic—symmetry for symmetry's sake? Or can the symmetry be tied to some functional purpose?
- Does the city present some kind of unified composition in which the elements of the city—its buildings, its open spaces, its blocks—fit together? It is said that the ancient Greek town, in line with the theories of Hippodamus, had everything in balance, so that one type of function didn't overwhelm the rest. Is there evidence of this balance?
- What level of control is indicated? If the city or town is large and also highly ordered, this likely involved an extraordinary level of control. And the more diagrammatic looking the new town is, the more it is an indication of being created all at once by the same hand: urban manipulation from on high.
- If city patterns and forms seem random, is it a sign that collective life is not particularly prioritized? Are places for collective life ordered in some discernible way?
- Are the ordered places in the city empty, or full? Is there evidence, as in the baroque, of exaggeration, in which "clarification gave place to regimentation, openness to emptiness, greatness to grandiosity"?[1]
- One way to assess order is to look at how strict and uniform the street pattern is. Are street and block patterns strictly rectilinear, or are they more relaxed

What Cities Say. Emily Talen, Oxford University Press. © Oxford University Press 2024. DOI: 10.1093/oso/9780197647769.003.0037

and curvilinear? How frequent are the interruptions of the street pattern? Is there an observable hierarchy, a division into primary and secondary streets?

- Did the order require starting with a clean slate, involving destruction, probably by force? Or did the order evolve over time, perhaps as the result of city-building rules, like zoning?
- What is surrounding an ordered space? Is order contextualized, creating a nice contrast to the diversity or variegation around it? Or is the order so vast that contrast is no longer possible? Bernini's small squares in Rome are thought to be particularly beautiful because they were small insertions of order that contrasted with a surrounding clutter.

Dominance

- Does city pattern reveal who or what is dominant, prioritized, or privileged? Is there a sense that space is being hoarded by a particular function? Benevolo wrote that the city was essentially a "vast discriminatory apparatus [that] confirmed the dominion of the strong over the weak."[2] How is this revealed in city pattern and form?
- Who/what has claim to the heart of the city? Is there a center of gravity, or are there multiple centers? How much of the nucleus of the city is given to civic purpose, as opposed to commercial or residential? Is there a public space at the center, as in the Greek city, where the centrality of the agora showed its function as the town's cultural, social, and economic heart?
- It has been said that cities changed from being public realm hegemonic in the mid-18th century to being private realm hegemonic by the early 20th century. What seems more elevated and dominant, the public or the private realm?
- Does residential use dominate, as in garden cities and suburbs? The amount of space given over to a particular function says something about what a society thinks life is supposed to be about.
- What space is given over to the productive life of the city, as opposed to its consumptive life?
- Is economic life connected to public places like squares and plazas, or is it only the streets that play an economic role?
- If the settlement is on water, what dominates the water's edge—recreation, housing, commerce, or industry? Is the water's edge beautified for aesthetic or civic enjoyment, or is the water a working harbor for employment? These two uses of the urban-water edge have long competed for domination.
- What is the strength of social institutions—like churches, marketplaces, or community centers—based on the density around them? Is their gravitational pull such that there is density, and presumably higher land prices, immediately around them? In New England villages, settlers were once required to live within

a half mile of a church so that they would not miss weekly services. Is there any evidence that people are vying to live closer to social and cultural assets?

- Do dominant institutions relate to each other? In some European cities, cathedrals were not randomly located but were placed near other prominent institutions to create a unit, sometimes even forming the pattern of a cross. In Salzburg, castle and cathedral formed a unified complex.

Choice Locations

- Are there increasingly smaller block and lots sizes or higher densities toward choice locations like the center—revealing the importance of access, land rents, and profit?
- Who/what has the choicest locations—near assets like waterfronts? In the Netherlands, the choicest sites were along the canals, and thus they are lined with elegant homes reserved for the wealthy.
- Does the public have protected access to natural features like lakes and rivers, or is it mostly a setting for industry or housing, with the public's access secondary or ignored?
- Do the means of production, and the commerce and transport they require, occupy the best locations? Land use in the United States is said to prioritize the needs of transport—is this in evidence?
- Where are the fixed and durable expressions of community located? What is the centrality and positioning of public buildings and civic spaces? Are choice locations, such as T-intersections or elevated ground, reserved for important civic buildings? Or are civic buildings located in unexalted ways?
- Are the poor forced into subpar locations, such as near industry or highways? What the poor live next to says something about how a society values people.

Social Connection

- What settings are provided for social gathering and social ritual?
- How easy is social encounter? Are there places for chance meeting? Is the density sufficient to make these encounters easy, even unavoidable?
- How spread out is the city? Does it reveal an open character in which buildings are detached and set back, or a more closed character in which buildings are attached and fronting the street?
- Are public spaces meant to impress people, or are they meant to provide a means for people to congregate and socialize?
- To what degree are places for sociability tied to consumption, as opposed to being explicitly civic, with no ulterior motive other than provision of space for social gathering and civic discourse?

- How connected is a separate and identifiable neighborhood to the rest of the city? Does the neighborhood turn its back and give an attitude that it does not want to connect with the city beyond it?

Diversity

- Is there a diversity of elements and forms and patterns, which can support a diversity of activities and people with different needs, desires, and life circumstances? Mumford summarized the goal: "The essential facilities and functions of the city—co-operation, communication, and communion, meeting, mixture, and mobilization—call for a container where a great diversity of activities can simultaneously take place."[3]
- Are there settings for nurturing interdependence, putting people of different backgrounds and life experiences in proximity? Are there places—plazas, squares, parks—with a diverse population close by?
- Does regularization, for example of housing type and lot size, bring a kind of egalitarianism to the city? Does it limit the outward expression of social difference and thereby limit social conflict—or does it support homogeneity and limit diversity?
- Consider the implications of size. For example, 500,000 square feet in a single tall building embodies a social order that is corporate, non-local, detached, uniform, global; 500,000 square feet in 50 small buildings embodies a social order that is local, diverse, and interconnected.[4]

Circulation

- What is the ratio of land for living (public space, residences, neighborhood functions) vs. movement (thoroughfares)? Is priority placed on destinations, or is priority placed on movement between destinations? The latter is characteristic of the baroque spirit: functions sacrificed to movement and vistas. It might also be said of the standard American subdivision, where the car dominates.
- Are diverse forms and speeds of travel accommodated? Olmsted and Vaux worked this out in their circulation plan for Central Park, using underpasses and overpasses, which allowed carriages at different speeds (depending on whether it was a pleasure drive or strictly getting across town), as well as pedestrians and people on horseback.
- Are thoroughfares differentiated, with the functions fronting them appropriately sized—for example where large buildings, which are more resilient, front large roads? Or are there smaller buildings and residences on wide, heavily trafficked streets and highways?

- Is the network of streets and the number of intersections appropriate, such that internal traffic is prioritized for neighborhoods and cross-city traffic occurs outside and around them?
- Under monarchical rule in Europe, the prince made sure that roads led to the castle. What do main roads lead to now? If there are diagonals cutting through, do they terminate into something, like an important building site, or do they just drift off into open space?

Notes

Introduction

1. Lefebvre, *The Production of Space*, 99.
2. Tonkiss, *Cities by Design*; Rotenberg and McDonogh, *The Cultural Meaning of Urban Space*.
3. Lefebvre, *The Production of Space*, 73.
4. Zaidman and Kark, "Garden Cities in the Jewish Yishuv of Palestine," 58, 73.
5. Davis, "Sand, Fear, and Money in Dubai," 52; see also Broudehoux, "Delirious Beijing: Euphoria and Despair in the Olympic Metropolis." On Menteng, see Silver, "Menteng: Heritage of a Planned Community in a Southeast Asian Megacity."
6. Braunfels, *Urban Design in Western Europe*, 81.
7. Mumford, *The City in History*, 208.
8. Wilson, *The City Beautiful Movement*.
9. Gallion and Eisner, *The Urban Pattern*, 385.
10. Mumford, *The City in History*, 53.
11. Golding, "Plato as City Planner," 361.
12. Lynch, *Good City Form*, 424.
13. Mumford, *The City in History*, 308, 311.
14. Kostof, *The City Shaped*, 214; Rykwert, *The Seduction of Place*, 5.
15. Blackwell and Kohl, "Varieties of Housing Finance in Historical Perspective."
16. Kostof, *The City Shaped*, 64; Bacon, *Design of Cities*; Stern et al., *Planned Paradise*; Conzen, "The Morphology of Nineteenth Century Cities in the U.S."
17. Unwin, *Town Planning in Practice*, 52.
18. Abercrombie, *Town and County Planning*; Braunfels, *Urban Design in Western Europe*, 61.
19. Low, *Why Public Space Matters*; Lipsitz, "Locked on This Earth: Movement and Stasis in Black Culture"; Tuan, *Space and Place*; Gallagher, *The Power of Place*.
20. Moody, *Wacker's Manual*.
21. Beauregard, *Planning Matter*; Campanella, "Jane Jacobs and the Death and Life of American Planning."
22. Morris, *History of Urban Form*.
23. Reps, *The Making of Urban America*.
24. Loukaitou-Sideris, "Addressing the Challenges of Urban Landscapes," 472.
25. Alexander, *A Pattern Language*.
26. This is something Venturi et al., in *Learning from Las Vegas*, discovered about architecture.
27. Mumford, *The City in History*, 198. Only a few planners are included, limited to where it is difficult to separate city forms from the main characters behind them: Sixtus V in Rome, Louis XIV in Versailles, Peter the Great in St. Petersburg. Fortunately, there is already a literature on the many colorful personalities of city planners, from Greek city planner Hippodamus of Miletus, to Biagio Rossetti, designer of Renaissance Ferrara, to military engineers, like Franz de Voland who planned a number of cities in southern Russia. There are the colonial cities of merchant kings, garden city designers like Raymond Unwin, industrialists with their company towns, idiosyncratic planners like James Oglethorpe and his design for Savannah, or Judge Augustus B. Woodward's baroque plan of Detroit.

28. Tunnard, *The City of Man*, 172.

29. Benevolo, *The History of the City*, 477.

30. Hayden, *Seven American Utopias*.

31. Zucker, *Town and Square*; Bacon, *Design of Cities*, 83.

32. See, e.g., Geoff Boeing's big-data approach to visualizing street layout: https://geoffboeing.com/2018/07/comparing-city-street-orientations/.

33. Adshead, "An Introduction to Civic Design."

34. Braudel, *Civilization and Capitalism*; Kostof, *The City Shaped*; Cherry, *Cities and Plans*, 11.

35. In a fifth chapter, "Skyline," Kostof presents another way of seeing the city, but not from the air.

36. Lynch, *Good City Form*; Hall, *Cities of Tomorrow*.

Chapter 1

1. Gallion and Eisner, *The Urban Pattern*, 19.

2. Benevolo, *The History of the City*, 73; Gutkind, 18.

3. Benevolo, *The History of the City*, 95.

Chapter 2

1. Mumford, *The City in History*, 302, 322.

2. Aldridge, *The Case for Town Planning*.

3. Benevolo, *The History of the City*, 310; Aldridge, *The Case for Town Planning*, 39.

4. Gutkind, *Urban Development in Western Europe*, 25, 27.

5. Jacobs, *The Death and Life of Great American Cities*, 375.

6. Miller et al., "Inscribing Minority Space in the Islamic City"; Mumford, *The City in History*, 302, 322.

Chapter 3

1. Adams, *Outline of Town and City Planning*, 80.

2. Braunfels, *Urban Design in Western Europe*; Krier, *Houses, Palaces, Cities*, 79.

3. Meinig, "Symbolic Landscapes," 165.

4. Kostof, *The City Shaped*, 196, 202.

5. Reps, *The Making of Urban America*.

Chapter 4

1. Sharp, *Town and Countryside*, 163.

2. Campanella, "Introduction: The Necessity for Congestion"; Faure, "Local Life in Working-Class Paris at the End of the Nineteenth Century."

3. Ward, "Environs and Neighbours in the 'Two Nations' Residential Differentiation," 162; Miller, *Visions of Place*.

4. Fishman, *The American Planning Tradition*; Elsheshtawy, "Urban Dualities in the Arab World."

5. Lynch, *Good City Form*, 95.

6. Kostof, *The City Assembled*, 45; Sieber, "Public Access on the Urban Waterfront."

7. Cohen, *A Consumer's Republic*.

Chapter 5

1. Clay, *Close-up: How to Read the American City*, 108.
2. Creese, *The Search for Environment*; Collins, "Linear Planning throughout the World."
3. Lynch, *Good City Form*, 86, 88.
4. Pedersen, "Peter Calthorpe Has a Plan."

Chapter 6

1. Lefebvre, *The Production of Space*, 151.
2. Kostof, *The City Shaped*, 207.
3. Price, "Introduction to Planning in Early American Cities."
4. Kostof, *The City Shaped*, 106.
5. Reps, *The Making of Urban America*; Dennis, *Temples and Towns*, 76. Urban planning historian John Reps studied the bastides of 13th-century Provence and documented their urban design qualities. Reps's bastides collection is publicly available at https://library.artstor.org/#/collection/87730275;browseType=undefined.
6. Kostof, *The City Shaped*, 110. Braunfels, *Urban Design in Western Europe*, 157.
7. Morosi, "La Plata: An Advanced Nineteenth Century New Town."
8. Busquets et al., *Urban Grids*, 202; Reps, *The Making of Urban America*, 30.
9. Rapoport, *The Meaning of the Built Environment*; see also Smith, "Form and Meaning in the Earliest Cities."
10. Hla, "Traditional Town Planning in Burma"; Lynch, *Good City Form*.
11. Gutkind, *Urban Development in Western Europe*, 35.
12. Lewis, *City of Refuge*.
13. Edwards, "City Design: What Went Wrong with Milton Keynes?," 93.
14. Blumenfeld, *The Modern Metropolis*, 49; on New Towns see Wakeman, *Practicing Utopia*.

Chapter 7

1. Alexander et al., *A Pattern Language*, 228–229.
2. Creese, *The Search for Environment*, 31.
3. Mumford, *The City in History*, pl. 41.
4. Eaton, *Ideal Cities*.
5. Dal Co, "From Parks to the Region."
6. Gans, "Letter," 183.
7. Mumford, *The City in History*.

Chapter 8

1. Culpin, *The Garden City Movement Up-to-Date*, 6.
2. Rego, "Brazilian Garden Cities and Suburbs," 279.
3. Dennis, *Temples and Towns*, 110.
4. Loudon, *Encyclopaedia of Gardening*.
5. Crinson, "Abadan: Planning and Architecture under the Anglo-Iranian Oil Company," 350.
6. Fishman, "The Open and the Enclosed," 37.
7. Stern et al., *Paradise Planned*, 14–15.
8. Abercrombie, *Town and Country Planning*, 99.

9. Crinson, "Abadan," 351.

10. Creese, *The Search for Environment*, 333; Rego, "Brazilian Garden Cities and Suburbs."

11. Creese, *The Search for Environment*, 14.

12. Pittari, "Sunnyside Gardens and Radburn," 223.

Chapter 9

1. Fishman, *Bourgeois Utopias*, 27, 137, 142.

2. Woods and Kennedy, *The Zone of Emergence*; Hayden, *Building Suburbia*.

3. Warner, *Streetcar Suburbs*, 19.

Chapter 10

1. Tunnard, *The City of Man*, 203.

2. Harvey, *Spaces of Hope*, 160, 168.

3. Unwin, "Building and Natural Beauty," 93.

4. Fishman, *Bourgeois Utopias*, 26, 34, 206.

5. Fishman, *Bourgeois Utopias*, 26; Gillem, *America Town*.

6. Masterman, *The Condition of England*; Sharp, *Town and Countryside*, 11, 69–70; Sharp, *English Panorama*, 98.

7. Fishman, *Bourgeois Utopias*, 153–154.

8. Fishman, *Bourgeois Utopias*, 61.

9. Meinig, "Symbolic Landscapes"; Fishman, *Bourgeois Utopias*, 4; see also Hayden, *Building Suburbia*.

Chapter 11

1. Stern et al., *Paradise Planned*, 961. Famous garden suburbs include Forest Hills Gardens, Queens, NY; Yorkship Village, NJ; Union Park Gardens, DE; Buchman Village, PA; Goodyear Heights, OH; and Billerica Garden Suburb, MA. There are also three federally funded Greenbelt towns in this genre—two iconic with organic loops, cul-de-sacs and superblocks intended to accentuate their ruralized ethos, and one (Greendale, WI) modeled in part on the historical precedent of Williamsburg, Virginia.

2. Jacobs, *The Death and Life of Great American Cities*, 17.

3. Bamberg, *Chatham Village*, 175.

4. Fishman, *Bourgeois Utopias*.

5. From Kostof, *The City Shaped*, 74. See also Stern et al., *Paradise Planned*, 295; Fishman, *Bourgeois Utopias*, 119.

6. Kreiger, *City on a Hill*.

7. Rybczynski, *A Clearing in the Distance*, 293; Fishman, *Bourgeois Utopias*, 146; Schuyler, "Riverside: The First Comprehensively Designed Suburban Community in the United States"; Hayden, *Building Suburbia*, 66; Fishman, *Bourgeois Utopias*.

8. Stern et al., *Planned Paradise*, 141.

9. Barnett, *The Elusive City*; Stilgoe, *Borderland*; Creese, *The Search for Environment*.

Chapter 12

1. Barnett, *The Elusive City*; see also Dennis, *Temples and Towns*.

2. Barnett, *The Elusive City*, 24; CNU, *The Charter of the New Urbanism*.

3. Yerolympos, "A New City for a New State," 253–254.
4. Le Corbusier quoted in Fishman, *Urban Utopias of the Twentieth Century*, 239.
5. Bamberg, *Chatham Village*; Gallion and Eisner, *The Urban Pattern*.
6. Le Corbusier, *The City of Tomorrow and Its Planning*; Barnett, *The Elusive City*. See also Dennis, *Temples and Towns*.
7. Boyer, *Dreaming the Rational City*, 282. See also Jencks, *Modern Movements in Architecture*.
8. Gutnov, *The Ideal Communist City*, 74.
9. Frolic, "The Soviet City," 292
10. Frolic, "The Soviet City," 302, 285.
11. The term was popularized by publication of the book *Sotsgorod: The Problem of Building Socialist Cities* by Nikolai Aleksandrovich Miliutin in 1930. See also the film *Sotsgorod: The Socialist "New Cities" and Planning for Utopia*, https://youtu.be/k1fFd4S9IBc.
12. Aman, *Architecture and Ideology in Eastern Europe*.
13. Cavalcanti, "Urban Reconstruction and Autocratic Regimes," 85, 86.
14. Gehan, "Instituting Order."
15. Jencks, *Modern Movements in Architecture*, 304. See also Hall, "The City of Towers"; Berman, *All That Is Solid Melts into Air*.
16. Kreiger, *City on a Hill*, 303.
17. Biles, "The Rise and Fall of Soul City," 60

Chapter 13

1. As discussed in Talen, *New Urbanism and American Planning*.
2. Marshall, *How Cities Work*.
3. Choay, *The Modern City*, 14; Lynch, *Good City Form*.
4. Murray, "The Quandary of Post-Public Space," 119, 133.
5. Schuman and Sclar, "The Impact of Ideology on American Town Planning," 447.

Chapter 14

1. Talen, *Neighborhood*; Reps, *The Making of Urban America*.
2. Reps, *The Making of Urban America*, 283; Bacon, *Design of Cities*, 319
3. Cooley, *Social Organization*.
4. Mehaffy et al., "The 'Neighborhood Unit' on Trial."
5. La Gory and Pipkin, *Urban Social Space*; Stone, *Nippur Neighborhoods*.
6. Keyvanian, "Concerted Efforts," 293.
7. Fischer, "Canberra," 183. Proudfoot, "The Symbolism of the Crystal."
8. Hayden, "The Potential of Ethnic Places for Urban Landscapes"; Suttles, *The Social Order of the Slum*.
9. Clay, *Close-up*, 49.
10. Jacobs, *Death and Life*.
11. Mehaffy, "The Neighborhood Unit on Trial."
12. Siembieda and Moreno, "Barrios and the Hispanic American City."
13. Mumford, *The City in History*, 308, 311.
14. Bacon, *Design of Cities*, 101.
15. Stieber, "Housing Design and Society in Amsterdam."
16. Whitehead, "Love Thy Neighbourhood"; see also Harvey, *Social Justice and the City* and *The Urban Experience*; Krase, "Italian American Urban Landscapes."

Chapter 15

1. Fleure, "Some Types of Cities in Temperate Europe"; Cherry, *Cities and Plans*.
2. Myers, "Designing Power: Forms and Purposes"; Macfarlane, "Planning an Arab Town"; Shiber, *The Kuwait Urbanization*.
3. Gillem, *America Town*, 8.
4. Hunter, *Westmoreland and Portland Place*, 9.
5. Keating et al., *Cleveland's Lakefront*, 152.
6. Mumford, *The City in History*, pl. 11, 12.
7. Gallion and Eisner, *The Urban Pattern*, 82; Kostof, *The City Assembled*, 155.
8. Robinson, *Modern Civic Art*, 82; Jacobs, *Death and Life*, 25.
9. Robinson, *Modern Civic Art*, 82.
10. Kostof, *The City Shaped*, 100; Dennis, *Temples and Towns*, 6.
11. Rasmussen, *The Unique City*, 282, 277.

Chapter 16

1. Jacobs, *Death and Life*; Rasmussen, *Towns and Buildings*, 117.
2. Mumford, *The City in History*, pl. 9, 162.
3. Kostof, *The City Shaped*; Zucker, "Space and Movement"; Burnham and Bennet, *Plan of Chicago*, 89; Reps, *The Making of Urban America*.
4. Irving, *Indian Summer*, 73, 76.
5. Kostof, *The City Shaped*; Mumford, *The City in History*, 198.
6. Boyer, *Dreaming the Rational City*, 32; Morley, "The Filipinization of the American City Beautiful."
7. Zucker, "Space and Movement"; Kostof, *The City Shaped*, 215, 97–98; Napier, "Bernini's Anthropology," 17.
8. Ashley, *Louis XIV and the Greatness of France*; Gallion and Eisner, *The Urban Pattern*, 84; Kostof, *The City Shaped*, 112; Braunfels, *Urban Design in Western Europe*; Hohenberg and Lees, *The Making of Urban Europe 1000–1950*, 154; Sutcliffe, *Towards the Planned City*.
9. Mumford, *The City in History*, 197, pl. 28.
10. Creese, *The Search for Environment*; Abercrombie, *Town and Country Planning*, 104.
11. Unwin, *Town Planning in Practice*, 69; Benevolo, *The History of the City*, 715.
12. Morris, *History of Urban Form before the Industrial Revolutions*, 145.
13. This issue was explored by Madanipour et al., "Master Plans and Urban Change."
14. Mumford, *The City in History*, 198; Krier, *The Architecture of Community*; Kostof, *The City Shaped*.

Chapter 17

1. Blumenfeld, *The Modern Metropolis*, 224.
2. Mumford, *The City in History*, pl. 9, 162.
3. Triggs, *Town Planning Past, Present and Possible*.
4. Speer, *Inside the Third Reich*, 69.
5. Mumford, *The City in History*, 201
6. Jeong et al., "Characteristics of Spatial Configurations in Pyongyang, North Korea"; Broudehoux, "Delirious Beijing," 99–100.
7. Scott, *American City Planning*, 53; Adams, *Outline of Town and City Planning*, 126; Pierre L'Enfant to George Washington, 1789, quoted in Krieger, *City on a Hill*, 191.

8. Speer, *Inside the Third Reich*; Cavalcanti, "Urban Reconstruction and Autocratic Regimes."
9. Anker, "Il Papa e Il Duce."
10. Kostof, *The City Shaped*, 220; Berman, *All That Is Solid Melts into Air.*
11. Lin, "From Megastructure to Megalopolis."

Chapter 18

1. Mumford, "Yesterday's City of Tomorrow."
2. Souther, "Acropolis of the Middle-West," 38.
3. James Baldwin made this remark in a 1963 interview with Kenneth Clark, https://youtu.be/T8Abhj17kYU; Stern and Massengale, *The Anglo-American Suburb*, 48
4. Stern and Massengale, *The Anglo-American Suburb*, 48; Stein, "Housing and the Depression."
5. Adde, *Nine Cities*, vii; Avila and Rose, "Race, Culture, Politics, and Urban Renewal," 337–338.
6. Mumford, *The City in History*, pl. 21.
7. Giedion, *Space Time and Architecture*, 832; Berman, *All That Is Solid Melts into Air*, 307–308.
8. Berman, *All That Is Solid Melts into Air*, 307–308.

Chapter 19

1. Silliman, *Architecture in the United States*, 255.
2. Cherry, *Cities and Plans*, 14; Bamberg, *Chatham Village.*
3. Whyte, *Organization Man.*
4. Gallion and Eisner, *The Urban Pattern*, 122; Lefebvre, *The Production of Space*, 98.
5. Kostof, *The City Shaped.*
6. Creese, *Search for Environment*, 122; Adams, *Outline of Town and City Planning*, 138
7. Gutkind, *Urban Development in Western Europe*, 32; Dennis, *Temples and Towns*, 222.
8. Kostof, *The City Shaped*, 101; Cerda, *Teoría General de la Urbanización* ("General Theory of Urbanization").
9. Davies, *Real Estate in American History*, 6; Creese, *The Search for Environment*, 35; Koolhaas, *Delirious New York*, 15.
10. Bauer, *Modern Housing*, 164.
11. Gallion and Eisner, *The Urban Pattern*, 86.
12. Burnham and Bennett, *Plan of Chicago*, 114.
13. Bluestone, "Detroit's City Beautiful and the Problem of Commerce."
14. Mumford, *The City in History*, 312; Koolhaas, *S,M,L,XL*; Mumford, "Yesterday's City of Tomorrow."
15. Abercrombie, "Era of Architectural Town Planning"; Sitte quoted in Triggs, *Town Planning*, 279.

Chapter 20

1. Saalman, *Medieval Cities.*
2. Barnett, *Towards Social Reform*, 333.
3. Lang, "The Design of Yorkship Garden Village"; Creese, *The Search for Environment*, 249; Schuyler, "Riverside," 47.
4. See Talen and Lee, *Design for Social Diversity*; Talen, *Neighborhood*; Lesger and Van Leeuwen, "Residential Segregation from the Sixteenth to the Nineteenth Century," 336, 337; Bardet, "Rouen au 17eme et 18eme siècle."

Chapter 21

1. Fishman, *Bourgeois Utopias*, 199.
2. Creese, *The Search for Environment*, 117; Parera, "Mormon Town Planning," 157.
3. Artz and Stone, "Revisiting WalMart's Impact on Iowa Small-Town Retail"; Mennel, "Victor Gruen and the Construction of Cold War Utopias," 128.
4. Cohen, *A Consumer's Republic*.
5. Roth, *Frederick Law Olmsted's First and Last Suburbs*.
6. Gillem, *America Town*.
7. Gruen cited in Mennel, "Victor Gruen and the Construction of Cold War Utopias."
8. Moudon, "Housing and Settlement Design Series Working Paper."
9. Hayden, *A Field Guide to Sprawl*, 151.
10. Reps, *The Making of Urban America*, 22.
11. Stübben, *City Building* (*Der Städtebau*).
12. Le Corbusier, *The City of Tomorrow*.
13. Gottdiener, *Planned Sprawl*; Fishman expounds on this point in; Kunstler, *The City in Mind*, 152
14. Frederick and Mehta, *101 Things I Learned in Urban Design School*, 15.
15. Mackin, *Americans and Their Land*; Williamson, *Sprawl, Justice, and Citizenship*; Kunstler, *The City in Mind*, 45, 63.
16. Webber, "Order in Diversity"; Jencks, *Modern Movements in Architecture*.
17. Fishman, *Bourgeois Utopias*, 201; Mumford, *The City in History*, 513; Creese, *The Search for Environment*, 91.
18. Sutcliffe, *Towards the Planned City*, 32, 41; for an interesting exploration of single family houses, see Comstock, *The Housing Book*.

Chapter 22

1. Blumenfeld, *The Modern Metropolis*.
2. Busquet et al., *Urban Grids*.
3. Benevolo, *The History of the City*; Mumford, *The City in History*, 172, 194, pl. 27; Lewis, *City of Refuge*; Jackson, "The Order of a Landscape," 162.
4. Parera, "Mormon Town Planning"; Reps, *The Making of Urban America*, 264.
5. Rykwert, *The Idea of a Town*; Dutt, *Town Planning in Ancient India*; Kostof, *The City Shaped*, 48, 104; Gaube, *Iranian Cities*; Busquets et al., *Urban Grids*, 22; Morris, *History of Urban Form*, 302.
6. Madeddu and Zhang, "Harmonious Spaces," 712; Schinz, *The Magic Square*; Mumford, *The City in History*, 207.
7. Argan, *The Renaissance City*; Busquets et al., *Urban Grids*.
8. Braunfels, *Urban Design in Western Europe*, 161; Rykwert, *The Seduction of Place*; Jäger, "The Art of Orthogonal Planning."
9. Kostof, *The City Shaped*; Arendt, *Crossroads, Hamlet, Village, Town*, 20.
10. Forster, *From "Rocca" to "Civitas"*; Braunfels, *Urban Design in Western Europe*, 150.
11. Le Corbusier, *The City of Tomorrow*.
12. Benevolo, *The History of the City*; Mumford, *The City in History*, 193; Reps, *The Making of Urban America*.
13. Kostof, *The City Shaped*, 148; Doug Allen Institute, "History of Urban Form Lecture Series."
14. Marcuse, "The Grid as City Plan"; Kostof, *The City Shaped*, 100 and 121.
15. Frederick and Mehta, *101 Things I Learned in Urban Design School*.
16. Koolhaas, *Delirious New York*, 15.
17. Grant, "The Dark Side of the Grid"; Benevolo, *The History of the City*, 109; Kreiger, *City on a Hill*, 24, 25.

18. Grant, "The Dark Side of the Grid"; Zad, "Spatial Discrimination in Tehran's Modern Urban Planning 1906–1979," 54.
19. Buras, *The Art of Classic Planning*, 242.
20. Mumford, *The City in History*, 193.
21. Kostof, *The City Shaped*, 153; Grant, "The Dark Side of the Grid."
22. Mullin, "The Reconstruction of Lisbon Following the Earthquake of 1755," 10–11; Campanella, "Straight Streets in a Curvaceous Crescent," 197.
23. Kostof, *The City Shaped*, 149, 152.
24. Kostof, *The City Shaped*; Gutkind, *Urban Development in Western Europe*.
25. Warner, *Streetcar Suburbs*, 21; Fishman, *Bourgeois Utopias*; Kostof, *The City Shaped*, 122.
26. Mumford, *The City in History*, 423.
27. Braunfels, *Urban Design in Western Europe*, 107.
28. Peterson, *The Birth of City Planning*, 9.
29. Angel, *Planet of Cities*; see also Kreiger, *City on a Hill*.

Chapter 23

1. Penther, *Lexicon Architectonicum*, quoted in Gutkind, *Urban Development in Western Europe*, 34; MacDonald, "Suburban Vision to Urban Reality."
2. Mumford, *The City in History*, 193.
3. Adams, *Outline of Town and City Planning*, 57.
4. Buras, *The Art of Classic Planning*.
5. Wilson, *Strange Island*, 245; Creese, *The Search for Environment*, 82.
6. Rykwert, *The Idea of a Town*, 91, 202.
7. See the *Lexicon of the New Urbanism*; Mumford, *The City in History*, 368, 369; Kostof, *The City Shaped*, 95.
8. Kostof, *The City Shaped*, 217.
9. Sitte, *City Planning According to Artistic Principles*; Mumford, *The City in History*, 391; Triggs, *Town Planning*, 242.
10. Mumford, *The City in History*.
11. Abercrombie, *Town and Country Planning*.
12. Argan, *The Renaissance City*, 102.
13. Mumford, *The City in History*.
14. Schmidt, "Cultural Influences and the Built Environment."
15. Argan, *The Renaissance City*.
16. Talen, *City Rules*.

Chapter 24

1. Lynch, *Good City Form*, 96.
2. Morris, *History of Urban Form*; Alberti, *De re aedificatoria*.
3. Platt, *The English Medieval Town*; Rasmussen, *Towns and Buildings*.
4. Charmes, "Cul-de-sacs, Superblocks and Environmental Areas," 360; Freestone and Nichols, "Pacific Crossing?"
5. Allen, *A History of Urban Form*; Duany, Plater-Zyberk & Co., *The Lexicon of the New Urbanism*; Creese, *Search for Environment*; Dal Co, "From Parks to the Region," 241; Southworth and Parthasarathy, "The Suburban Public Realm I."
6. Abu-Lughod, "The Islamic City"; Kheirabadi, *Iranian Cities*; Gutkind, *The Twilight of Cities*.

Chapter 25

1. Gutkind, *The Twilight of Cities*, 15; McCann, "Planning and Building the Corporate Suburb."
2. Vitruvius, *The Ten Books on Architecture*; Mumford, *The City in History*, 163.
3. Rybczynski, *A Clearing in the Distance*; Olmsted, Vaux and Co., "Preliminary Report upon the Proposed Suburban Village at Riverside," 25; Kostof, *The City Shaped*, 74.
4. Frederick and Mehta, *101 Things I Learned in Urban Design School*, 14, 60.
5. Mumford, *The City in History*, 303; Morris, *History of Urban Form*.
6. Rasmussen, *Towns and Buildings*, 33.
7. Barnett, *The Elusive City*; Kostof, *The City Shaped*, 76.
8. Le Corbusier, *The City of Tomorrow*.
9. Otto, "City-Planning Theory in Nationalist-Socialist Germany," 72; Blumenfeld, *The Modern Metropolis*

Chapter 26

1. Darin, "Designating Urban Forms."
2. Kostof, *The City Shaped*; Kling, "Wide Boulevards, Narrow Visions."
3. Navapan, "Absolute Monarchy and the Development of Bangkok's Urban Spaces," 14; Capolino, "Tirana," 600.
4. Fishman, *Bourgeois Utopias*, 116.
5. Berman, *All That Is Solid Melts into Air*, 194, 204; Gutkind, *Urban Development in Western Europe*, 49.
6. Berman, *All That Is Solid Melts into Air*, 194, 204.
7. Choay, *The Modern City*, 17.
8. Fishman, *Bourgeois Utopias*.
9. Berman, *All That Is Solid Melts into Air*, 307–308.

Chapter 27

1. Cavaglieri, "Outline for a History of City Planning."
2. Tunnard, *The City of Man*, 78.
3. Gallion and Eisner, *The Urban Pattern*.
4. Kickert, *Dream City*, 17; Reps, *The Making of Urban America*.
5. Kostof, *The City Shaped*, 185. Kostof, *The City Assembled*, 106; Lewis, *New Orleans*.
6. Lynch, *Good City Form*, 283; Stevens, "Masterplanning Public Memorials," 60.
7. Abercrombie, *Town and Country Planning*, 91; Berman, *All That Is Solid Melts into Air*, 229.
8. Brand, "Crossing the Roads," 442.
9. Yglesias, "To Build a Metaphor," 172.

Chapter 28

1. Gutkind, *Urban Development in Western Europe*, 16.
2. Archer, *Architecture and Suburbia*.
3. Hall, *Cities of Tomorrow*, 108.
4. Foster, "What Is Home without a Golf Course?," 3.
5. Stein, *Toward New Towns for America*, 169; see also Dahir, "Greendale Comes of Age"; Dal Co, "From Parks to the Region"; https://www.jamescolincampbell.com/village-green/.

6. Jacobs, *Death and Life.*

7. Quoted in Girling and Helphand, *Yard Street Park*, 66.

Chapter 29

1. Duany, Plater-Zyberk & Co., *Lexicon of the New Urbanism*; note that some urbanists add a third type, the piazza. See https://www.smartcitiesdive.com/ex/sustainablecitiescollective/defining-piazza-and-why-it-s-not-plaza/23003.

2. Price, "Introduction to Planning in Early American Cities," 169.

3. Unwin, *Town Planning in Practice*, 13; Aldridge, *The Case for Town Planning*, 63.

4. Mumford, *The City in History*, 150, 162; Low, *Why Public Space Matters.*

5. Keyvanian, "Concerted Efforts," 293.

6. Zucker, *Town and Square*, 3; Blumenfeld, *The Modern Metropolis*, 229; Sitte, *City Planning According to Artistic Principles.*

7. Busquets et al., *Urban Grids*, 185.

8. Madanipour, "Whose Public Space?"; Zucker, *Town and Square*; Kostof, *The City Assembled*, 150.

9. Braunfels, *Urban Design in Western Europe*, 149.

10. Reps, *The Making of Urban America*; Kostof, *The City Shaped*, 133

11. Mumford, *The City in History*, 27; Alexander et al., *A Pattern Language*, 312–313.

12. Tunnard, *The City of Man*, 72; Reps, *The Making of Urban America.*

13. Braunfels, *Urban Design in Western Europe*, 339; Triggs, *Town Planning*, 21.

14. Triggs, *Town Planning*, 21; Hedman and Jaszewski, *Fundamentals of Urban Design*, 53–54.

15. Rasmussen, *Towns and Buildings,* 60; Stern et al., *Planned Paradise.*

16. Busquets et al., *Urban Grids*, 184; Rasmussen, *London, the Unique City*; Barnett, *The Elusive City.*

Chapter 30

1. Mumford, *The City in History*, pl. 2; Kim, "Making Cities Global," 330, 336; see also Roy and Aihwa, eds., *Worlding Cities.*

2. Dennis, *Temples and Towns.*

3. Adams, *Outline of Town and City Planning*, 76; Morris, *History of Urban Form*, 25; Wycherley in Mumford, *The City in History*, 150.

4. Le Corbusier, *When the Cathedrals Were White*; Lefebvre, *The Production of Space.*

5. Quoted in Benevolo, *The History of the City*, 628.

6. Kostof, *The City Shaped*, 115

7. Hall, *Cities of Tomorrow*, 104.

8. Mumford, *The City in History*, 303; Abercrombie, *Town and Country Planning*, 47.

9. Mumford, *The City in History*, 268, 9.

10. Veselka, *The Courthouse Square in Texas*, 145–147; Reps, *The Making of Urban America*; Argan, *The Renaissance City*; Mumford, *The City in History*, 307; Benevolo, *The History of the City.*

11. Veselka, *The Courthouse Square in Texas*, 145–147.

12. Krier, *The Architecture of Community*; Larice, "Great Neighborhoods."

13. Bluestone, "Detroit's City Beautiful and the Problem of Commerce," 246; Gutkind, *Urban Development in Western Europe*, 48.

14. Alonso, *Location and Land Use*; Blumenfeld, *The Modern Metropolis*, 31.

15. See Loukaitou-Sideris and Banerjee, "Downtown Urban Design"; Berman, *All That Is Solid Melts into Air*, 289.

16. Ruggeri, " 'Palm Springs,' " 103.

17. Fishman, *Bourgeois Utopias.*

Chapter 31

1. King, "Re-writing the City," 131.
2. Kostof, *The City Shaped*, 96.
3. Busquets et al., *Urban Grids*.
4. Reps, *Monumental Washington*; Kreiger, *City on a Hill*.
5. Taylor, "City Form and Capital Culture," 80–82.
6. Argan, *The Renaissance City*, 105.
7. Argan, *The Renaissance City*.

Chapter 32

1. Barnett, *The Elusive City*; Braunfels, *Urban Design in Western Europe*, 47, 49.
2. Le Corbusier, *When the Cathedrals Were White*.
3. Braunfels, *Urban Design in Western Europe*, 109; Jacobs, *Death and Life*, 22, 23, 436; Fishman, *Bourgeois Utopias*, 203; Mumford, "Megalopolis as Anti-City."
4. Alexander et al., *A Pattern Language*, 210.
5. Summerson, *Heavenly Mansion*; Le Corbusier, *The City of Tomorrow*.
6. Le Corbusier, *The City of Tomorrow*; Irazábal, "Localizing Urban Design Traditions," 80; Avery-Quinn, "Cities of Zion."
7. Newman, *Defensible Space*.
8. Trancik, *Finding Lost Space*; Rykwert, *The Seduction of Place*, 6.
9. Corner, "Terra Fluxus"; Wall, "Programming the Urban Surface"; Mostafavi, *Ecological Urbanism*; Waldheim, *The Landscape Urbanism Reader*.
10. Kim, "Making Cities Global," 330, 336; see also Roy and Aihwa, eds., *Worlding Cities*.

Chapter 33

1. Vitruvius, *The Ten Books on Architecture*, 31; Mumford, *The City in History*, 204.
2. Barnett, *The Elusive City*.
3. Zucker, *Town and Square*, 65.
4. Argan, *The Renaissance City*.
5. Kostof, *The City Shaped*; Reps, *The Making of Urban America*, 5.
6. Garnier quoted in Hegemann and Peets, *American Vitruvius*, 7, 10; Sitte quoted in Ladd, "Urban Aesthetics and the Discovery of the Urban Fabric"; Stübben, *City Building (Der Städtebau)*, 47.
7. Kostof, "The Emperor and the Duce."
8. See Mostafavi and Doherty, eds., *Ecological Urbanism*.
9. Braunfels, *Urban Design in Western Europe*, 225.
10. Draper, "The Art and Science of Park Planning."

Chapter 34

1. Langdon, "How Urbanism, Density, and Spatial Enclosure Are Related"; Sitte, *City Planning According to Artistic Principle*; Maertens, as reported in Gallion and Eisner, *The Urban Pattern*, 395.
2. Morris, *History of Urban Form*, 124; Gallion and Eisner, *The Urban Pattern*, 48.
3. Choay, *The Modern City*, 32.

4. Scruton, "Public Space and the Classical Vernacular."

5. Fishman, "The Open and the Enclosed," 37.

6. Adams, *Outline of Town and City Planning*, 69; Peets, "Famous Town Planners IV," 24.

7. Mumford, "Home Remedies for Urban Cancer."

Chapter 35

1. Fishman, "The Bounded City"; for an interesting perspective on walled communities, see Ruggeri, "'Palm Springs'"; Mumford, *The City in History*, 304.

2. Krier, *The Architecture of Community*; Gutkind, *Urban Development in Western Europe*.

3. Rykwert, *The Idea of a Town*; Alexander et al., *A Pattern Language*, 278, 334.

4. Kostof, *The City Shaped*, 19, 111; Argan, *The Renaissance City*.

5. Argan, *The Renaissance City*.

6. Schorske, *Fin-de-siècle Vienna*, 33; Braunfels, *Urban Design in Western Europe*, 303, 306; Dennis, *Temples and Towns*, 6.

7. Henderson, "Römerstadt," 327.

8. Bamberg, *Chatham Village*, 108.

9. Clay, *Close-up*.

10. Fishman, *Bourgeois Utopias*; Gillem, *America Town*; Clay, *Close-up*.

11. Clay, *Close-up*, 167; Hwang et al., "The Intensifying Gated Exclusiveness of Apartment Complex Boundary Design in Seoul, Korea."

12. Barnstone, "Between the Walls," 287.

Conclusion

1. Mumford, *The City in History*, 350.

2. Benevolo, *The History of the City*.

3. Mumford, *The City in History*, pl. 48.

4. This example is inspired by Frederick and Mehta, *101 Things I Learned in Urban Design School*, 28.

Bibliography

Abercrombie, Sir Patrick. 1914. The Era of Architectural Town Planning: A Study of Certain Influences of Work during the Renaissance. *Town Planning Review* 5: 195–213.

Abercrombie, Sir Patrick. 1943. *Town and Country Planning*. London: Oxford University Press.

Abu-Lughod, Janet L. 1987. The Islamic City—Historic Myth, Islamic Essence, and Contemporary Relevance. *International Journal of Middle East Studies* 19, 2: 155–176. doi:10.1017/S0020743800031822.

Adams, Thomas. 1935. *Outline of Town and City Planning: A Review of Past Efforts and Modern Aims*. New York: Russell Sage Foundation.

Adde, Leo. 1969. *Nine Cities: The Anatomy of Downtown Renewal*. Washington, DC: Urban Land Institute.

Adshead, S. D. 1910. An Introduction to Civic Design. *The Town Planning Review* 1, 1: 3–17.

Alberti, Leon Battista. 1988. *De re aedificatoria. On the Art of Building in Ten Books*. Translated by Joseph Rykwert, Robert Tavernor, and Neil Leach. Cambridge, MA: MIT Press.

Aldridge, Henry R. 1915. *The Case for Town Planning*. London: National Housing and Town Planning Council.

Alexander, Christopher, Sara Ishikawa, Murray Silverstein, Max Jacobson, Ingrid Fiksdahl-King, and Shlomo Angel. 1977. *A Pattern Language*. New York: Oxford University Press.

Allen, Douglas C. "A History of Urban Form." YouTube, https://youtu.be/4QigggmU1ME.

Alonso, William. 1964. *Location and Land Use*. Cambridge, MA: Harvard University Press.

Aman, Anders. 1992. *Architecture and Ideology in Eastern Europe during the Stalin Era*. Cambridge, MA: MIT Press.

Angel, S. 2012. *Planet of Cities*. Cambridge, MA: Lincoln Institute of Land Policy.

Anker, A. 1996. Il Papa e Il Duce: Sixtus V's and Mussolini's Plans for Rome. *Journal of Urban Design* 1, 2: 165–178.

Archer, John. 2005. *Architecture and Suburbia: From English Villa to American Dream House, 1690–2000*. Minneapolis: University of Minnesota Press.

Arendt, Randall. 2004. *Crossroads, Hamlet, Village, Town: Design Characteristics of Traditional Neighborhoods, Old and New*. Rev. ed. Planning Advisory Service Report, no. 523/524. Chicago: American Planning Association.

Argan, Giulio Carlo. 1969. *The Renaissance City*. New York: George Braziller.

Artz, Georgeanne M., and Kenneth E. Stone. 2012. Revisiting WalMart's Impact on Iowa Small-Town Retail: 25 Years Later. *Economic Development Quarterly* 26, 4: 298–310. https://doi.org/10.1177/0891242412461828.

Ashley, Maurice. 1965. *Louis XIV and the Greatness of France*. New York: Free Press.

Avery-Quinn, Samuel. 2018. Cities of Zion: Methodist Camp Meeting Associations and Vernacular Town Planning. *Journal of Planning History* 17, 1: 42–66.

Avila, Eric, and Mark H. Rose. 2009. Race, Culture, Politics, and Urban Renewal: An Introduction. *Journal of Urban History* 35, 3: 335–347.

Bacon, Edmund. 1976. *Design of Cities*. New York: Penguin Books.

Bamberg, Angelique. 2011. *Chatham Village: Pittsburgh's Garden City*. Pittsburgh: University of Pittsburgh Press.

Bardet, Jean-Pierre. 1995. *Rouen au 17eme et 18eme siècle*. Paris: Sedes.

Barnett, Canon and Mrs. S. A. 1909. *Towards Social Reform*. London: T. Fisher Unwin.

Barnett, Jonathan. 1986. *The Elusive City: Five Centuries of Design, Ambition and Miscalculation*. New York: Harper & Row.

Barnstone, Deborah Ascher. 2016. Between the Walls: The Berlin No-Man's Land Reconsidered. *Journal of Urban Design* 21, 3: 287–301.

Bauer, Catherine. 1934. *Modern Housing*. New York: Houghton Mifflin.

Beauregard, Robert A. 2015. *Planning Matter. Acting with Things*. Chicago: University of Chicago Press.

Benevolo, Leonardo. 1980. *The History of the City*. Cambridge, MA: MIT Press.

Berman, Marshall. 1982. *All That Is Solid Melts into Air: The Experience of Modernity*. New York: Penguin Books.

Biles, Roger. 2005. The Rise and Fall of Soul City: Planning, Politics, and Race in Recent America. *Journal of Planning History* 4, 1: 52–72.

Blackwell, Timothy, and Sebastian Kohl. 2017. "Varieties of Housing Finance in Historical Perspective: The Impact of Mortgage Finance Systems on Urban Structures and Homeownership." MPIfG Discussion Paper, No. 17/2. Cologne: Max Planck Institute for the Study of Societies. https://hdl.handle.net/11858/00-001M-0000-002C-6801-F.

Bluestone, Daniel M. 1988. Detroit's City Beautiful and the Problem of Commerce. *Journal of the Society of Architectural Historians* 47, 3: 245–262.

Blumenfeld, Hans. 1967. *The Modern Metropolis: Its Origins, Growth, Characteristics, and Planning*. Cambridge, MA: MIT Press.

Boyer, M. Christine. 1983. *Dreaming the Rational City: The Myth of American City Planning*. Cambridge, MA: MIT Press.

Brand, Diane. 2011. Crossing the Roads: Urban Diagonals in New Zealand and the Nineteenth Century Anglo-Colonial World. *Planning Perspectives* 26, 3: 423–444.

Braudel, Fernand. 1992. *Civilization and Capitalism, 15th–18th Century*, Vol. I: *The Structure of Everyday Life*. Berkeley: University of California Press.

Braunfels, Wolfgang. 1990. *Urban Design in Western Europe: Regime and Architecture, 900–1900*. Translated by Kenneth J. Northcott. Chicago: University of Chicago Press.

Broudehoux, Anne-Marie. 2011. "Delirious Beijing: Euphoria and Despair in the Olympic Metropolis." In Mike Davis and Daniel Bertrand Monk, Eds., *Evil Paradises*. New York: The New Press. Pp. 87–101.

Buras, Nir Haim. 2019. *The Art of Classic Planning: Building Beautiful and Enduring Communities*. Cambridge, MA: Belknap Press of Harvard University Press.

Burnham, Daniel H., assisted by Edward H. Bennett. 1909. *Plan of Chicago*. Chicago: Commercial Club.

Busquets, J., D. Yang, and M. Keller. 2019. *Urban Grids: Handbook for Regular City Design*. Cambridge, MA: ORO Editions.

Calthorpe, Peter, and Jerry Walters. 2017. Autonomous Vehicles: Hype and Potential. *Urban Land* January/February: 58–62.

Campanella, Richard. 2019. Straight Streets in a Curvaceous Crescent: Colonial Urban Planning and Its Impact on Modern New Orleans. *Journal of Planning History* 18, 3: 196–211.

Campanella, Thomas. 2011. "Jane Jacobs and the Death and Life of American Planning." In Max Page and Timothy Mennel, Eds., *Reconsidering Jane Jacobs*. Chicago: Planners Press. Pp. 141–160.

Campanella, Thomas J. 2023. "Introduction: The Necessity for Congestion." In Charles Downing Lay, Eds., *The Freedom of the City*. Washington, DC: Island Press. Pp. 1–18.Capolino, Patrizia. 2011. Tirana: A Capital City Transformed by the Italians. *Planning Perspectives* 26, 4: 591–615.

Cavaglieri, Giorgio. 1947. Outline for a History of City Planning. From Prehistory to the Fall of the Roman Empire. *Journal of the Society of Architectural Historians* 6, 3/4: 22–34.

Cavalcanti, Maria de Betânia Uchôa. 1997. Urban Reconstruction and Autocratic Regimes: Ceausescu's Bucharest in Its Historic Context. *Planning Perspectives* 12: 71–109.

Cerda, Ildefons. 1867. *Teoría General de la Urbanización* ("General Theory of Urbanization"). Madrid: n.p.

Charmes, Eric. 2010. Cul-de-sacs, Superblocks and Environmental Areas as Supports of Residential Territorialization. *Journal of Urban Design* 15, 3: 357–372.

Cherry, Gordon E. 1988. *Cities and Plans: The Shaping of Urban Britain in the Nineteenth and Twentieth Centuries*. New York: E. Arnold.

Choay, Françoise, 1969. *The Modern City: Planning in the 19th Century*. New York: George Braziller.

Clay, Grady. 1980. *Close-up: How to Read the American City*. Chicago: University of Chicago Press.

Cohen, Lizbeth. 2003. *A Consumer's Republic: The Politics of Mass Consumption in Postwar America*. New York: Knopf.

Collins, George R. 1959. Linear Planning throughout the World. *Journal of the Society of Architectural Historians* 18, 3: 74–93.

Comstock, W. Phillips. 1919. *The Housing Book: Containing Photographic Reproductions, with Floor Plans of Workingmen's Homes*. New York: William T. Comstock Co.

Conzen, Michael. 1980. "The Morphology of Nineteenth Century Cities in the U.S." In Woodrow Borah, Jorge Hardoy, and Gilbert A. Stelter, Eds., *Urbanization in the Americas*. Ottawa: National Museums of Canada. Pp. 119–141.

Cooley, Charles Horton. *Social Organization*. New York: Charles Scribner's Sons, 1912.

Corner, J. 2006. "Terra Fluxus." In Charles Waldheim, Ed., *The Landscape Urbanism Reader*. New York: Princeton Architectural Press. Pp. 21–33.

Creese, Walter L. 1992. *The Search for Environment*. Baltimore: Johns Hopkins University Press.

Crinson, Mark. 1997. Abadan: Planning and Architecture under the Anglo-Iranian Oil Company. *Planning Perspectives* 12: 341–359.

Culpin, Ewart G. 1913. *The Garden City Movement Up-to-Date*. London: Garden Cities and Towns Planning Association.

Dahir, James. 1958. *Greendale Comes of Age: The Story of Wisconsin's Best Known Planned Community as It Enters Its Twenty-First Year, a Manuscript Prepared for the Milwaukee Community Development Corporation*. Milwaukee, WI: Milwaukee Community Development Corp.

Dal Co, Francesco. 1979. "From Parks to the Region: Progressive Ideology and the Reform of the American City." In Giorgio Ciucci, Francesco Dal Co, Mario Manieri-Elia, and Manfredo Tafuri, Eds., *The American City: From the Civil War to the New Deal*. Cambridge, MA: The MIT Press. Pp. 143–291.

Darin, Michaël. 2004. Designating Urban Forms: French *boulevards* and *avenues*. *Planning Perspectives* 19: 133–154.

Davies, Pearl J. 1958. *Real Estate in American History*. New York: Public Affairs Press.

Davis, Mike. 2007. "Sand, Fear, and Money in Dubai." In Mike Davis and Daniel Bertrand Monk, Eds., *Evil Paradises*. New York: The New Press. Pp. 48–68.

Denman, D. S. 2019. Machiavelli and the Fortress City. *Political Theory* 47, 2: 203–229. https://doi.org/10.1177/0090591718772546.

Dennis, Michael. 2022. *Temples and Towns: The Form, Elements, and Principles of Planned Towns*. New York: ORO Editions.Doug Allen Institute. n.d. History of Urban Form Lecture Series. https://dougalleninstitute.notion.site/9e6df33b6b234c5cb8cd8373857159b3.

Draper, Joan E. 1996. "The Art and Science of Park Planning in the United States." In Mary Corbin Sies and Christopher Silver, Eds., *Planning the Twentieth-Century American City*. Baltimore: Johns Hopkins University Press. Pp. 98–119.

Duany, Andrés, Paul Roberts, and Emily Talen. 2015. *A General Theory of Urbanism*. Miami: DPZ.

Duany, Plater-Zyberk & Co. 2014. *The Lexicon of the New Urbanism*. Miami: DPZ. https://www.dpz.com/wp-content/uploads/2017/06/Lexicon-2014.pdf.

Dutt, B. B. 2009. *Town Planning in Ancient India*. Delhi: Isha Books.

Eaton, Ruth. 2002. *Ideal Cities: Utopianism and the (Un) Built Environment*. New York: Thames & Hudson.

Edwards, Michael. 2001. City Design: What Went Wrong with Milton Keynes? *Journal of Urban Design* 6, 1: 87–96.

Elsheshtawy, Yasser. 2011. "Urban Dualities in the Arab World: From a Narrative of Loss to Neo-Liberal Urbanism." In Michael Larice and Elizabeth Macdonald, Eds., *The Urban Design Reader*. 2nd ed. London: Routledge. Pp. 475–496.

Faure, Alain. 2006. Local Life in Working-Class Paris at the End of the Nineteenth Century. *Journal of Urban History* 32, 5: 761–772. doi:10.1177/0096144206287098.

Fischer, K. F. 1989. "Canberra: Myths and Models." *The Town Planning Review* 60, 2: 155–194. doi:10.2307/40112789.

Fishman, Robert. 1977. *Urban Utopias of the Twentieth Century: Ebenezer Howard, Frank Lloyd Wright and Le Corbusier*. New York: Basic Books.

Fishman, Robert. 1987. *Bourgeois Utopias: The Rise and Fall of Suburbia*. New York: Basic Books.

Fishman, Robert. 2000. *The American Planning Tradition: Culture and Policy*. Washington, DC: Woodrow Wilson Centre Press.

Fishman, Robert. 2002. "The Bounded City." In Kermit C. Parsons and David Schuyler, Eds., *From Garden City to Green City: The Legacy of Ebenezer Howard*. Baltimore: Johns Hopkins University Press. Pp. 58–66.

Fishman, Robert. 2011. "The Open and the Enclosed: Shifting Paradigms in Modern Urban Design." In Tridib Banerjee and Anastasia Loukaitou-Sideris, Eds., *Companion to Urban Design*. London: Routledge. Pp. 30–40.Fleure, H. J. 1920. Some Types of Cities in Temperate Europe. *Geographical Review* 10, 6: 357–374. https://doi.org/10.2307/207531.

Forster, K. W. 1969. *From "Rocca" to "Civitas": Urban Planning at Sabbioneta*. Milan: Istituto Editoriale Italiano.

Foster, Elene. 1919. What Is Home without a Golf Course? *New-York Tribune*, September 28, 1919. https://chroniclingamerica.loc.gov/lccn/sn83030214/1919-09-28/ed-1/seq-79/.

Frederick, Matthew, and Vikas Mehta. 2018. *101 Things I Learned in Urban Design School*. New York: Three Rivers Press.

Freestone, Robert, and David Nichols. 2012. Pacific Crossing? From the American Bungalow Court to the Australian Cul-de-sac. *Journal of Planning History* 12, 1: 3–27.

Frolic, B. Michael. 1964. The Soviet City. *The Town Planning Review* 34, 4: 285–306. doi:10.2307/40102409.

Gallagher, Winifred. 1994. *The Power of Place: How Our Surroundings Shape Our Thoughts, Emotions, Actions*. New York: Perennial.

Gallion, Arthur B., and Simon Eisner. 1963. *The Urban Pattern: City Planning and Design*. Princeton, NJ: D. Van Nostrand Co.

Gans, Herbert. 1967. Letter. *Journal of the American Institute of Planners* 33: 183.

Gaube, Heinz. 1979. *Iranian Cities*. New York: New York University Press.

Gehan, Selim. 2014. Instituting Order: The Limitations of Nasser's Post-colonial Planning Visions for Cairo in the Case of the Indigenous Quarter of Bulaq (1952–1970). *Planning Perspectives* 29, 1: 67–89. doi:10.1080/02665433.2013.808580.

Giedion, Sigfried. 1941. *Space Time and Architecture*. Cambridge, MA: Harvard University Press.

Gillem, Mark L. 2007. *America Town: Building the Outposts of Empire*. Minneapolis: University of Minnesota Press.

Girling, C. L., and K. Helphand. 1994. *Yard, Street, Park: The Design of Suburban Open Space*. New York: John Wiley & Sons.

Golding, Naomi H. 1975. Plato as City Planner. *Arethusa* 8, 2: 359–371.

Gottdiener, Mark. 1977. *Planned Sprawl: Private and Public Interests in Suburbia*. Beverly Hills, CA: Sage.

Grant, Jill. 2001. The Dark Side of the Grid: Power and Urban Design. *Planning Perspectives* 16: 219–241.Gutkind, Erwin A. 1962. *The Twilight of Cities*. New York: Free Press.

Gutkind, Erwin A. 1971. *Urban Development in Western Europe: The Netherlands and Great Britain*. New York: Free Press.

Gutnov, A. É. 1971. *The Ideal Communist City*. I Press Series on the Human Environment. New York: George Braziller.

Hall, Peter. 2002. *Cities of Tomorrow*. London: Wiley-Blackwell.

Harvey, David. 1973. *Social Justice and the City*. Baltimore: Johns Hopkins University Press.

Harvey, David. 1989. *The Urban Experience*. Baltimore: Johns Hopkins University Press.

Harvey, David. 2000. *Spaces of Hope*. Berkeley: University of California Press.

Hayden, Dolores. 1976. *Seven American Utopias*. Cambridge, MA: MIT Press.

Hayden, Dolores. 1991. The Potential of Ethnic Places for Urban Landscapes. *Places* 7, 1: 11–17.Hayden, Dolores. 2003. *Building Suburbia: Green Fields and Urban Growth, 1820–2000*. New York: Pantheon Books.

Hayden, Dolores. 2004. *A Field Guide to Sprawl*. New York: W. W. Norton.

Hedman, Richard, and Andrew Jaszewski. 1984. *Fundamentals of Urban Design*. Chicago: American Planning Association.

Hegemann, Werner, and Elbert Peets. 1922. *American Vitruvius: An Architects' Handbook of Civic Art*. New York: Architectural Book Publishing Co.

Henderson, Susan R. 2010. Römerstadt: The Modern Garden City. *Planning Perspectives* 25, 3: 323–346.

Hla, U Kan. 1978. Traditional Town Planning in Burma. *Journal of the Society of Architectural Historians* 37, 2: 92–104.

Hohenberg, Paul M., and Lynn Hollen Lees. 1985. *The Making of Urban Europe 1000–1950*. Cambridge, MA: Harvard University Press.

Hunter, Julius K. 1988. *Westmoreland and Portland Place: The History and Architecture of America's Premier Private Streets, 1888–1988*. Columbia: University of Missouri Press.

Hwang, Soe Won, and Hyo-Jin Kim. 2020. The Intensifying Gated Exclusiveness of Apartment Complex Boundary Design in Seoul, Korea. *Planning Perspectives* 35, 4: 719–729.

Irazábal, Clara. 2006. Localizing Urban Design Traditions: Gated and Edge Cities in Curitiba. *Journal of Urban Design* 11, 1: 73–96.

Irving, R. G. 1981. *Indian Summer: Lutyens, Baker and Imperial Delhi*. New Haven, CT: Yale University Press.

Jackson, J. B. 1979. "The Order of a Landscape." In D.W. Meinig, Ed., *The Interpretation of Ordinary Landscapes*. New York: Oxford University Press. Pp. 153–163.

Jacobs, Jane. 1961. *The Death and Life of Great American Cities*. New York: Vintage Books.

Jäger, Thomas. 2004. The Art of Orthogonal Planning: Laparelli's Trigonometric Design of Valletta. *Journal of the Society of Architectural Historians* 63, 1: 4–31.

Jencks, Charles. 1973. *Modern Movements in Architecture*. New York: Anchor Press.

Jeong, Sang Kyu, Tae Ho Lee, and Yong Un Ban. 2015. Characteristics of Spatial Configurations in Pyongyang, North Korea. *Habitat International* 47: 148–157. https://doi.org/10.1016/j.habitatint.2015.01.010.

Kacar, Duygu. 2010. Ankara, a Small Town, Transformed to a Nation's Capital. *Journal of Planning History* 9, 1: 43–65.

Keating, Dennis, Norm Krumholz, and Ann Marie Wieland. 2005. Cleveland's Lakefront: Its Development and Planning. *Journal of Planning History* 4, 2: 129–154.

Keyvanian, Carla. 2005. Concerted Efforts: The Quarter of the Barberini Casa Grande in Seventeenth-Century Rome. *Journal of the Society of Architectural Historians* 64, 3: 292–311. doi:10.2307/25 068166.

Kheirabadi, Masoud. 1991. *Iranian Cities: Formation and Development*. Austin: University of Texas Press.

Kickert, Conrad. 2019. *Dream City: Creation, Destruction, and Reinvention in Downtown Detroit*. Cambridge, MA: MIT Press.

Kim, Jung In. 2014. Making Cities Global: The New City Development of Songdo, Yujiapu and Lingang. *Planning Perspectives* 29, 3: 329–356.

King, Ross. 2007. Re-writing the City: Putrajaya as Representation. *Journal of Urban Design* 12, 1: 117–138.

Kling, Samuel. 2013. Wide Boulevards, Narrow Visions: Burnham's Street System and the Chicago Plan Commission, 1909–1930. *Journal of Planning History* 12, 3: 245–268.Koolhaas, Rem. 1995. *S,M,L,XL*. New York: Monacelli Press.

Koolhaas, Rem. 1997. *Delirious New York*. New York: Monacelli Press.Kostof, Spiro. 1978. "The Emperor and the Duce: The Planning of the Piazzale Augusto Imperatore in Rome." In H. A. Millon and L. Nochlin, Eds., *Art and Architecture in the Service of Politics*. Cambridge, MA: MIT Press. Pp. 270–305.

Kostof, Spiro. 1991. *The City Shaped*. London: Thames & Hudson.

Kostof, Spiro. 1992. *The City Assembled*. London: Thames & Hudson.

Krase, Jerome. 2004. Italian American Urban Landscapes: Images of Social and Cultural Capital. *Italian Americana* 22, 1: 17–44. doi:10.2307/29776910.

Kreiger, Alex. 2019. *City on a Hill: Urban Idealism in America from the Puritans to the Present*. Cambridge, MA: Belknap Press of Harvard University Press.

Krier, Léon. 1984. *Léon Krier, Houses, Palaces, Cities*. AD Profile 54. London: Architectural Design AD Editions.

Krier, Léon. 2011. *The Architecture of Community*. Washington, DC: Island Press.

Kunstler, James Howard. 2001. *The City in Mind*. New York: Free Press.

Ladd, Brian K. 1987. Urban Aesthetics and the Discovery of the Urban Fabric in Turn-of-the-Century Germany. *Planning Perspectives* 2, 3: 270–286. doi:10.1080/02665438708725644.

La Gory, Mark, and John Pipkin. 1981. *Urban Social Space*. Belmont, CA: Wadsworth.

Lang, Michael H. 1996. "The Design of Yorkship Garden Village." In Mary Corbin Sies and Christopher Silver, Eds., *Planning the Twentieth-Century American City*. Baltimore: Johns Hopkins University Press. Pp. 120–144.

Langdon, Philip. 2023. How Urbanism, Density, and Spatial Enclosure Are Related. *Public Square*, April 18, 2023. https://www.cnu.org/publicsquare/2023/04/18/how-urbanism-density-and-spatial-enclosure-are-related.

Larice, Michael Angelo. 2005. Great Neighborhoods: The Livability and Morphology of High Density Neighborhoods in Urban North America. PhD diss., University of California, Berkeley.

Le Corbusier. 1929. *The City of Tomorrow and Its Planning*. New York: Dover.

Le Corbusier. 1964 (1937). *When the Cathedrals Were White*. New York: McGraw-Hill.

Lefebvre, Henri. 1991. *The Production of Space*. Translated by Donald Nicholson-Smith. Malden, MA: Blackwell.

Lesger, Clé, and Marco H. D. Van Leeuwen. 2012. Residential Segregation from the Sixteenth to the Nineteenth Century: Evidence from the Netherlands. *Journal of Interdisciplinary History* 42, 3: 333–369.

Lewis, Michael J. 2016. *City of Refuge: Separatists and Utopian Town Planning*. Princeton, NJ: Princeton University Press.

Lewis, Pierce F. 2018. *New Orleans: The Making of an Urban Landscape*. Charlottesville: University of Virginia Press.

Lin, Zhong-Jie. 2007. From Megastructure to Megalopolis: Formation and Transformation of Mega-projects in Tokyo Bay. *Journal of Urban Design* 12, 1: 73–92.

Lipsitz, George. 2004. "Locked on This Earth: Movement and Stasis in Black Culture." Paper presented at the symposium Constructing Race: The Built Environment, Minoritization, and Racism in the United States. University of Illinois, Urbana-Champaign, March 5–6.

Loudon, J. C. 1982. *An Encyclopaedia of Gardening; Comprising the Theory and Practice*. London: Longman, Rees, Orme, Brown, Green, and Longman, based on 1834 revisions. Facsimile repr., New York: Garland.

Loukaitou-Sideris, Anastasia. 2012. Addressing the Challenges of Urban Landscapes: Normative Goals for Urban Design. *Journal of Urban Design* 17, 4: 467–484.

Loukaitou-Sideris, Anastasia, and Tridib Banerjee. 2011. "Downtown Urban Design." In Tridib Banerjee and Anastasia Loukaitou-Sideris, *Companion to Urban Design*. London: Routledge. Pp. 345–355.Low, Setha. 2023. *Why Public Space Matters*. New York: Oxford University Press.

Lynch, Kevin. 1981. *Good City Form*. Cambridge, MA: MIT Press.

MacDonald, Elizabeth. 2005. Suburban Vision to Urban Reality: The Evolution of Olmsted and Vaux's Brooklyn Parkway Neighborhoods. *Journal of Planning History* 4, 4: 295–321.

Macfarlane, Patrick W. 1954. Planning an Arab Town: Kuwait on the Persian Gulf. *Journal of the Town Planning Institute* 40, 5: 110–113.

Machiavelli, Niccolò. 2005. *The Prince*. Translated by Peter Bondanella. Oxford: Oxford University Press. Originally published 1532.

Mackin, Anne. 2006. *Americans and Their Land*. Ann Arbor: University of Michigan Press.

Madanipour, Ali, ed. 2010. *Whose Public Space?: International Case Studies in Urban Design and Development*. London: Routledge.

Madanipour, A., K. Miciukiewicz, and G. Vigar. 2018. Master Plans and Urban Change: The Case of Sheffield City Centre. *Journal of Urban Design* 23, 4: 465–481. https://doi-org.proxy.uchicago.edu/10.1080/13574809.2018.1435996.Madeddu, Manuela, and Xiaoqing Zhang. 2017. Harmonious Spaces: The Influence of Feng Shui on Urban Form and Design. *Journal of Urban Design* 22, 6: 709–725.

Marcuse, Peter. 1987. The Grid as City Plan: New York City and Laissez-Faire Planning in the Nineteenth Century. *Planning Perspectives* 2: 287–310.

Marshall, Alex. 2000. *How Cities Work: Suburbs, Sprawl, and the Roads Not Taken*. Austin: University of Texas Press.Masterman, C. F. G. 1909. *The Condition of England*. London: Methuen.

McCann, L. D. 1996. Planning and Building the Corporate Suburb of Mount Royal, 1920–1925. *Planning Perspectives* 11: 259–301.

Mehaffy, Michael W., Sergio Porta, and Ombretta Romice. 2014. The "Neighborhood Unit" on Trial: A Case Study in the Impacts of Urban Morphology. *Journal of Urbanism: International Research on Placemaking and Urban Sustainability* 8, 2: 1–19. doi:10.1080/17549175.2014.908786.

Meinig, D. W. 1979. "Symbolic Landscapes: Some Idealizations of American Communities." In D. W. Meinig, Ed., *The Interpretation of Ordinary Landscapes*. New York: Oxford University Press. Pp. 164–192.

Mennel, Timothy. 2004. Victor Gruen and the Construction of Cold War Utopias. *Journal of Planning History* 3, 2: 116–150.

Miller, Susan Gilson, Attilio Petruccioli, and Mauro Bertagnin. 2001. Inscribing Minority Space in the Islamic City: The Jewish Quarter of Fez (1438–1912). *Journal of the Society of Architectural Historians* 60, 3: 310–327.

Miller, Zane L. *Visions of Place: The City, Neighborhoods, Suburbs, and Cincinnati's Clifton, 1850–2000*. Urban Life and Urban Landscape Series. Columbus: Ohio State University Press, 2001.

Moody, Walter D. 1916. *Wacker's Manual of the Plan of Chicago*. 2nd ed. Chicago: Chicago Plan Commission.

Morley, Ian. 2018. The Filipinization of the American City Beautiful, 1916–1935. *Journal of Planning History* 17, 4: 251–280.

Morosi, Julio Angel. 2003. La Plata: An Advanced Nineteenth Century New Town with Ancient Roots. *Planning Perspectives* 18: 23–46.

Morris, A. E. J. 1979. *History of Urban Form before the Industrial Revolutions*. London: George Goodwin.

Mostafavi, Mohsen, and Gareth Doherty, eds. 2010. *Ecological Urbanism*. Zurich: Lars Muller Publishers.

Moudon, Anne Vernez. "Housing and Settlement Design Series Working Paper: Spatial Structures." Cambridge, MA: Massachusetts Institute of Technology, 1978.

Mullin, John R. 1992. The Reconstruction of Lisbon Following the Earthquake of 1755: A Study of Despotic Planning. *Journal of the International History of City Planning Association* 45: 1–18.

Mumford, Lewis. 1961. *The City in History: Its Origins, Its Transformations, and Its Prospects*. New York: Harcourt Brace Jovanovich.

Mumford, Lewis. 1962. Megalopolis as Anti-City. *Architectural Record*, December. Pp. 101–108.

Mumford, Lewis. 1962a. Home Remedies for Urban Cancer. *The New Yorker*, December 1. Pp. 1–32.

Mumford, Lewis.1962b. Yesterday's City of Tomorrow. *Architectural Record*, November. Pp. 139–144.

Murray, Martin J. 2013. The Quandary of Post-Public Space: New Urbanism, Melrose Arch and the Rebuilding of Johannesburg after Apartheid. *Journal of Urban Design* 18, 1: 119–144.

Myers, Garth Andrew. Designing Power: Forms and Purposes of Colonial Model Neighborhoods in British Africa. *Habitat International* 27, 2: 193–204.

Napier, David A. 1988. Bernini's Anthropology: A "Key" to the Piazza San Pietro. *Res: Anthropology and Aesthetics* 16: 17–32.

Navapan, Nattika. 2014. Absolute Monarchy and the Development of Bangkok's Urban Spaces. *Planning Perspectives* 29, 1: 1–24.

Newman, Oscar. 1972. *Defensible Space: Crime Prevention through Urban Design*. New York: Macmillan.

Olmsted, Vaux & Co. 1868. "Preliminary Report upon the Proposed Suburban Village at Riverside, near Chicago." New York.

Otto, Christian F. 1965. City-Planning Theory in Nationalist-Socialist Germany. *Journal of the Society of Architectural Historians* 24, 1: 70–74.

Parera, Cecilia. 2005. Mormon Town Planning: Physical and Social Relevance. *Journal of Planning History* 4, 2: 155–174.

Pedersen, Martin C. 2023. Peter Calthorpe Has a Plan for More Housing in California. Common Edge. https://commonedge.org/peter-calthorpe-has-a-plan-for-more-housing-in-california/.

Peets, Elbert. 1930. Famous Town Planners IV. The Plans for Rebuilding London in 1666. *Town Planning Review* 14, 1: 13–30.

Peterson, Jon A. 2003. *The Birth of City Planning in the United States, 1840–1917*. Baltimore: Johns Hopkins University Press.

Pittari, John J. "Sunnyside Gardens and Radburn." In Mary Corbin Sies, Isabelle Gournay, and Robert Freestone, Eds., *Iconic Planned Communities and the Challenge of Change*. Philadelphia: University of Pennsylvania Press. Pp. 217–237.

Platt, C. 1976. *The English Medieval Town*. London: Secker & Warburg.

Price, Virginia. 2019. Introduction to Planning in Early American Cities. *Journal of Planning History* 18, 3: 169–171.

Proudfoot, Peter R. 1996. The Symbolism of the Crystal in the Planning and Geometry of the Design for Canberra. *Planning Perspectives* 11: 225–257.

Rapoport, Amos. 1990. *The Meaning of the Built Environment: A Nonverbal Communication Approach*. Rev. ed. Tucson: University of Arizona Press.

Rasmussen, Steen Eiler. 1934 (1967). *London: The Unique City*. Cambridge, MA: MIT Press.

Rasmussen, Steen Eiler. 1969. *Towns and Buildings*. Cambridge, MA: MIT Press.

Rego, Renato Leão. 2014. Brazilian Garden Cities and Suburbs: Accommodating Urban Modernity and Foreign Ideals. *Journal of Planning History* 13, 4: 276–295.

Reps, John. 1965. *The Making of Urban America: A History of City Planning in the United States*. Princeton, NJ: Princeton University Press.

Reps, John. 1967. *Monumental Washington*. Princeton, NJ: Princeton University Press.

Robinson, Charles Mulford. 1903. *Modern Civic Art*. New York: G. P. Putnam's Sons.

Rotenberg, Robert, and Gary McDonogh. 1993. *The Cultural Meaning of Urban Space*. Westport, CT: Bergin & Garvey.

Roth, Darlene R. 1993. *Frederick Law Olmsted's First and Last Suburbs: Riverside and Druid Hills*. National Association for Olmsted Parks Workbook 4. Bethesda, MD: National Association for Olmsted Parks.

Roy, Ananya, and Ong Aihwa, eds. 2011. *Worlding Cities*. West Sussex: Wiley-Blackwell.

Ruggeri, Laura. 2007. "'Palm Springs': Imagineering California in Hong Kong." In Mike Davis and Daniel Bertrand Monk, Eds., *Evil Paradises*. New York: The New Press. Pp. 102–113.

Rybczynski, Witold. 1999. *A Clearing in the Distance: Frederick Law Olmsted and America in the Nineteenth Century*. New York: Scribner.

Rykwert, J. 1970. *The Idea of a Town: The Anthropology of Urban Form in Rome, Italy and the Ancient World*. London: Faber & Faber.

Rykwert, Joseph. 2000. *The Seduction of Place: The History and Future of the City*. New York: Vintage.

Saalman, Howard. 1968. *Medieval Cities*. New York: George Braziller.

Schinz, A. 1996. *The Magic Square: Cities in Ancient China*. Stuttgart: Edition Axel Menges.

Schmidt, Stephan. 2005. Cultural Influences and the Built Environment: An Examination of Kumasi, Ghana. *Journal of Urban Design* 10, 3: 353–370.

Schorske, Carl. 1980. *Fin-de-siècle Vienna: Politics and Culture*. New York: Vintage.

Schuman, Tony, and Elliott Sclar. 1996. "The Impact of Ideology on American Town Planning." In Mary Corbin Sies and Christopher Silver, Eds., *Planning the Twentieth-Century American City*. Baltimore: Johns Hopkins University Press. Pp. 428–448.

Schuyler, David. 2019. "Riverside: The First Comprehensively Designed Suburban Community in the United States." In Mary Corbin Sies, Isabelle Gournay, and Robert Freestone, Eds., *Iconic Planned Communities and the Challenge of Change*. Philadelphia: University of Pennsylvania Press. Pp. 40–60.

Scott, Mel. 1969. *American City Planning since 1890*. Berkeley: University of California Press.

Scruton, R. 1987. "Public Space and the Classical Vernacular." In N. Glazer and M. Lilla, Eds., *The Public Face of Architecture: Civic Culture and Public Spaces*. New York: Free Press. Pp. 13–25.

Sharp, Thomas. 1932. *Town and Countryside: Some Aspects of Urban and Rural Development*. London: Humphrey Milford.

Sharp, Thomas. 1936. *English Panorama*. London: Dent.

Shiber, Saba George. 1964. *The Kuwait Urbanization: Documentation, Analysis, Critique*. Published by the author.

Sieber, Timothy R. 1993. "Public Access on the Urban Waterfront: A question of Vision." In Robert Rotenberg and Gary McDonogh, Eds., *The Cultural Meaning of Urban Space*. Westport, CT: Bergin & Garvey. Pp. 173–193.

Siembieda, W. J., and E. L. Moreno. 1998. Barrios and the Hispanic American City: Cultural Value. *Journal of Urban Design* 3, 1: 39–52. https://doi-org.10.1080/13574809808724415.

Silliman, Benjamin, ed. 1830. Architecture in the United States. *American Journal of Science and Arts* 17: 249–273. https://www.biodiversitylibrary.org/item/97104#page/311/mode/1up.

Silver, Christopher. "Menteng: Heritage of a Planned Community in a Southeast Asian Megacity." In Mary Corbin Sies, Isabelle Gournay, and Robert Freestone, Eds., *Iconic Planned Communities and the Challenge of Change*. Philadelphia: University of Pennsylvania Press. Pp. 111–131.

Sitte, Camillo. 1889. *City Planning According to Artistic Principles*. Translated from the German by George R. Collins and Christiane Crasemann Collins. New York: Random House.

Smith, Michael E. 2007. Form and Meaning in the Earliest Cities: A New Approach to Ancient Urban Planning. *Journal of Planning History* 6, 1: 3–47.

Souther, J. Mark. 2011. Acropolis of the Middle-West: Decay, Renewal, and Boosterism in Cleveland's University Circle. *Journal of Planning History* 10, 1: 30–58.

Southworth, M., and B. Parthasarathy. 1996. The Suburban Public Realm I: Its Emergence, Growth and Transformation in the American Metropolis. *Journal of Urban Design* 1, 3: 245–264.

Speer, A. 1997. *Inside the Third Reich*. New York: Simon & Schuster.

Stein, Clarence. 1933. Housing and the Depression. *Octagon: A Journal of the American Institute of Architects* 5, 6: 3–5.

Stein, Clarence. 1951. *Toward New Towns for America*. Liverpool: University Press of Liverpool.

Stern, Robert A. M., David Fishman, and Jacob Tilove. 2013. *Planned Paradise: The Garden Suburb and the Modern City*. New York: Monacelli Press.

Stern, Robert A. M., and John M. Massengale. 1981. *The Anglo-American Suburb*. London: Architectural Design.Stevens, Quentin. 2015. Masterplanning Public Memorials: An Historical Comparison of Washington, Ottawa and Canberra. *Planning Perspectives* 30, 1: 39–66.

Stieber, Nancy. 1998. *Housing Design and Society in Amsterdam: Reconfiguring Urban Order and Identity, 1900–1920*. Chicago: University of Chicago Press.

Stone, Elizabeth C. 1987. *Nippur Neighborhoods*. Chicago: Oriental Institute of the University of Chicago.

Stübben, Joseph. 1980 (1890). *City Building (Der Städtebau)*. Repr. ed. Braunschweig: Vieweg. https://uchicago.app.box.com/s/nequkaloacwqv8p382qc13htvbldmafc.

Summerson, John. 1963. *Heavenly Mansion*. New York: W. W. Norton.

Sutcliffe, Anthony. 1981. *Towards the Planned City: German, Britain, the United States and France 1780–1914*. New York: St. Martin's Press.

Suttles, G. D. 1968. *The Social Order of the Slum: Ethnicity and Territory in the Inner City*. Chicago: University of Chicago Press.

Talen, Emily. 2005. *New Urbanism and American Planning: The Conflict of Cultures*. New York: Routledge.

Talen, Emily. 2015. *City Rules*. Washington, DC: Island Press.

Talen, Emily. 2019. *Neighborhood*. London: Oxford University Press.

Talen, Emily, and Sungduck Lee. 2018. *Design for Social Diversity*. New York: Routledge.

Taylor, John H. 1989. City Form and Capital Culture: Remaking Ottawa. *Planning Perspectives* 4, 1: 79–105.

Tonkiss, Fran. 2013. *Cities by Design: The Social Life of Urban Form*. Cambridge: Polity Press.

Trancik, Roger. 1986. *Finding Lost Space*. New York: Van Nostrand Reinhold.

Triggs, H. Inigo. 1909. *Town Planning: Past, Present and Possible*. London: Methuen & Co.

Tuan, Yi-Fu. 1981. *Space and Place: The Perspective of Experience*. Minneapolis: University of Minnesota Press.

Tunnard, Christopher. 1953. *The City of Man*. New York: Charles Scribner's Sons.

Unwin, Raymond. 1901. "Building & Natural Beauty." In *The Art of Building a Home*. London: Longmans. Pp. 83–89.

Unwin, Raymond. 1909. *Town Planning in Practice*. London: T. Fisher Unwin.

Venturi, Robert, Steven Izenour, and Denise Scott Brown. 1977. *Learning from Las Vegas: The Forgotten Symbolism of Architectural Form*. Cambridge, MA: MIT Press.

Veselka, Robert E. 2000. *The Courthouse Square in Texas*. Austin: University of Texas Press.

Vitruvius, Marcus. 1960. *The Ten Books on Architecture*. Dover Publications. First published in the first century BCE. https://lexundria.com/vitr/1.5.2/cf.

Wakeman, Rosemary. 2016. *Practicing Utopia: An Intellectual History of the New Town Movement*. Chicago: University of Chicago Press.

Waldheim, Charles. 2006. *The Landscape Urbanism Reader*. New York: Princeton Architectural Press.

Wall, A. 1999. "Programming the Urban Surface." In Corner, James, Ed., *Recovering Landscape: Essays in Contemporary Landscape Theory*. New York: Princeton Architectural Press. Pp. 233–249.

Ward, David. 1980. Environs and Neighbours in the "Two Nations" Residential Differentiation in Mid-Nineteenth-Century Leeds. *Journal of Historical Geography* 6, 2: 133–162.

Warner, Sam Bass. 1962. *Streetcar Suburbs: The Process of Growth in Boston, 1870–1900*. Cambridge, MA: Harvard University Press.

Webber, M. M. 1963. "Order in Diversity: Community without Propinquity." In L. Wingo, Ed., *Cities and Space: The Future Use of Urban Land*. Baltimore: Johns Hopkins University Press. Pp. 23–56.

Whitehead, Mark. 2003. Love Thy Neighbourhood—Rethinking the Politics of Scale and Walsall's Struggle for Neighbourhood Democracy. *Environment and Planning A* 35, 2: 277–300. doi:10.1068/a35127.

Whyte, William H. 1956. *Organization Man*. New York: Simon & Schuster.

Williamson, Thad. 2010. *Sprawl, Justice, and Citizenship: The Civic Costs of the American Way of Life*. New York: Oxford University Press.

Wilson, Francesca M. 1955. *Strange Island*. London: Longmans.

Wilson, William H. 1989. *The City Beautiful Movement*. Baltimore, MD: Johns Hopkins University Press.

Woods, Robert A., and Albert J. Kennedy. 1962. *The Zone of Emergence: Observations of the Lower Middle and Upper Working Class Communities of Boston, 1905–1914*. 2nd ed. Cambridge, MA: MIT Press.

Yerolympos, Alexandra. 1993. A New City for a New State: City Planning and the Formation of National Identity in the Balkans (1820s–1920s). *Planning Perspective* 8, 3: 233–257.

Yglesias, Caren. 2019. To Build a Metaphor: L'Enfant's Design for the City of Washington. *Journal of Planning History* 18, 3: 172–195.

Zad, Vahid Vahdat. 2012. Spatial Discrimination in Tehran's Modern Urban Planning 1906–1979. *Journal of Planning History* 12, 1: 49–62.

Zaidman, Miki, and Ruth Kark. 2016. Garden Cities in the Jewish Yishuv of Palestine: Zionist Ideology and Practice 1905–1945. *Planning Perspectives* 31, 1: 55–82.

Zucker, Paul. 1955. Space and Movement in High Baroque City Planning. *Journal of the Society of Architectural Historians* 14, 1: 8–13.

Zucker, Paul. 1959. *Town and Square: From the Agora to the Village Green*. New York: Columbia University Press.

Index